IN
DISTURBING THE SLEEPING BUFFALO

Sally Thompson's dramatic stories show us a Montana too few know. Similar to her popular *People Before the Park*, the tales in *Disturbing the Sleeping Buffalo* reverse perspective on regional history by respectfully sharing Native American accounts. Whether describing a neglected Crow chief or a native child buried in Missoula, Thompson is a gifted storyteller who uncovers the revelatory power of the past. This is a must-have book for anyone interested in Montana and Western American history.

— **Ken Egan Jr.,** author of *Montana 1864* and *Montana 1889*

These stories are planting seeds from which people will benefit. They bring a sense of belonging, wholeness, and connection for greater insight into the emotional history we carry.

— **Leon Rattler,** Blackfeet elder, Brave Dog Society

Vivid, untold stories. Back country adventures. Explorations of Montana's buried histories. Sally Thompson offers surprise and delight in this collection of trails untrodden in Indian Country and beyond. If you like discovering hidden treasures, you will love this book!

— **Annick Smith,** author of *Homestead, Big Bluestem:*
  A Journey into the Tallgrass, and *In This We are Native: Memoirs and Journeys;*
  co-editor of *The Last Best Place: A Montana Anthology*

Disturbing the Sleeping Buffalo is a delight. Sally Thompson's tales from the past break open new vistas and understandings about our state. With grace, authority, and humor, Thompson separates truth from myth. Her deep research, human connections, and plain old common sense lend the history she recounts a sense of rightness—at last. Along the way, we share in the obsession, sleuthing, and serendipity of the historian's quest.

— **Beth Judy,** author of *Bold Women in Montana History*

Sally Thompson possesses a remarkable knowledge of the archaeological and cultural history of the beautiful place now called Montana, including her extensive research with tribal elders into their deep-rooted oral history of this land. In *Disturbing the Sleeping Buffalo*, Thompson highlights some of the most fascinating—and lesser-known—stories she has uncovered in her years of inquiry, stories that give us a fuller, richer, and deeper picture of the past. A must-read and totally engaging book for anyone who loves Montana!

— **Peter Stark,** author of *Gallop Toward the Sun:*
 Tecumseh and William Henry Harrison's Struggle for the Destiny of a Nation

DISTURBING
◆—THE—◆
SLEEPING BUFFALO

23 Unexpected Stories that Awaken Montana's Past

SALLY THOMPSON

FARCOUNTRY
PRESS

ISBN: 978-1-56037-839-6

Text © 2024 by Sally Thompson

Design by Steph Lehmann

Cover: Bison painting by Antoine-Louis Barye. *PUBLIC DOMAIN.*

Back cover: Sketch of Indians and Sleeping Buffao Rock. *PHOTOGRAPH BY SALLY THOMPSON, FROM* LAND OF NAKODA, *WORKS PROGRESS ADMINISTRATION WRITERS' PROJECT, FIRST EDITION.*

For more information about our books, write Farcountry Press, P.O. Box 5630, Helena, MT 59604;
call (800) 821-3874; or visit www.farcountrypress.com.

Produced and printed in the United States of America.

29 28 27 26 25 24   1 2 3 4 5 6

CONTENTS

STORY MAPS

AN EAR TO THE GROUND
LISTENING FOR THE HEARTBEAT OF HISTORY

A while back, my longtime friend Joyce Hocker suggested that I write the stories that I often tell. She felt sure that other Montanans—and readers far and wide—would enjoy them as much as my family and circle of friends have. I liked the idea. My career as an anthropologist has provided me the good fortune to delve deeply into Montana's past through research and field-work. Retired now, I can look back on the many unusual opportunities that gave me a different picture of Montana history than is commonly held.

My archaeological work included digging in the ground and surveying the land, all across the state. I also met and talked with a wide variety of people of different backgrounds and cultures. I learned different perspectives from Native Montanans about our shared history, our values, and our ways of knowing. I learned to respect the important truths held in oral history. Descendants of homesteaders taught me about the decades of transition, when the dominant story shifted from Native to White. Their grandparents had come to this vast land of opportunity in the 1880s, just after the buffalo were gone.

From the historical record, I learned to dig deep, to read between the lines, and to question what was missing. And to better understand it all, I meandered along the old trails and tried to imagine Montana as it was, long before we were born. After more than four decades, I have accumulated some uncommon insights and a large trove of stories that are as enlightening as they are entertaining.

Having decided to write this book, my first task was to figure out which tales to tell. I began the cumbersome task of excavating through my ample files and field journals looking for compelling stories. Like finely flaked projectile points found during a dig, topics revealed by my mental trowel sorted themselves into folders. Content came from both written and oral histories and from my own experiences. The process stirred up old memories, many of them unrelated to the focus of the work. For instance, from a long-ago summer spent surveying on the Tongue River, I remembered seeing three colors of rattlesnake—green like the prickly pear, red like the sandstone, and beige like the sere soil. In my mind's eye, the colors are still vivid, as are the ridgetops and bottomlands where I walked. Near Townsend, one June, I was delighted by an unexpected field of blooming bitterroots along an old Salish trail to the Musselshell River. These ancillary experiences return me to the places where they happened. These kinds of experiences—like the first time one sees fireflies or witnesses a large owl glide silently past—are the ones that carry the memories forward. I believe we remember these times because of the emotional responses that take us beyond data collecting. We all have had such moments. Montana's varied and magnificent character provides a wealth of opportunity for such memories to form, and always has. Sharing our stories about her is part of what it means to belong here.

Digging through the piles of notes, I remember asides expressed during interviews, and often not caught on tape. A Coeur d'Alene elder, Felix Aripa told me that his grandmother, whom he had known as a child, had been baptized by one the Jesuits who came to the Rockies with Father De Smet. For him, as someone whose people had never left their homeland, that history was not so long ago. I will always remember when Darrell Martin stood more proudly when he told me the name his people call themselves, A'aninin, meaning "upright person." French fur traders called them Gros Ventre, meaning "Big Bellies," because the traders misunderstood the sign language for "The Falls," referring to the Falls of the Saskatchewan.

One pile concerned my archaeological work and stories of thousands of years of human history still buried under the Big Sky. The stories address cultural continuity and long-term trends on a scale that individual lives are too short to encompass. Mixed with the physical evidence are stories of ingenuity, intelligence, adaptability, resilience, and the finely tuned connectedness of those who came before. Original place names hold such stories and etch the history into the land—like the tipi-shaped Deer's Lodge and the Two Medicine River, where two Medicine Lodge ceremonies were held during the same summer. Indigenous experiences and connections to the land carry these memories, as do ties from more recent times, as told in names like Yankee Jim Canyon and Confederate Gulch.

Another pile of stories held clues about mostly forgotten or misunderstood people and events. The vast majority of Montana history has been written by White men, either those who came into the country in the nineteenth century as newcomers, or historians, writing from the record put down by the men who preceded them. The results have been influenced by their worldview, experiences, and priorities, which began with the Lewis and Clark journals and resounded with the publication of *Progressive Men of Montana* in 1902. *Disturbing the Sleeping Buffalo* aims to expand and balance our points of view.

One large pile of stories focused on unexpected—in some cases unexplainable—events I experienced while following old trails, especially those of Lewis and Clark, Father De Smet, and government surveyors. Serendipity often led me to unusual finds. Sometimes I found needles in haystacks, like when I stumbled upon a map important to the Blackfeet in a mistitled U.S. government document in the stacks at the National Archives. A Blackfeet friend said that her ancestors were dragging me around by the nape of the neck to find what was needed.

My piles of potential stories grew too large for a single book. One solution I considered was to create multiple volumes, organized by chronology, topic, or geography but, ultimately, I decided to write just this one volume. I dug deeper through the piles to see which stories were most relatable and realized that the memories I wanted to share had more to do with my own experiences of preparing for and conducting research and fieldwork and less with the results. Like new facets on flaked stone, some stories emerged simply because they offered unusual glimpses into moments of Montana history. In the end, my treasure box contained the stories that most called to me, the ones that still moved me, the ones that have lingered. These are the nuggets gleaned from the pan.

The result, in your hands, is twenty-three stories derived from my experiences as an anthropologist in Montana. The compilation spans twelve millennia, arranged into five geographical areas. Several of the stories address lives of Native Montanans before the arrival of Euro-Americans, and many others tell of adjustments Native communities made as their worlds changed afterward. Some stories tell of harrowing journeys across the land, and others recount my own tracking of the journeys of historical figures, both Native and Euro-American. My favorites are those that bridge across cultures and centuries.

For many readers, most of the stories will be unknown. Aspects of others will be recognized by history buffs, but the renditions offered here will be new. My hope is for this book to serve as a lens into a truer and more inclusive version of our shared history. At times, these stories act like a magnifying glass, revealing details about people and events often glossed over in the sweep of more general histories. At other times, these stories provide an eagle-eye view from the heights of Mistakis, the mountains that form "the Backbone of the World," enabling us to survey along mighty rivers and quiet streams through the varied landscapes of this treasured state, Montana. ✛

PART I

OVERLAND JOURNEYS

MONCACHT-APÉ'S INCREDIBLE JOURNEY

What if Thomas Jefferson's scientific speculation about a northwest route to the Pacific was based on the account of someone who had already made the trip? Imagine how much less risky the cross-country expedition of Lewis and Clark might have been, had some predecessor traveled along those Indian trails up the Missouri, across the Continental Divide, and down the Columbia, and lived to tell about it. The famous explorers' situation would have been that much better, if they'd had a map to follow and knew about how long the trip might take. Well, in fact, they did.

Lewis and Clark carried with them an account attributed to a Yazoo Indian named Moncacht-apé (say Moan-kahsht-ah-pay), who reportedly traveled all the way from the Mississippi Delta to the Pacific Ocean more than a century before the 1804–1806 Corps of Discovery expedition.

During the Lewis and Clark Bicentennial, my position at the University of Montana's Regional Learning Project provided me with the opportunity to focus deeply on the subject of tribal communities along the trails that the expedition had followed. I heard someone mention Moncacht-apé at a conference and decided to look into it. Having heard many tales of remarkable journeys taken by Native people, I liked how the story of Moncacht-apé puts a different spin on the Lewis and Clark story. This is not to say the Corps' journey wasn't a remarkable accomplishment—it surely was—but indigenous people of this continent have their remarkable stories as well.

A description of Moncacht-apé's trek was told in the 1720s to French ethnographer, historian, and naturalist Antoine-Simon Le Page du Pratz. The story, along with a rough map, was included in Le Page's 1758, multi-volume history of colonial Louisiana, *L'Histoire de la Louisiane*. The account shared here stems from that source, the only known record of this man called Moncacht-apé.

The name Moncacht-apé, given to him by his own people, translates as "the killer of pain and fatigue." The French called him "the Interpreter" because he understood so many Indian languages. Moncacht-apé was so knowledgeable of the manners and customs of different nations, Le Page compared him to early Greeks who traveled into the east to examine foreign cultures and then returned to share their newfound knowledge. The Frenchman reports that he spent three days recording Moncacht-apé's remarkable story of his five-year solo trip up the Missouri to its headwaters, then across the divide to "the Beautiful River,"

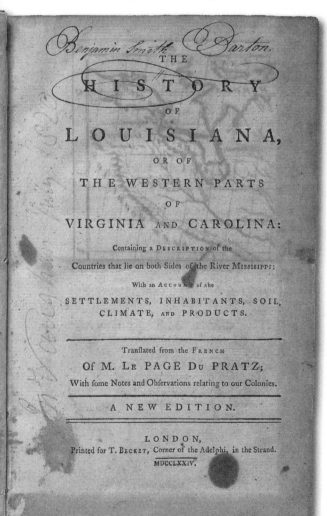

Left: Title page from the 1874 edition of Antoine-Simon Le Page du Pratz's The History of Louisiana, *originally published in 1757. Photograph courtesy of the Library Company of Philadelphia.*

and on to the Pacific. The impetus for his travels was to find the place from which his forebears had originated. His journey was a pilgrimage.

It is surprising that most Montanans have never heard the story of Moncacht-ape's northwestern exploration because it is known that Thomas Jefferson kept a copy of Le Page's history in his library, and that Meriwether Lewis carried the 1774 English edition of Moncacht-ape's story with him all the way to Oregon and back.[1] They would have done better with the French publication, which gave important details not included in the English version.[2] Moncacht-ape's accomplishment may have provided the impetus for Jefferson to imagine the trip and, certainly, for Lewis and Clark to believe that such a trip was possible.

Why Moncacht-ape's name and his story remain virtually unknown is a question that needs to be asked. Did Lewis and Clark suppress information about this journey? Have American historians neglected information that doesn't fit with the grand narrative of Manifest Destiny? Or, perhaps, the Corps of Discovery didn't find the Yazoo man's observations useful?

I wish I could tell you that I am going to lead you in the footsteps of Moncacht-apé all the way from the Mississippi Delta to the Pacific Ocean. I really wanted to. Although the record is remarkable for a journey taken without paper, pen, and a compass, many details remain unknown. We are left to look for clues in the changing seasons, geographical landmarks, and cultural observations. Some temporal and cultural clues are provided with reference to bearded men. By 1700, Europeans had already caused radical dislocations of Native people along the Eastern Seaboard and throughout the Southeast. Countless Indians had already died through disease and warfare, while a quarter of a million Europeans were settling on abandoned lands. West of the Appalachian Mountains and north of Spanish Territory, however, the world remained generally as it had been for centuries, except for exploration by Europeans along the Pacific Coast.

Moncacht-apé's story is worth knowing, despite its obvious limitations. Here is what we know.

The young man, after losing his wife and children, set off on a personal journey of discovery, heading northwest from his home in the Mississippi Delta. On an earlier trip, he had met with some Chickasaw elders to learn about their shared origins, or at least their migration story. They were recognized as elders of the Yazoo, "since from them came the language of the country," Muskogean. Their elders, the Choctaw, to this day, retain a creation story of being led to the lower Mississippi by two brothers, Chata (Choctaw) and Chickasah, from their home in the far west because it "had ceased to prosper." They were guided by a magical rod or staff. They carried with them the bones of their ancestors in buffalo sacks from their original land.[3] Among the Chickasaw, after several days of searching, Moncacht-apé found no one who could provide him the particulars he sought. He was directed to continue his journey, traveling from nation to nation, "until he should find himself in the country from which his ancestors emigrated, being persuaded that he could there learn many things which they had forgotten in their travels."[4]

Moncacht-apé started his journey "when the grain was ripe," following the high land on the east bank of the Mississippi, till he reached the Ohio River (across from present-day Cairo, Illinois). Grasses were just beginning to green up. He had to travel some six hours upstream from the confluence in order to cross it without being carried into the Mississippi. At that place he used canes to make a raft and a paddle and was able to cross the Ohio. On the very next day, he managed to kill a fat buffalo cow and harvest the prime meat—the tenderloin, hump, and tongue—and soon reached a village of Tamaroas, part of the Illinois nation. There, he rested for several days.

Off again, he headed north beyond the point opposite the mouth of the Missouri (just north of present-day St. Louis). Crossing the Mississippi, he needed plenty of room for his raft to drift so that he could land on the north side of the Missouri. As he neared the bank, he allowed himself to drift with the current until reaching the sandy point at the confluence. At that place he paused to witness the mingling together of "the two waters." He thrilled at the sight of the two waters flowing side by side, the west side being muddy and the east side clear. Later, he told Le Page how the Mississippi had been muddy all the way to the Missouri, then "very clear" above it, where he had crossed.

Moncacht-apé traveled several days along the north bank of the Missouri, marveling at the bison herds through which he passed. Probably somewhere in the vicinity of Columbia, Missouri, he arrived at the nation of the Missouris and stayed with them through the winter, while snow fell "deep as a man's waist." He made his journey close to the peak of the Little Ice Age (which lasted from approximately 1300 to 1850). During these long winter months, he was able to learn the language spoken by people living farther upriver.[5]

"When the cold was past, and the snows were melted," he traveled up the Missouri to a village of the Kansa nation. Their territory extended from today's Kansas City area up to around what became the border between Kansas and Missouri. From them, presumably because he had learned to speak their language, he was able to gather much-needed information about what to expect and how to plan for the next phase of his journey. The Kansa told him that after about a month, he would need to bear to the right and head directly north. Several days beyond that turn he would find a river opposite the Missouri that would take him toward the setting sun. He should follow that river until he met "the nation of the Otters." There, he could rest, and learn what he needed to continue toward his nation's original lands. He might find some willing persons to accompany him on his journey. From the place of the Otters, he would be able to descend "this river in a dug-out and travel a great distance without fatigue."

Moncacht-apé reported that he followed northwestward along the Missouri's "sinuosities" because he was traveling through unknown countries and did not want to get lost and wasn't sure where a cut-off might lead. He knew this river route took longer than need be, but it was the safest bet. One obvious omission in his account is mention of any of the dozens of earth lodge villages that lined the Missouri between the Kansas and Knife Rivers. Perhaps the original editor deemed these details unnecessary to the point of the story, but it's hard to explain their omission. Moncacht-apé told Le Page that he "travelled faster than red men ordinarily do." According to Le Page, the usual rate for a heavily laden man was about six leagues (eighteen miles) per day. The Frenchman figured that the Yazoo man's relatively light load of about 100 pounds or less—considered half a load—allowed him to make nine or even ten leagues, that is, twenty-seven or thirty miles, a day.

Moncacht-apé reported that he traveled "constantly for one moon." Even traveling thirty miles a day, he would not have been close to the mountains of Montana in a month. He wouldn't even have made it to Williston, North

Dakota, about a thousand miles up the Missouri from the Kansa (or Kaw) village. If the story is true, he must have traveled longer than he remembered. His Kansa advisors might have been assuming he would follow the cut-off trail when they provided him the timing for his journey. Or maybe they said it would take two months, not one, and the old man had forgotten. The only specific landmark he had to go on, besides the river itself, was a north-trending trail when he was nearing the headwaters. As he approached the mountains of what is now central Montana, he equivocated about his route because the rocky terrain before him made him fear wounding his feet. Finally, afraid that he would miss his turn, he decided to stop, build a fire, and camp. With time to think through his situation, he resolved to head northward the following day.

That very evening, help arrived.

> While watching the sun, which already had nearly set, I saw some smoke at some distance off. I did not doubt that this was a party of hunters who proposed to pass the night in this place, and it entered my mind that they might belong to the Otters. I imme-diately left in order that I might be guided to them by the smoke while it was yet daylight. I joined them and they were surprised to see me arrive alone. They were a party of thirty men and some women. Their language was unknown to me and we were only able to communicate by signs. Nevertheless, although surprised, they received me well enough, and I remained three days with them. At the end of this time one of the wives told her husband that she believed herself ready for lying in.[6] Upon that the others sent this man and his wife to the village, and told them to take me with them in order that I might travel by an easier road than that which I was on the point of taking.

Moncacht-apé told Le Page that he and his new companions continued their journey along the Missouri for nine short days beyond their meeting place before arriving at the awaited junction.

At a place recognized by his guides, but for which Moncacht-apé reported no geographical clues, they "turned directly North." He doesn't provide

Map of Louisiana, showing the course of the Mississippi and Missouri Rivers, and Moncacht-apé's route, from Du Pratz's History of Louisiana. *PHOTOGRAPH COURTESY OF THE LIBRARY COMPANY OF PHILADELPHIA.*

any evidence for how long they traveled that direction. After five days or northward travel, they arrived at what the Otter people called "The Beautiful River," a river running toward the west. He says nothing about traveling across mountains to get there. When they arrived at this river, his friends bathed

and, by signs, invited him to clean up as well. He did so only after being assured there were no crocodiles.

Although the Yazoo's travelogue would have been of little use to Lewis and Clark, it helps us to understand Lewis' great despair when he first caught sight of the snow-covered barrier of the Bitterroot Mountains. From Moncacht-apé's account, Lewis would have expected smooth sailing after an easy ascent of the main chain of the Rockies.

So, where might Moncacht-apé have been, and how do we explain the omissions and discrepancies in his tale? I won't presume to question his knowledge of directions. Native people have many methods to orient themselves in ways that would put most modern people to shame. We are left to question the particulars of his memory or the authenticity of the story. Presuming the tale is true, he told of his journey many decades after his return. Even this I am hesitant to question, though, knowing that American Indians, before writing, employed a variety of mnemonic devices to retain important information. If the tale is a yarn of Le Page's spinning, he concocted a rather convincing account about territory unexplored by non-Native people at the time.

To speculate as to Moncacht-apé's location, we might assume his group turned northward before the Great Falls, since he makes no mention of these ear-splitting cataracts. (Remember, however, he also fails to mention the Mandan villages and crossing through mountains.) They might have taken an old trail that veered north from the Missouri toward the Sweet Grass Hills until it reached a westward intersection toward the main chain of the Rockies.

None of the travel options for crossing the Continental Divide quite fit the description. Whichever pass they crossed, Moncacht-apé and his guides and "a troop of hunters" traveled along that beautiful westward-flowing river for the rest of the day. When they arrived at a certain stream, he reported that his companions retrieved their concealed dugout canoes. They arrived at his companions' village that night, where the visitor "was as well received by this nation as if [he] had been one of them."

Who were the Otters? From geography alone, the best options for cultural identification are Salish, Pend d'Oreille, or Kootenai. Not enough indicators are provided to know for sure.

During his travels with the Otters, and then while in their village, Moncacht-apé learned to communicate in their language. This happened, he explained, because he was always in the company of old men "who love to instruct the young, as the young love to be instructed and converse freely with each other." He would gladly have stayed longer among these fine people, and they made clear that they also wished it, but he could not let go of the desire that fired this mission from the start, to find the origin place of his people.

When an opportunity arose for him to make progress toward his destination, he joined a small party of Otters who were heading downriver. Moncacht-apé bid farewell to those at the village with whom he had spent several enjoyable weeks. The departing group carried a calumet (a ceremonial pipe) to be delivered to a neighboring nation as a sign of peace. Traveling by canoe, which he referred to as a pirogue, they let the Beautiful River carry them toward the ocean. They traveled for eighteen days, stopping as needed to hunt, and they experienced no hunger.

When the peacemakers arrived at their destination, Moncacht-apé thought he would press on. Travel was pleasant and he was making good progress toward his goal. But his companions convinced him otherwise, offering compelling reasons. First, they explained that the serpents were dangerous in that season when the heat was great and the grass was high. He would risk being bitten while out hunting. Their other reason was that he should learn the language of the nation where he was headed. These people spoke a language nearly the same as the Otters, which provided him a means to learn the language of their neighbors. He chose to spend the winter with them, and to learn the language of the people beyond them. He had been assured that he would be able to make himself understood by all the people that he would encounter all the way to the "Great Water."

Moncacht-apé stayed through the winter and well into the summer before he was ready to continue his quest. Our hero headed down the river, his boat stocked with his meager provisions—his bow and arrow, a pot, a bowl, and his bedding—and plenty of dried meat. He was sorry not to have corn but noted that the kind people who had housed him through the winter did not cultivate maize except "a little as a curiosity." He floated with ease down the river until he came upon a very small nation. When he pulled ashore, he was not made to feel welcome. These people were unsure of a short-haired stranger, traveling alone. The chief faced him as he pulled up on the riverbank, asking, "Who are you? Where do you come from? What do you want here with your short hair?" Moncacht-apé explained himself, telling that he came from the Otters and hoped that he could learn the knowledge he sought from them. His words did not seem to relieve the hostility conveyed by the leader of this village. Moncacht-apé went on to assure the chief that he had not come to ask for food and would not impose on them. In case the man didn't understand him, he put his thoughts into metaphor. "During winter, like the bear, I seek a c[ul]vert," he said, "and in summer I imitate the eagle, who moves about to satisfy his curiosity."

Because of his obvious courage and his peaceful intentions, he was permitted to stay. Why, though, the chief asked, was Moncacht-apé able to speak their language, since the people east of them spoke otherwise. Moncacht-apé told him that an old man called Salt Tear had taught him. Salt Tear had told him to ask for "Big Roebuck." His interrogator immediately sent for Big Roebuck, his own father, as luck would have it. The old man received Moncacht-apé as if he were his own son and took him and his few belongings into his lodge, where the visitor soon learned the reason for their hesitancy about him. Regarding hair, they "look upon those who wear it short as slaves whose hair has been cut in order that they may be recognized." He remained with them only two days, learning what he needed to in order to proceed. Big Roebuck provided him with "some gruel from certain small grains, smaller than French peas, which are very good, which pleased me all the more that it was so long that I had eaten only meat." With his new stock of provisions, he "descended the Beautiful River without stopping more than one day with each nation" that he met along the way.

Although clues are sparse, he appears to have transitioned from Salish- or Kootenai-speaking territory, or perhaps Sahaptin, and entered the world of Chinookan speakers, somewhere in the vicinity of The Dalles, Oregon. Coastal Chinook and Clatsop made raids on groups to the north and acquired slaves whose hair was short. The traveler makes no mention of the series of falls along the mid-Columbia that required portaging. His description is that of a long, easy glide to the ocean. Once again, Lewis and Clark would have found themselves sorely disappointed by the very real challenges of travel, once they discovered the inadequacy of Moncacht-apé's account.

The last group he would meet, who lived "a day's journey from the Great Water" and a few miles away from the river, according to what he had been told, were forced to "remain in the woods to conceal themselves" because of "the bearded men." When Moncacht-apé arrived among them, he was received again as if he were among family. He delighted in a food they served, made of the same grain that Big Roebuck had made into a gruel. He found this grain, which "springs up without being sowed," was better than any he had ever tasted. Other foods of these people included some large blue birds, which they killed when they came in to eat the grain and meat from the water. Moncacht-apé was intrigued by an animal these people killed to eat when it came ashore to eat grass, which he remembered as having "a head shaped like a young buffalo, but not of the same color." It's difficult to imagine what this animal might have been. Fish and a variety of shellfish from the Great Water provided much of their diet.

Although the foods were plentiful and delicious, life had become difficult for these people because of being on alert for the bearded men who did all they could "to carry away the young persons." These men were white, the people told Moncacht-apé, with "long, black beards which fell upon their breasts." The strangers were "short and thick, with large heads, which they covered with cloth." They wore coats that "fell to the middle of the legs." Both their coats and the cloth that covered their feet were dyed red or yellow. The Natives thought it strange that these men wore their clothes no matter the temperature, even in the hottest weather. (More than a century later, the Chinookan people would have a similar reaction to Lewis and Clark, who never shed their soggy clothes and moccasins.) These Indians had never approached the bearded men because they were afraid, due to "their arms making a great noise and a great flame." The White strangers would return to their boat whenever they saw "more red men than their own numbers."

The bearded White men arrived from the west "to seek upon this coast a yellow and bad-smelling wood which dyes a beautiful yellow." They would arrive each year soon after the cold of winter had retreated. So greedy were these men that they had destroyed all these trees along the coast. The remnants, which still existed in small quantities up the rivers, were reserved for the tribe's own people, who also used the yellow dye.

What might this tree have been? An internet search for trees from the Pacific Coast used to obtain a yellow dye turns up empty, as does a broader search for yellow dyes. When the textile industry was beginning to boom in Europe, from the early sixteenth and into the eighteenth century, the red brazilwood tree (*Paubrasilia echinata*) was in high demand for the powdered red dye that could be extracted from it. So important was this dye that the Portuguese, who had a monopoly on this precious substance, named a country after it. Over-exploitation finally collapsed the market, and the tree is now endangered. Perhaps something similar happened to trees of the Pacific Northwest that provided a yellow dye.

Moncacht-apé told Le Page of the plan made with two neighboring nations to drive off these marauders who were expected soon after Moncacht-apé's arrival. Our traveler was eager to see these bearded, beturbaned men who arrived from the sea. Their descriptions did not correspond to the French, English, or Spaniards whom he had seen, whose beards were more trimmed and their clothing other than what these Natives had described. Their five-day journey to intercept the tree thieves took them to a place near two high and long cliffs, connected with the mainland, where these raiders would moor their large boat. The Natives established a camp away from the shore and waited. Seventeen days passed before they saw the bearded men appear in two large vessels. They watched them for four days before the White men finally went ashore to cut the wood. The Natives' attack was only a partial success. They managed to kill eleven of the marauders, leaving a greater number to run back to their boats and leave. Of the eleven, only two had firearms with powder and balls. Moncacht-apé and the others examined the bodies of the dead.

They were much smaller than we were, and very white. They had large heads, and bodies sufficiently large for their height. Their hair was only long in the middle of the head. They did not wear hats like you [meaning Frenchmen], but their heads were twisted around with cloth; their clothes were neither of wool nor bark [he meant to say silk] but something similar to your old shirts [no doubt cotton] very soft and of different colors. That which covered their limbs and their feet was of a single piece.

At the end of this skirmish, Moncacht-apé chose not to return with his companions. It was time for him to continue his quest. He "joined with those who lived further toward the Sunsetting, on the coast" who had come to help drive off the bearded men. They traveled together, "following closely the coast of the Great Water." He rested for several days at their village. While there, he sought to learn about the path he would travel. The elders advised him not to continue. They explained that the coast extended a great distance farther and conveyed that it was not possible for him to accomplish his goal. He should return home.

Moncacht-apé headed home along the same general route by which he had come. The journey to the Pacific Coast had taken three years. His return trip was shorter because he took some of the shortcuts that avoided the big loops of the Missouri. When he reached the Mississippi Delta after five long years—if this trip was more than a fantasy concocted in the mind of Le Page du Pratz—we can be sure he was grateful to see the faces of his relations.

I believe at least part of the story might be true, despite the many gaps. But I keep going back to the bag of buffalo bones his ancestors carried from their homeland. Moncacht-apé claimed their homeland was somewhere in the northwest, well beyond the Rockies and far removed from buffalo country. Gordon Sayre, an English professor at the University of Oregon and an expert on the subject, thinks the story sprang from the pen of the very imaginative and creative Le Page.[7] What do you think?

Regardless of whether it be fact or fiction, Le Page's telling of Moncacht-apé's travels shaped a belief in an easy route to the Pacific that influenced the launching of America's most lauded overland expedition, the Corps of Discovery. The Bitterroot Mountains convinced them otherwise. ✢

THE MOCCASIN TELEGRAPH, 1805

The history of Montana is often told as if it began with Lewis and Clark, the first White men to pass through the state. You can imagine that the Native people of these lands hold a different point of view, yet the story commonly known of the explorers' initial journey up the Missouri River and across much of present-day Montana is still told from Lewis and Clark's point of view. In all those miles, the Corps of Discovery failed to see a single soul. The Moccasin Telegraph tells the flipside of the story. Lewis and Clark were observed all along the way. Why wouldn't they be?

Villages across the upper Missouri country and even across the mountains had been told of the scores of White men traveling upriver with a black man and an Indian woman with a baby. Traders from these tribal communities had visited the Mandan villages during the winter of 1804–1805 and had seen these strangers with their own eyes. They were familiar with white-skinned people from the north, but this group was different. Of course, the Native travelers told their people about them.

During the winter layover at Fort Mandan, William Clark worked with both Indian and White traders and travelers to compile a map and list of the tribes they would meet as they headed west. The expedition leaders knew they would pass through the extensive homelands of the Assiniboine after leaving Hidatsa territory, then perhaps they would encounter the Gros Ventre. Eventually they would enter the homeland of the Blackfeet before reaching Sacagawea's people, a northern band of Shoshones.

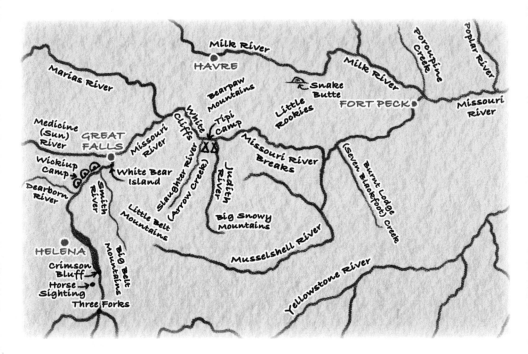

They left Fort Mandan in early April and rowed past the last Hidatsa village on April 11. Not for four months would they meet another person. Given the active trade network in the region, we can guess that there was much communication about the strangers' passage through the country with no awareness on their part. Rather than the classic image of explorers confidently pointing the way, they might better be portrayed scratching their heads or demonstrating another classic sign for confusion, holding both arms out from the elbows, with hands up and shoulders shrugged, like a human question mark.

Traveling by water, Lewis and Clark missed much of the life of the place. Montana Indians were not canoe people except in the far northwestern part of the state, where Pend d'Oreille and Kootenai people plied their canoes along waterways. Little in the way of a human presence caught the explorers' eyes until May 2, when one of the hunters found several yards of scarlet cloth suspended on a tree branch near an old hunting camp, the sign of a prayer offering. A little farther on, above Big Muddy Creek, they encountered a curious cylindrical bundle of sticks, about ten feet in diameter and standing on end to a height of about thirty feet. The travelers supposed it was some kind of sacrifice.[1] (Today, this area is near Brockton and Haystack Butte in Richland County, at the southern edge of the Fort Peck Indian Reservation, home to Assiniboine and Sioux.)

Upriver from Poplar, Montana, on May 4, Lewis reported passing several old Indian hunting camps. One, which was fortified, consisted of two large lodges surrounded by a five-foot-tall circular fence, laid out horizontally, with overlapping driftwood and fallen timber. Lewis referred to the structure as a "pound." They had seen several, some as large as thirty feet across and "covered over with the trunks and limbs of old timber." The lodges were constructed of "three or more strong sticks the thickness of a man's leg or arm and about 12 feet long." These were wrapped together at one end, then set up and spread out at the other end to form a circular base, ten to fourteen feet in diameter. More random poles were added to help support the conic structure. Lewis went on to describe these lodges as imperfect shelters because they had no straw on them. This type of three-pole lodge frame was characteristic of the Assiniboine and Sioux, in contrast to the four-pole frame of the Blackfeet. They would leave their lodge poles there to be used year after year. The same poles might have been put to good use by a war party. Of course, these are just speculations from this distant perch of two centuries later. Clark named the creek there "Indian Fort Creek" (now Nickwall Creek, in McCone County).

The travelers reached the Milk River on May 8. The distance from the Poplar River to the Milk is only about fifty miles by road but at least twice that by the course of the winding river. A few days before, they had seen a place "where an Indian had recently grained, or taken the hair off of a goat-skin," meaning a pronghorn. Lewis noted that they did "not wish to see those gentlemen just now as we presume they would most probably be the Assinniboine and might be troublesome to us." Their concern was based on information provided by the Mandan and Hidatsa about a fierce band of Assiniboines known as the "Red Devils."

As they continued past the pronghorn processing location, Captain Clark got a good look up the Milk River where he noticed smoke and what he believed were some Indian lodges in the distance.[2] The explorers camped a little upriver from the mouth of Milk River. What they didn't know as they set up their camp that night was that they had been seen by scouts from the village Clark had glimpsed. The village was on Porcupine Creek, which merges

Pencil illustration, "Assiniboines Observe the Corps of Discovery from the Hills," May 1805. ARTWORK BY DON GREYTAK, USED WITH PERMISSION.[3]

with the Milk River a short distance above the Missouri. From a well-hidden vantage point on the bluff above the river, these men of the Assiniboine Nation, or, more appropriately, Nakota, had watched two large boats and six canoes pass. According to their oral history, this sighting happened during the time of the "Idle Moon." The scouts reported what they saw to their village leader, Rosebud. He directed them to send out smoke signals to alert other Nakota bands of the intruders coming up the river. That was the smoke that William Clark had seen as they passed by the Milk River.

On the morning of May 10, at a location now under Fort Peck Reservoir, a dog came into the expedition's camp. Suspecting that Indians were close, Lewis sent out scouts, but they returned having found no recent evidence.[4]

A week later, near a big bend in the Missouri, the expedition members saw a fortified Indian camp "in the upper part of a Small timbered bottom" where they, themselves, were camped. They named that tributary Burnt Lodge Creek (now Seven Blackfoot Creek, in the Charles M. Russell National Wildlife Refuge, the bottomland long ago flooded by Fort Peck Reservoir). Clark surmised that the fortified camp was evidence of a Hidatsa war party of about fifteen men who had left from their village two months before, while the explorers still remained at Fort Mandan. The Hidatsa had gone on a raid against the Blackfeet.[5]

On May 24, the weary travelers entered the rough country of the Missouri Breaks. Once the Little Rockies came into view, Lewis reported seeing "more or less old stick lodges of the Indians" at timbered points all along the way. The next day, two and a half weeks after passing the mouth of the Milk River where they had seen signs of smoke, the Corps passed to the south of the Little Rockies (near the town of Hays on the Fort Belknap Reservation). On the far side of those mountains lay Snake Butte, sacred site to people of the Assiniboine and Gros Ventre Nations.

Two centuries after Chief Rosebud sent scouts to follow the Lewis and Clark Expedition, his grandson, Jerome Four Star, told the story as it had been passed down to him.[6] He was told that everyone gathered at the council lodge to discuss what should be done about the strangers who were poling their boats up the river. A medicine man told them that these were the people he had seen in his dreams. "One day they will cover the earth like buffalo. They will come and go," he told them. More importantly, though, they should remember that "the Nakodabi [Nakota people] will always be here."[7] Each man, in turn, spoke his mind. Some thought to leave them be. Since they were traveling with a woman and baby, the intruders must have meant no harm. Others thought maybe they should be taught a lesson for stealing their food, for they had hunted without permission. The chief thought them to be peaceful, but to be certain, he told scouts to keep an eye on the travelers until they were out of their territory. They should be left alone unless the strangers drew their weapons. Once the travelers had passed beyond the Little Rockies, the scouts should go atop Snake Butte, make a fire, and send a status report by smoke signal to the people.[8]

⊕ ⊕ ⊕

The explorers remained unaware that they had been tracked by scouts who were watching for any signs of aggression. After the travelers were on their way, the scouts' smoke signals from Snake Butte would send a message that could be seen for 100 miles. Lewis and Clark's party pulled their boats ashore that night on the south side of the river, downstream from Cow Island, and camped near two of the stick lodges that were so prevalent through this stretch of river.

In the Missouri Breaks country near present-day Judith Landing, Lewis reported on May 28 of finding "a new Indian lodge pole today which had been brought down by the stream, it was woarn at one end as if draged by dogs or horses."[9] Other items, including a "football," also washed downstream. This would have been a round or oblong rawhide ball, likely stuffed with buffalo hair or sand, that was used in a traditional game of kickball. The men took these objects as strong evidence of Indians upriver from them, "and probably at no great distance."

Their supposing was well-founded. The very next day they found evidence of 126 lodges on the south side of the river, based on the remains of hearths they counted. The men estimated the camp had been abandoned about two weeks before. Its occupants must have been alerted by the message sent out from the camp on Porcupine Creek. Vestiges of another large encampment, just above the confluence with the Judith River, was of an older date. From moccasins found at these camps, Sacagawea confirmed that they were not of her people. Clark reported that she "believed they were some of the Indians who inhabit the country on this side of Rocky Mountains and North of the Missoury." These would be the Gros Ventre (Falls Indians) or one of the tribes of the Blackfoot Confederacy—the Piegan Blackfeet (Pikunni), Blood (Kainai), and Blackfoot (Siksika).[10] The name Gros Ventre (Big Bellies in French) comes from a misinterpretation of the sign for "The Falls," referring to the Falls of the Saskatchewan River, which were the center of their homeland. They call themselves A'aninin, meaning "upright person."[11]

Later that day, according to Lewis, they witnessed "the remains of a vast many mangled carcases of Buffalow" at the base of a cliff. The men set up their camp by a tributary stream not far past this huge pile of wasted buffalo. They assumed the bison had been driven off the cliff by Indians and so named the stream Slaughter River. Nearly two centuries later the area was investigated by MSU archaeologists who concluded that this carnage had been caused by accidental drowning while trying to cross the river on weak ice. Spring runoff washed their carcasses onto the bank, one atop another. No tools or other cultural evidence were associated with their deaths. Floaters on the Wild and Scenic Missouri River today can camp at Arrow Creek, the Slaughter River of 1805.

Entering the White Cliffs area, the exhausted travelers struggled to move their boats upriver against the raging springtime flow. They passed several Indian encampments, none of which had been inhabited within the last month. These may have been winter camps that had been abandoned after the last big storm, always expected by the Blackfeet during the Leaves Coming Out Moon, when the Buffalo Flowers grow. The people knew better than to be on the move when Wind Maker sent the snow sideways.

On June 1, they passed Coal Banks Landing where boaters today put in for their river adventure. The expedition camped upriver of an old crossing at the site of today's Virgelle Ferry. Along the way they saw an unspecified number of recently abandoned "Indian camps made of Sticks & bark Set up on end."[12] These lodges were distinctive from those they had passed downriver. Similar sightings continued until June 3, when they reached the Marias River and pulled their boats ashore. During their overland explorations the following week, they continued to encounter abandoned encampments in every well-timbered bottomland. Along the Marias, they camped in one of the old bark-covered stick lodges that provided them "a dry and comfortable shelter" during a miserable rainstorm.[13] These were likely to have been some of the simple dwellings Blackfeet scouting parties constructed out of saplings and brush, or short lodge poles and bark, known as "war lodges."

They continued through Blackfeet Country, passing by what would become Fort Benton. This area was an important crossroads because of the good ford just above there. Blackfeet travelers, back then, knew this as a place "where the Missouri River could be crossed in waters little over knee deep."[14] Lewis explored up the Marias to a place where he could see the Sweet Grass Hills, significant landmarks to travelers and sacred hills of the tribes. This entire area was central to the Blackfeet tribes, yet Lewis saw nobody on this journey. If he was watched, the story did not survive.

After cautiously opting for the left fork—the Missouri rather than the Marias—they continued upriver. Their choice was confirmed when they arrived at the Great Falls, a key location they had been told to watch for by the Hidatsa. They were sure they had found the right spot when they witnessed bald eagles perched in a cottonwood tree nest on an island in the midst of mist. The only time in the entire journey when Lewis claimed to be beyond words was here, so moved by the beauty, at this "truly magnificent and sublimely grand object" of the falls.[15]

After their grueling portage in mid-June, the party spent a month in the vicinity of White Bear Island, south of what is now the city of Great Falls, fending off grizzly bears and reconfiguring their boat situation, while some of the party explored the area. On July 13, Lewis noted the frame of "a very extraordinary Indian lodge," south of modern Great Falls. Sixteen posts of cottonwood trunks were arranged in a circle, seventy feet across, with an opening for the doorway on the east side. Each post was about fifty feet long, and their bases, which rested upon the ground, were about the girth of a man's body. The tops of the posts were "united in a common point above and secured with large wyths of willow brush."[16] Ash from a large fire marked the center. Some eighty tipis—"leather lodges"—surrounded the massive structure. Clearly this lodge served some ceremonial purpose. Gary Moulton, editor of the Lewis and Clark journals, notes that Lewis' description has similarities with a Blackfoot medicine lodge, particularly the use of stout cottonwood posts.[17] It also has significant differences. The medicine lodge ceremony, held during the moon When the People Move Together (July), has a central pole as its predominant feature and no central hearth.

Small hunting parties for the expedition explored the lower reaches of the Sun River, where they continued to see evidence of abandoned Indian camps and trails. It may be that these camps were empty because the Indians were simply making their seasonal rounds, but it is possible that news of the

Raising the pole in a medicine lodge. PHOTOGRAPH BY WALTER MCCLINTOCK, COURTESY OF THE YALE COLLECTION OF WESTERN AMERICANA, BEINECKE RARE BOOK AND MANUSCRIPT LIBRARY.

approaching party of White men traveled faster than the Corps, and tribal groups avoided the area rather than chance an encounter. We know that a trade tomahawk made it to Nez Perce country before the expedition, so surely news would have traveled right along with it.

Throughout these weeks of encampment-studded travels in Amskapi Pikunni (Blackfeet) territory, no members of the Lewis and Clark party saw any people outside of their own crew, but they were observed by at least one small camp. A woman named Sikey-kio, or Black Bear (*sik* means black, *kiááyo* means bear), was in a camp near the mouth of the Sun River during the Long Rains Come Moon (June). It was during that time that she saw several members of the Lewis and Clark Expedition. These were the first White men she ever saw.[18] Six and a half decades later, she was living on the Sun River cattle ranch of Edward A. Lewis, within a few miles of this first sighting. She told many old stories to the family while she helped care for their eight children.[19] In 1899, twenty years after her passing, Mr. Lewis repeated the brief account to Robert Vaughn, who made note of it in his book, *Then and Now*.[20] Unfortunately, either Vaughn or Edward Lewis, or both, failed to include any more details of this historic event. No one from the Lewis and Clark party reported seeing signs of an active Blackfeet camp during their stay in that area upriver and south of Great Falls.

Having to abandon their large boats to continue up the river meant that some of the Corps would go on foot. Clark's group set out overland and found Indian evidence everywhere, but still they saw no people. Based on the presence of wickiup frames, some of the camps appeared to be those of Shoshones, whom the explorers called "Snakes," such as the one they had seen on July 16 about halfway between the Smith and Dearborn Rivers. On that day, Lewis noted that they "passed about 40 little booths formed of willow bushes to shelter them from the sun; they appeared to have been deserted about 10 days; we supposed that they were snake Indians." The camp was an encouraging sight, especially the tracks left behind by their many horses, which the Corps needed for transportation.

The overland party spent much of their time following an Indian road that skirted the western side of the Missouri valley. This direct route over a

Wickiup. PHOTOGRAPH COURTESY OF THE NATIONAL PARK SERVICE.

low mountain made for excellent travel and cut off miles along the winding river. The road was wide and well-traveled. (See Chapter 21, "Prayer Rocks and Sacred Paint along the Old North Trail.") All along the way they saw Shoshone camps that had been inhabited several months before, when the sap was running in the ponderosa pines, as evidenced by all the peeled trees in the area. The sweet cambium layer of inner bark provided a nourishing and welcome springtime treat.

From the river, on the morning of July 20, the Lewis party saw smoke coming from one of the valleys (probably the Prickly Pear) "as if the contry had been set on fire." Lewis reported that he couldn't be sure who set the fire—the Clark party might have caused the situation by accident or Indians might have set it "as a signall among themselves." In fact, it had been set by Indians who must have seen one or the other party, or both. Lewis, probably through information provided by Sacagawea (whom he still referred to as "the Indian woman"), concluded that they "had set the plain on fire to allarm the more distant natives and fled themselves further into the interior of the mountains." When Clark noticed the fire, he "left Signs to Shew the Indians if they Should come on our trail that we were not their enemeys."[21]

By July 22, Sacagawea knew she was in familiar territory and that they were nearing the Three Forks. Two days later, south of where Townsend sits today, Clark's party was following the Indian road up a creek when he spotted a horse out in the Missouri valley about six miles away. He and his men set out in pursuit, but the healthy horse wouldn't let Clark or anybody else get anywhere close.

When Clark's party reached the Three Forks on July 25, although they saw recent sign of Indians in the form of the track of a single horse headed up the river, they saw no people. This was the place Sacagawea had been captured by the Hidatsa several years before. When the Lewis party arrived at that location on July 27, Sergeant Ordway recorded in his journal their disappointment at not finding Sacagawea's people there. She told them they might be farther up the river, or salmon fishing on the other side of the mountains.

The thirty-three men and one woman of the Lewis and Clark Expedition traveled some 600 miles through what is now Montana, and progressed into Idaho, before their first encounter with a Native person since leaving the last

Hidatsa village four months before. On August 13, just below Lemhi Pass, the expedition finally met the Shoshone. Although the unusual travelers had been observed all along the Missouri, the Shoshones seemed unaware of their presence until they were face-to-face. Clearly, they were not part of the communication network of tribes along the Missouri.

The two oral histories shared here, from the Assiniboine and the Blackfeet, about the unusual people traveling upriver in their boats, are precious remnants of history from the vantage point of the people whose homelands the trespassers traversed. Such stories are a drop in the vast history bucket holding thousands of pages written about the Lewis and Clark story. I wish more Native stories had survived. ✣

Never Give Up
The Story of Marie Dorion

You might never have heard of Marie Dorion, born in St. Louis in 1786, the daughter of an Iowa mother and French father. No portrait of her exists. Her remarkable life, like that of countless other courageous Indian women, has not been the focus of biographers except for her role in the death-defying expedition sent west by John Jacob Astor in 1811.[1] Marie's greatest challenge actually came two years later. Although she may never have stepped foot in what would become Montana, her amazing story deserves to be remembered by those of us who occupy what was then known as the Oregon Country.

⊕ ⊕ ⊕

John Jacob Astor's American Fur Company needed a good interpreter to help them get through Sioux Country and beyond as they set out from St. Louis in February of 1811. They hired Pierre Dorion, Jr., the son of one of Lewis and Clark's interpreters on the Missouri. Dorion agreed to go on the condition that his wife Marie and their two young sons be allowed to accompany him. Like her husband, who was half Sioux and half French, Marie had good language skills. Opposed to going, she attempted to flee the scene, but her husband beat her into submission. Powerless to choose otherwise, Marie and her children joined a party of some sixty men on their way to the mouth of the Columbia River and what would become Astoria, Oregon. The location was key in the competition between America and England for control of the region.

The expedition left St. Louis by keelboat and headed for their winter camp a few hundred miles upriver. Their plan was to reverse the route Meriwether Lewis took back to St. Louis in 1806. They would follow the Missouri to the Sun River and then cross the mountains and follow the Blackfoot River to the Clark Fork River, through the Missoula Valley, and continue downstream to the Columbia. This plan came into question when they encountered John Colter, who had been in the Rockies since soon after Lewis and Clark's return. He told of his harrowing escape from hundreds of Blackfeet warriors somewhere in the Jefferson River valley the previous year. Ironically, most people today who read the history of this region know of Colter's famous flight, when he reportedly ran five miles in his bare feet before hiding in a logjam or beaver den to evade his pursuers, then walked some 200 miles to safety. Marie Dorion would survive an ordeal just as life-threatening, lasting four months and covering nearly 300 snow-covered miles, all the while caring for her two young sons. First, though, she would have to survive the journey to the mouth of the Columbia.

Colter advised the party to change their route. Undecided, Wilson Price Hunt, the leader of the expedition, continued upriver toward the mouth of the Grand River (across the Missouri from what is now Pierre, South Dakota), where they were to meet up with their competitor Manuel Lisa. En route, three more survivors of the Blackfeet threat arrived at their camp. These men also encouraged Hunt to opt for a route that skirted the Upper Missouri. In mid-June, Hunt's party reached the Grand River and learned that Manuel Lisa agreed—the Upper Missouri was too dangerous. Some of his employees, including Lewis and Clark's interpreter, George Drouillard, had lost their lives at the Three Forks. It seems that nobody thought the expedition should continue with their original plan.

While the men from these competing companies haggled, Marie Dorion must have been thrilled to learn that Sacagawea, the only woman in America known to have traveled to the mouth of the Columbia River, was there for her to talk with. Not surprisingly, no one recorded their conversation.

What might Sacagawea have told Marie of what she would encounter along the way? They were about the same age and had much in common. They might have already known each other in St. Louis, where both had been living with their interpreter husbands. I imagine Sacagawea told Marie about foods and medicines and where to find them, and what she could use to line the bottom of her baby's cradleboard when cattail fluff wasn't available. Marie might have expressed concern that she was pregnant. As the only woman in her party, the prospect of birthing a child must have felt daunting. Sacagawea would have told her stories about traveling with a baby through these unknown places, with no relatives—no women—to help out. Did they also swap stories of their husbands' tempers?

The Lower Columbia is vastly different from the prairie lands that had shaped the lives of these women. Sacagawea probably told Marie how leather moccasins never dry in that world of canoes, rivers of salmon, and giant cedars. Like the local people, she would learn to wear pounded cedar bark clothing to keep herself and her family dry and free from bugs. She might get to see a whale. The Astorians would be too late for camas and cous roots on the west side of the mountains, but they might arrive in time for late berries. On the coast she would feast on blackberries and salal, and shoots of fiddle-leaf ferns would augur the welcome of spring.

It was August and time to go. To avoid the Blackfeet, the Astorians would travel overland, rather than by river. Besides, the Missouri was too low to travel that late in the season, even if they had wanted to. They traded their two large keelboats to the Arikaras, and received horses in exchange. The five dozen men, one woman, and two children followed a route that met up with what would eventually become the Oregon Trail.

Their travels made Lewis and Clark's expedition look easy, especially once across the Continental Divide when they made the decision to abandon their horses for canoes to navigate down the Snake River. If you ever wondered why Lewis and Clark didn't follow the Snake River from Shoshone Country, read Peter Stark's recounting of the Astorians' travails in his book *Astoria*. After one drowning and the loss of one third of their canoes, they split into four pedestrian teams. Marie, well along in a third pregnancy, kept pace with her group with two-year-old Paul on her back and four-year-old Jean Baptiste walking beside her. Eventually they got some horses from an Indian village and were able to rest their aching feet. On a cold day at the end of December, after a twenty-seven-mile ride through snow into the Baker Valley of southeastern Oregon, Marie dropped behind, alone, to give birth. The following day she rode twenty miles through rough country into the Grand Ronde, where she met up with her party. About a week later, Marie buried "Little Lark" in an unmarked grave along a ridge on the north side of the Blue Mountains.[2]

They reached their destination on February 15, 1812, a half-year later than originally hoped, and established Fort Astor. Throughout this winter journey, Marie Dorion demonstrated great courage, resilience, and tenacity. As reported by Washington Irving, based on the journals and records of Astor's Pacific Fur Company, Marie "displayed a force of character that won the respect and applause of the white men."[3] She would need all these qualities and more to face the challenges that still lay ahead.

Two years after they arrived at the mouth of the Columbia, the Dorion family was headed back to the Snake River country with a small group of trappers. Fort Astor had been sold to the British, due to complications caused by the War of 1812. The group, led by John Reed, recrossed the Blue Mountains, probably retracing their route along what is now Interstate 84, and traveled some 500 miles into the basin country of southeastern Oregon and adjacent parts of Idaho. They built a small post on the lower Malheur River but didn't stay there long. When some Shoshones warned them of unfriendly Bannocks in the area, they moved the post across the Snake River, near the mouth of the Boise River.[4] Marie and her children stayed at the post, where she worked at preparing skins and cooking for the crew. Her husband and two other trappers set up a trapping camp about a day's ride to the southeast.[5] One evening, while she was alone with her children, an Indian man stopped by to tell Marie that the Bannocks had burned the abandoned post across the Snake. She loaded the boys, then seven and four, onto a horse, and left immediately to warn her husband. It took her three days of trudging through some twenty miles of snow to reach their cabin, but she was too late. The Bannocks had preceded her. She found her husband and another trapper dead. Shallow breath told her the third man was still alive, but just barely. This is where Marie Dorion's depth of character was defined.

Accounts vary somewhat, but the most reliable sources tell that she somehow managed to hoist the injured man onto a horse, hoping to get him to Reed's place for help. The man's injuries were too great, though. He fell from the horse. Unable to load him back up, Marie stayed with him until he died. She covered his body with snow and sagebrush and, with her children and a small amount of dried salmon she found in the cabin, headed the miles back to Reed's post. As they neared the cabin, exhausted and famished, she hid her children in a safe place, then proceeded on her own to face her worst fears. Again, she was too late. All the men had been killed.

Needing to warm her half-frozen children, she took the risk of making a fire in a protected area of trees. Next, she had to find food, for they had eaten little since this nightmare began. She returned to her boys empty-handed. The killers had ransacked the post. She scavenged a couple of knives, a few substandard skins, and some random supplies. For three days she stayed put, not knowing what to do. Drawing strength from her vast willpower, she collected herself and her children, loaded up two pathetic horses, and headed toward the Columbia where some help might be found. She traveled north along the east side of the Snake River to a crossing, where she improvised a way to float her sad little party across. She scavenged whatever food she could find along the way. The pitiful little family struggled their way up the Burnt River and into the snow-covered Blue Mountains. After nine days, a storm forced them to stop.

They spent the rest of the winter near a spring in the vicinity of present-day La Grande, Oregon. For their makeshift camp, she put up a small lodge frame and covered it with pine bark and cedar branches.[6] Marie caught mice and squirrels with a snare made of hair from the horses' manes. She found frozen berries around the spring, and managed to keep herself and the two boys alive. In mid-February, as the sap began to thaw, she removed sweet cambium from pines to take the edge off her children's hunger.[7] Finally, when starvation closed in, she smoked the meat of her horses—what little remained on their gaunt carcasses—and readied to leave.

With hints of spring in the air, Marie and the boys headed toward help. She packed up her meager supplies and what dried meat remained and put this load along with her featherweight four-year-old son on her back, took her seven-year-old by the hand, and headed toward help, not knowing if and when that might be found. There were no towns or trading forts in the region, only Indian villages and Bannock raiders. They traversed a ridge of the Blue Mountains along the trail where she had buried her infant two years before.

When snow-blindness forced her to stop for several days, she might have thought they wouldn't survive, but giving up was not in her vocabulary. In her world, there was no word for betraying the life Creator had given her.[8] She proceeded on. Emerging from the mountains, the sight of distant campfire lights offered her a modicum of hope. Knowing her children were too weak to journey on, she tucked them into a safe spot to wait, lined it with furs, and then this despairing woman headed toward hope. Thoroughly exhausted, Marie was reduced to crawling on her hands and knees toward what turned out to be a Walla Walla village. Too weak to cover the distance, she collapsed and, no doubt, would have died there had not the people of the village rescued her and her children and nursed them back to health.[9]

Two weeks later, on April 3, 1814, they were camped with the Walla Wallas on the Columbia near Walula Gap, when a party of Northwest Company traders arrived. All agreed that Marie's best option was to go with them to Fort Okanagan, where she would be safe and could figure out the next steps for herself and her sons.[10] The place they departed from was at or near the land now designated as the Marie Dorion Historical Park.

"Madam Dorian," as she is remembered, lived a full life. After Pierre's death, she would marry twice more, and her descendants spread throughout the Northwest, including Montana. She and her last husband settled in the Willamette Valley, where she died at about age sixty-four in September 1850. Her firstborn child Jean Baptiste had been killed by a White man a year or so earlier. Although the record is sketchy, his young son David, born around 1844, was raised by a relative in Montana. The trail regarding David's Cayuse mother, Josephine, is cold, leaving us only to wonder why this young boy came to live with others. He died in Missoula in 1924 and was buried in St. Mary's Cemetery in an unmarked grave. The brief obituary published by the *Missoulian* on January 11, 1924, tells that "O. D. Dorion, 86 years old, died at a local hospital yesterday morning as a result of the infirmities of age. Mr. Dorion was a resident of the Flathead reservation for many years and came to

Missoula about three years ago. There are no known relatives in this section."
I wonder if O. D. Dorion knew the story of what his father had endured as a
little boy and how his father survived only because of the heroic actions and
phenomenal tenacity of this amazing woman, Marie Dorion. ✛

*Monument to Marie Dorion at St. Louis Catholic Church near Woodburn, Oregon. PHOTOGRAPH BY ANDREW
PARODI, CC 2.0.*

WILLIAM HAMILTON'S
QUESTIONABLE ADVENTURE

Williliam T. Hamilton is often cited as the first White man in Missoula,
before it was a town. Local history remembers him as a trader there
from 1859 to 1864, while unofficial history whispers of his life as a distributor
of alcohol to the Indians on the Flathead Reservation. The earliest records
of Missoula County, Territory of Idaho, show him as the second sheriff,
appointed in 1861. Very little is known about him other than what he wrote
about himself.

When Hamilton published *My Sixty Years on the Plains* at the age of eighty-
five, background provided by the *Billings Gazette* claimed that, in the early days
of what would become Montana, he "was located on the Flathead lake, where
he hunted and traded with the Indians." Later, the article stated, "he moved
to the Bitter Root country," before moving to Fort Benton.[1] One might ask
why these locations don't match what has been reported elsewhere. Why
wouldn't he mention having been sheriff of Missoula County, and why didn't
John Owen ever mention his name in his journals or trading logs from Fort
Owen? It seems that history has taken Hamilton's words at face value. Perhaps
we should look again.

Hamilton was a man who could talk himself up so high that he was not
infrequently appointed to positions beyond his merit. In 1864, having sold his
little Missoula cabin near the mouth of Rattlesnake Creek, he moved to Fort

Benton, the only town in the enormous Chouteau County, home to thousands of Native people. He opened a hotel and butcher shop to serve travelers as well as the forty-five White residents. The next spring, Sidney Edgerton, the first territorial governor, appointed Hamilton as Chouteau County sheriff. What did it mean to be sheriff of the newly minted Montana county at that time, when most of the White men had little regard for the law, and Indians were fed up with unmet treaty promises and increasing numbers of interlopers? In April, some Kainai (one of the tribes of the Blackfoot Confederacy) had stolen several dozen horses from White residents of Fort Benton. Something needed to be done with the Indians, the townsfolk understood, seemingly unconcerned that they occupied Indian lands, guaranteed by treaty. "Wildcat Bill" Hamilton was an obvious choice to protect them. He had many years under his belt as an Indian fighter.

Hamilton's qualifications appear to have been nothing more than extreme self-confidence and quickness with a gun. In 1886, when the small town of Billings felt threatened by a daring gang of angry young Indians who had attacked Fort Custer, people remembered that "Old Indian fighters like 'Uncle Billy'

William T. "Billy" Hamilton. PHOTOGRAPH COURTESY OF THE BILLINGS PUBLIC LIBRARY.

William Hamilton's cabin in Missoula, built in 1858, shown circa 1903. PHOTOGRAPH COURTESY OF THE BILLINGS PUBLIC LIBRARY.

Hamilton and 'Liver Eating' Johnson appeared on the scene allured by the prospect of picking off a few Indians."[2] (I find it difficult not to veer off topic here to talk about how appalling it seems that such words would be printed in a respected newspaper. The good news is that progress has been made since then.) In the few snippets remembered of Hamilton by others, he is noted as a picturesque character, a drunk, and, as reported in a 1927 article in the *Billings Gazette*, "one of the most fearless fighters of Indians known in this part of the country." Hamilton himself bragged about the number of Native people he had turned into "good Indians," a euphemism for dead Indians. An article in the *Butte Daily Post* went so far as to say, "In the death of 'Uncle Billy' Hamilton the United States loses its greatest Indian fighter and the most skillful Indian sign talker and sign reader that this country ever produced."

Hamilton served in the role of Chouteau County sheriff for two years. One of his tasks that first year was to bring in the various tribes for a peace treaty to be negotiated by Acting Governor Thomas Meagher and Indian Agent Gad Upson. As Hamilton remembered in his written account several decades later, his amazing skills of communication and persuasion were, in no small part, responsible for accomplishing the work of delivering tribes to Fort Benton. This was not the only incredible accomplishment he wrote about. Another tale he put to ink was of a two-week, battle-filled odyssey in 1858 involving the Tobacco Plains Kootenai and the Pikunni Blackfeet. Hamilton plays the starring role in this lengthy and detailed autobiographical record published by the Montana Historical Society in 1900.[3]

Many years ago, while doing research at the Newberry Library in Chicago, I read a series of newspaper articles written by the brother of a member of the Mullan road crew and published in their hometown newspaper in Indiana. At that time, I didn't know much about the terrible winter of 1859–1860 at Cantonment Jordan, near Superior, but my eyes popped out as I read about the lions, wolves, and bears that lay down beside the river and died right in front of the men. Then I started to wonder. If such a thing had happened, I probably *would* have read about it. The reporting turned out to have been wildly exaggerated. Something about William Hamilton's story strikes me the same way.

Most of us over the age of twenty grew up accepting at face value things we read in print. After all, the story was right in front of us in "black-and-white," and in this case, it was published by the prestigious Montana Historical Society. Their stamp of approval gave Hamilton's story authenticity. But in the Old West, where Hamilton's witnesses were Indians, an illiterate traveling companion, and a Canadian fur trader, what were the chances he would get caught if he exaggerated, embellished, or just concocted a good tale? Or, what if after forty years, he truly couldn't remember? "Uncle Bill," as he came to be known, was a storyteller. Perhaps he had come to believe his own tales.

Secret Mission to the Blackfeet

Hamilton's most heroic story is about an expedition into Blackfeet country. At the end of the Plateau Wars between Native people and the U.S. Army in what is now eastern Washington (1856–1858), William T. Hamilton accepted an assignment "as secret Indian detective with pay as scout." As directed by Colonel George Wright, from Fort Walla Walla, Hamilton would "proceed through the different tribes of Indians to the Blackfoot Nation, east of the Rocky Mountains" and return at the earliest possible moment with a report on "the condition and disposition of the different tribes visited." He and a one-eyed, mixed-blood Nez Perce named Alex McKay would pose as traders.

They left in late September of 1858, and a couple of weeks later found themselves crossing the Continental Divide with the Salish hunting camp, led by Chief Victor, and entered Blackfeet territory. They crossed Cadotte Pass and landed near the Sun River Agency, where they spent time trading with some friendly Pikunni of Little Dog's band. Hamilton had several meetings with Alfred Vaughn, the Indian agent, who provided the information sought about "the disposition and condition" of the different bands of Indians in his jurisdiction, from which Hamilton completed his report for Col. Wright. With that task accomplished, he and McKay were free to move along, and happy to do so, as they were always on guard, afraid of losing their trade goods and stock to the Blackfeet. Also, the season was late. They needed to get back across the mountains before winter set in.

Chief Little Dog's son told them they might be able to cross the mountains with some Kootenai who were camped by St. Mary's Lake, which was within a day's ride. On October 26, they organized their stock of nineteen horses and mules and headed out. Pikunni guides escorted them much of the way. They caught their first glimpse of the Kootenai village after several hours of travel, and they were soon greeted by dozens of men, who escorted them to the lodge of the head chief, "old chief Black Bear."

While the men got settled, Kootenai women unpacked and stored the visitors' robes, built a corral for the visitors' stock, and prepared a meal. Hamilton asked the chief to have the women cut plenty of grass for their horses and mules. A dozen women left immediately, "each with a cord and large knife, and they proved themselves experts in cutting bunch grass." The capable women returned with "fully a thousand pounds," and Hamilton paid them for their services. He also arranged for these women to make some of their fine heavy caribou moccasins for himself and McKay. Their own moccasins were heavily worn, and the season was changing.

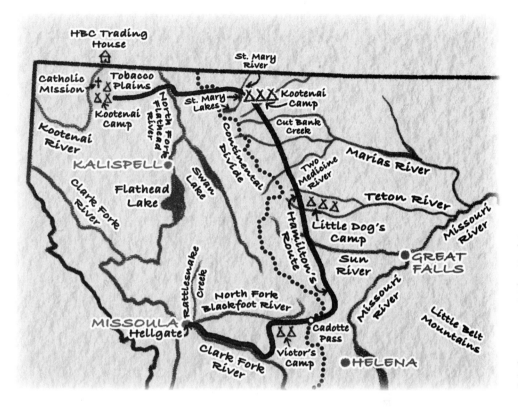

In the chief's lodge, the faux traders settled in to get to know these "noble, pleasant looking" Indians, including the "two noble looking sons" of Black Bear. They conversed through sign language. Hamilton, in his own estimation, was a better sign-talker than most of the Indians. He learned from them that three days before they had battled with some Blackfeet. One Kootenai had died and three were wounded. The leaders expressed their pleasure to have these two well-armed men join them. They were especially heartened to learn of all the ammunition the traders carried. Any young warriors who were out of ammunition were called to the chief's lodge for powder and balls, "with warnings not to waste any of it." A woman entered the lodge with six pairs of caribou-skin moccasins, three pairs each for the traders.

Two young scouts came to report they had discovered Blackfeet in the vicinity of the village. The headmen had to decide which route to take across the mountains through what are now Glacier and Waterton National Parks.

They had three options, according to Hamilton: two a little northwest of their camp and one to the south. They decided to take the southern route.[4]

They would post guards all night and leave early in the morning. Just before dawn, the village was attacked by what turned out to be a small contingent of six Blackfeet. As reported by Hamilton, "Upon count after the uproar it was found that five Blackfeet had been made good Indians, two being credited to McKay." Hamilton had been an Indian fighter in California and Oregon before taking this assignment. In his way of thinking, "good Indians" were dead Indians, except, of course, those he was with. The Kootenai had taken one prisoner and then debated how to punish him. They decided to strip him, cut his hair, and subject him to thirty lashes before telling him to run for his life. Hamilton credits himself for suggesting this option.

As daylight dawned, Black Bear was anxious to leave. He ordered the lodges to be packed up, and everyone made ready. The chief with one group of warriors would follow along behind the camp, while an advance guard would ride about a half-mile ahead. The two traders joined this vanguard of fifty warriors, led by Young Black Bear. When they reached a rise, about fifteen miles along, they looked to the rear of the long traveling village, where they saw "fully two hundred Blackfeet." Young Black Bear signaled to those in the rear to close up. The moving village instantly formed a compact circle.

A group of about 100 Blackfeet gave forth a "thrilling yell" as they rushed forward, firing their "Hudson Bay flint lock, muzzle-loading guns" from too great a distance to do any harm. The better mounted Kootenai drove back their attackers. Kootenai who understood Blackfeet ways knew their enemies would take revenge as they crossed the mountains, so Black Bear called off his warriors and kept the village moving. Some of the Kootenai gathered up robes, blankets, and about fifty Blackfeet horses from the battlefield. Hamilton counted thirty-five Blackfeet scalps. Travois were prepared to carry the four Kootenai dead and twenty wounded across the divide.

At about 3 P.M. they reached a good camp, with water, grass, and wood. Here they could bury their dead. The chief sent young men on a shortcut route across the mountains to call for recruitments. They would leave early in the morning. Black Bear hoped to get across the pass the following day, although some of the men thought it best to remain in their camp until reinforcements arrived.

Our storyteller, once again, takes credit for concocting the best plan for their success. He advised them to move the village by sunup with the goal of getting through the canyon and timber before they were outnumbered. Hamilton was so self-enthralled, it didn't occur to him that they would already have thought of this strategy as an option.

By daylight on October 28, the wounded had been tended, people had been fed, and the lodges were packed. Hamilton reports that he took the lead of about sixty warriors with Young Black Bear, while Chief Black Bear and his hand-picked warriors brought up the rear. The trail passed through a gorge, "wide enough for two abreast, but rocky and somewhat steep in places." Having to transport the wounded slowed them down. The Kootenai were not concerned that Blackfeet were lurking at the edge of the trail because, according to the chief, "the Blackfeet were afraid of timber and the Kootenai were their superiors in mountain warfare."

The vanguard made it out of the wooded canyon and into open country without any sign of their enemies when suddenly about fifty horses carrying battle-ready warriors cantered toward them. Another skirmish was about to begin, as Hamilton writes:

> As fortune would have it there were about forty Kootenais coming over the mountain, and at sight of what was going on they sent forth their war whoop with a will and were answered by the Kootenais still engaged with the Blackfeet. It evidently appeared to the Blackfeet that the reinforcements were many times greater than they really were, from the manner in which they were scattered out with the best horses in advance. Accordingly, the Blackfeet were quick to take action and called all their warriors off and beat a retreat and got into the timber, taking a number of their wounded with them.

By the time Chief Black Bear emerged from the timber, the Blackfeet were gone. Nine more Kootenai died that day and many more were wounded. Hamilton was sorry to see that one of the young boys who had been responsible for his pack animals had been killed and two others were wounded. He wrote that "those little boys fought more bravely than many of the grown Indians." He went on to tell of all the ways that he personally saved the day and explained how much more successful the Kootenai would have been if he had been in charge.

Once they arrived at their camp for the night, Hamilton was put into action dressing wounds. According to him, he was so proficient that "their medicine men were told to stand back." Of course, Hamilton was not only a better warrior and better sign-talker, he was also a better doctor.

The next morning, the third day of this perilous journey, was cloudy and cold. The Kootenai needed to get clear of the mountains before snow fell and before the Blackfeet attacked again. At least they had an additional hundred warriors. By the time they reached the summit of the mountains, snow was falling. All were relieved to reach a small prairie with a creek running through, where they efficiently set up and secured their camp. Black Bear ordered two dozen young warriors to act as lookouts, "as Blackfeet pay no attention to storms." In fact, according to what Hamilton was told, stormy weather was their preferred time to attack.

On the morning of October 30, they were greeted by frost. The sun was a welcome visitor while they packed up camp and made ready, once again, to travel. They could smell home. On the alert the entire way, they made good time and by midday "arrived on the south side of Tobacco Plains, where a beautiful location was selected alongside a small lake and a good spring of water." Warriors from other bands of Kootenai began to arrive, responding to the call for help. For the first time since Hamilton and McKay joined this group, the mood at camp was light. Young people spent the afternoon and into the night singing and dancing their scalp dance, while their elders pondered the threat level of the Blackfeet.

In the morning they packed up and traveled to the site of "the Mission" on the banks of the Kootenai River at the southwest end of Tobacco Plains. This mission was a rustic cabin from an earlier Hudson's Bay Company post, where priests stayed when they visited the Kootenai. Mice were the only occupants on that Halloween of 1858. The chief and his headmen selected a favorable place to raise the lodges "in a circle, leaving an abundance of room

"The Mission" at Tobacco Plains, an old Hudson's Bay Company cabin. PHOTOGRAPH COURTESY OF THE LIBRARY OF CONGRESS, LC-USZC4-11427.

inside the circle for all the stock." Since the chiefs expected the Blackfeet to return with reinforcements, they set the women to work digging rifle pits around the village. That night a strong guard watched over the camp.

On the morning of November 1, fifty well-mounted young warriors were sent out to search the surrounding countryside for signs of the enemy. Hamilton told Chief Black Bear that he was going to the trading post for some groceries. The chief directed his son to go along. This Hudson's Bay trading post was to the north, about six miles up the river from their camp. Although the 49th parallel had been determined as the dividing line between Canada and the United States in 1846, the boundary survey was not completed until 1860; at the time of this story nobody was sure whose territory the post was in.

Hamilton and Young Black Bear were greeted at the post by John Linklater, a Scotsman who had been the trader at this location for five years.[5] Because of trouble with the Blackfeet in 1853, his predecessor had moved the fort to this location on the west side of the river. Hamilton and Linklater discussed the boundary line, with Linklater "claiming the whole country as Hudson Bay territory, and I [Hamilton] claiming the whole of Tobacco Plains for Uncle Sam.[6]

Hamilton set down a double eagle as payment for the list of goods he desired. Linklater asked him how much that was worth. These gold coins, at the time, were worth $20. The trader would keep the coin himself, because the employees weren't allowed to trade for money but only for furs. Hamilton doesn't explain how they remedied the situation, but "Scotty" was able to provide everything on Hamilton's list at "Walla Walla prices" instead of the higher prices normally charged at these distant outposts. He also gifted Hamilton with a quart of Hudson Bay rum "as thick as cream." Scotty then told his assistant that he would accompany his visitors to the village and requested him "to put up sufficient provisions for a great feast." They loaded up Hamilton's acquisitions and the food for the feast and headed out.

The women had the food prepared within a couple of hours of their arrival, and the chief's lodge was made ready to serve the visitors and headmen. Others would sit outside, where hides had been spread for them. Afterward, the chiefs met with Mr. Linklater, while Hamilton checked on the wounded and then attended his horses.

The scouts returned at sundown and reported having seen signals (smoke) on the summit of the mountains. That meant that the Blackfeet were calling their warriors together for another round of fighting. The Kootenai expected to see them within three days.

In the morning, scouts were once again sent to check for threats before the stock was turned loose. Nothing was amiss. The next day was the same, although some signs of the Blackfeet were discovered. That night, they brought in the stock and attended to the rifle pits. On the third morning, evidence that Blackfeet had been close by came in the form of two wolf skins found near camp. The Kootenai expected an attack to come soon. Some 200 scouts searched the area and, through the course of the day, reported numerous signs. The chiefs knew that the favorite time for the Blackfeet to attack was with the rising sun, but they could come anytime during the day, if the opportunity arose.

Mr. Linklater arrived with his fast little war horse. He would stay to fight with them. The night was quiet, but the next morning revealed numerous signs of Blackfeet. The Kootenai turned out their stock with a strong guard to protect them, while scouts did their work outside of the village. About an hour later, three of the scouts approached at a full run, making the sign for Blackfeet. The animals were brought in and protected and "inside of five minutes fully three hundred mounted warriors were ready to go to the front."

The vanguard, including Hamilton, McKay, and Linklater, soon faced about 100 Blackfeet emerging from the timber, "shouting their war whoop and sending some lead" at them. The Kootenai charged and drove them to retreat to a small grove where they joined other Blackfeet. Even more waited in a nearby narrow draw. The Kootenai circled around the Blackfeet at a safe distance while they assessed the situation. Then the leaders held a council of war. After they had expressed their own thoughts about the situation, they asked their guests for their opinions. First, Scotty said he had come to fight, not to talk. McKay, in his "crude" sign language, told them that half of the Kootenai should dismount, that the footmen should charge the grove and the mounted warriors charge the draw, and thus get through with the fight. Hamilton went last and, at least according to his report, proposed the plan that would be followed:

> I told them that as there was a light breeze which was favorable and as the grass was dry, to burn or smoke out the Blackfeet from their stronghold; that they should bring up fifty or sixty squaws with wet blankets to put out the fire when the Blackfeet were routed. At the suggestion of this method many of the leading men brightened up, some of the Indians approving my measure and others opposing it, but finally it was adopted.

Hamilton tells his readers that the women soon arrived with wet blankets, just before a "cluster of Blackfeet showed themselves." Shots were fired and one of the enemies dropped. The Blackfeet returned fire as they retreated. About fifty Kootenai warriors then crawled within twenty-five yards of their enemies, "forming a half circle on the windward side of them." Hamilton and the others covered the young Kootenai while they set the grass afire. The bone-dry grass quickly swept toward the Blackfeet. Once the fire had a good start, the Blackfeet "sent forth a yell," as they retreated to the cover of the woods. A skirmish ensued.

Although the Kootenai were clearly winning, it was not without cost. Hamilton stopped to help "Scotty," who had an arrow stuck through the fleshy part of his thigh. The ever-ready Hamilton cut off the feather end, then grabbed the arrow end and jerked it through. Women carried the dead to the village. There were three, and many others wounded. The fighting continued, but with less vigor. The flames, too, had lost their gusto as the women's fire brigade did its job. When it was over, they found three Blackfeet who had not escaped the fire.

The next morning dawned clear and quiet. After breakfast, Hamilton and McKay said their goodbyes to Scotty, whom the women had placed in a travois to take home. It would be a while before his leg was healed. Hamilton and McKay told the chiefs they would soon be leaving. They were eager to return to Walla Walla before more winter weather arrived.

Before they left, though, they traded their remaining goods for marten and fisher skins, highly valued furs. Afterwards, they organized their scaled-down belongings, while women cut grass for their stock. Before leaving, these comrades-in-arms exchanged gifts with their Kootenai companions. Black Bear sent two young men along with them to show them the trail to Lake Pend d'Oreille. The Kootenai "marked out a map" for the travelers to show the route to reach the lower (western) end of the lake, and into country they would recognize.

Checking for Facts

Shouldn't a story such as this November 6, 1858, Tobacco Plains battle, involving hundreds of warriors, have been remembered by somebody other than William Hamilton? A man as extraordinary as this sign-talking, quick-drawing, war-strategizing medicine man was surely worthy of note by others, yet neither written nor oral history includes reference to him or the events he describes. It would be expected that John "Scotty" Linklater, the trader at Tobacco Plains, would at least mention Hamilton in his accounts book, and that Linklater would note his own participation in a battle where he was shot in the leg with an arrow.

However, anthropologist David Chance reviewed the evidence and could find no corroboration of Hamilton's story, either in the Hudson's Bay Company records or the writings of other travelers through the area in those years.[7] He found that a year after Hamilton's visit, two members of a British exploring expedition—James Hector and Augustus Thibido—met with Linklater.[8] Both men reported on history of the area, but neither of them mentioned Hamilton or the events he described. Although Thibido reported that two priests regularly paid visits to their little mission outpost at the location reported by Hamilton (citing Linklater as his source), he mentions nothing of a Blackfeet attack just a year before.[9]

David Chance questioned whether Linklater would abandon his tiny post to the care of an assistant "while taking part not only in the battle but in its preliminaries and aftermath, while there were hundreds of Blackfeet lurking about, advertising their presence with signals from the mountaintops." I question why they didn't locate their camp by the trading post across the Kootenai River, instead of the vulnerable site of the old mission. After all, the Hudson's Bay Company folks had moved across the river a few years earlier because of marauding Blackfeet.[10]

Perhaps most importantly, no mention of this battle or the events that led up to it has ever appeared in Kootenai oral history accounts. Tobacco Plains elder Ambrose Gravelle told anthropologist Claude Schaeffer that the last battle between his people and the Blackfeet had been in 1850 southeast of Lethbridge, with no mention of a later battle right in the middle of their homeland.[11] Another discrepancy is that the name Black Bear is not remembered as a chief. Head chief at that time was either Michelle or Aeneas. Many Tobacco Plains elders still tell stories of those years, as they have been passed down through the generations. If Hamilton's story were true, it seems like someone in the area at the time would have remembered the story of an amazing White man who helped the Kootenai defeat the Blackfeet with fire and wet blankets.

⊕ ⊕ ⊕

After his time in Fort Benton, William T. Hamilton fought in the wars against the Sioux and then finally settled down in a little cabin on the Yellowstone at what became Columbus.

He is reported to have lived "a quiet, independent life," which may be construed as lonely. Although he suffered "reduced circumstances," Uncle Billy "never begged," according to the *Butte Daily Post* reporter who wrote the lengthy and glowing 1908 article about him following Hamilton's death from cancer. He had eked out a living as "a trapper." The reporter mentioned that he trapped in the summertime. Since fur-trapping is done in winter, we can assume that Uncle Billy spent his later years killing wolves and coyotes for the bounty paid. In the 1890s, he could get $5 for every wolf pup he could kill. So-called wolfers commonly used strychnine-laced cattle to accomplish their work. The stench of strychnine might have kept people away, or maybe the people who knew him well had started to suspect his honesty. All these years later, we can only wonder. ✢

Right: William Hamilton's will, published in the June 5, 1908, Billings Weekly Gazette. PHOTOGRAPH COURTESY OF NEWSPAPERS.COM.

Friday, June 5, 1908.

W. T. HAMILTON WILL IS FILED

J. D. LOSEKAMP AND J. I. ALLEN NAMED AS EXECUTORS.

THREE BENEFICIARIES

Bequeaths John D. Losekamp Book "My Sixty Years on the Plains" and Other Writings—Leaves Personal Effects to Columbus Men.

From Thursday's Daily.

The holographic will of the late William T. Hamilton, the author, pioneer and scout, who died in Billings recently, was filed for probate in the district court yesterday. Accompanying it was a petition of J. D. Losekamp and J. I. Allen, who are named as executors, asking that the will be admitted to probate.

The petition states that "Uncle Bill's" estate consists of the book, "My Sixty Years on the Plains," a buggy and harness valued at $50, watch and other personal effects valued at $100 and one lot in the town of Columbus valued at $100.

Following is the will:

I, W. T. Hamleton, of Columbus, Yellowstone county, state of Montana, being of sound and disposing mind and memory do make, publish and declare this my last will and testament.

First: I give and bequeath book, "My Sixty Years on the Plains" and all other writings whatsoever to John D. Losekamp of Billings, state of Montana.

Second: I give and bequeath all of my personal property, buggy, harness and what horses I may possess at the time of my death to Albert Myers.

Third: I give and bequeath all of my personal effects, viz: clothes, trunks, watch, pipes, bedclothes, etc., to J. I. Allen of Columbus, Mont.

Fourth: What property I may be possessed of at my death to be sold and the proceeds of the same to be applied to pay my funeral expenses.

I hereby nominate and appoint J. D. Losekamp and J. I. Allen as executors, without bonds.

Dated this 10th day of March, A. D. 1908.

(Signed)   W. T. HAMILTON.

PART II
NORTHWEST MONTANA

5

KOOTENAI ORAL HISTORY AND GLACIAL LAKE GEOLOGY

Reconsidering Deep History

In graduate school in the 1970s, I was taught to disregard tribal oral histories. They were not considered to be a source of reliable information. When I would hear a tale of long ago, I listened with my ear toward quaintness, not truth. Since then, I have had numerous occasions to change my opinion on this subject, especially regarding the Kootenai. My attitude first began to shift when I heard their account of ashfall that accumulated so deeply as to choke the life out of the plants, causing widespread catastrophe for all living beings. The only ash deposits in the region of the magnitude described are those resulting from the eruption of Mount Mazama around 7,700 years ago.[1] Then, when I read the Kootenai creation story (shared below), I found myself in the realm of deep history, not what I had learned to hear as quaint myth.

The Kootenai story was like a chink in the armor of my schooling. Who was I to say where people came from, when we academics know so little about the buried history of this continent, and new theories emerge with some regularity? The narrative seemed to address the flood cycles that came with the melting glaciers of the last major ice age. On many occasions I heard Kootenai people state unequivocally that they never crossed the Bering land bridge, that they have lived in their origin place since the Creator prepared it. They have no migration story. Shouldn't researchers defer to them until such a time that concrete evidence proves otherwise?

For those of us with short memories, shallow roots, and a reliance on the written word, it is hard to imagine having such an unbroken connection to a place as what the Kootenai stories convey. The Kootenai origin story thrives in the homeland prepared for them at the beginning of time, the region they have always occupied. As a scientist, I started thinking about comparing their origin myth with documented geological processes and archaeological evidence.

I spoke with a Kootenai friend about my intentions and heard back from him a few days later. In an email, he included a list of dictionary definitions of "myth," used both as an adjective and a noun. He was concerned about how "mythic" stories get trivialized as being imaginary, "without foundation in fact." He was right to be concerned. The power of myth has been lost to the "age of enlightenment," when knowing became limited to the five senses. Intuition, dreams, visions, and mythology fell into the realm of the unreal. With the new emphasis on reason and fact, the Western world was left bereft of a means to relate to life's mysteries. The mysteries themselves were closeted, and myths were relegated to the world of fantasy. We corresponded about the truths held in the Kootenai origin story and how this writing might help regain something of what has been lost to rationalism.

Thinking about all of this, I wondered how I could bridge the gulf between the two worldviews without seeming too biased toward one viewpoint or the other. I might need my own land bridge to get me through the depths of this topic. Was I capable of suspending judgment and trying to be open to the two realities, or was I too stuck in the Age of Reason? Can the ancient Kootenai creation story actually be reconciled with geological evidence? Does it matter if this account of their origins is both myth and history? Maybe this attempt to reconcile the two was misdirected; perhaps what truly matters is to understand the underlying teachings held in the narrative and the way they guide behavior.

I could feel my heels dig into the shifting sands of my reality where I could cling to the evidence of geology to help me make sense of the world as I knew it. At the same time, I sensed that I had been led to the edge of this European way of knowing so that I could glimpse the world of indigenous knowing. I owed it to all the teachers who so patiently have shared their worlds with me, beginning in Navajo country in 1977. I had to release myself from a belief in the Bering land bridge theory and my need for a smoking gun.

I decided to move ahead with the plan, using a published version of the story. However, I would need to discuss this idea with some Kootenai colleagues before proceeding. This story is their cultural heritage, their spiritual legacy, and their intellectual property. I needed permission to use it. This isn't a legal imperative, it's a moral one. Since the version I intended to use came from the Ktunaxa First Nations—Kootenai of Canada—I asked historian Viola Birdstone, a Ktunaxa herself, to review what I wrote. She did, and with a few editorial recommendations, she approved the approach I had taken, and since this version was already published, I wasn't revealing any restricted cultural information.

One caution for the reader is to recognize that the story shared here can easily be misinterpreted because it is just a small part of a series of overlapping and interconnected stories that create a continuing saga, a living story. The closest example from the European world that comes to my mind is Wagner's Ring Cycle, based on the legends of Norse sagas. This Ktunaxa story should not be thought of as mythic or philosophical, but as a way of life, an understanding of the world. People who have left their homeland behind, myself included, have trouble thinking this way.

As I said, the Kootenai have no migration story. According to their origin story, Creator made their homeland ready with the help of the animals. The creation story shared here has been shortened from the version shared by former chief of the St. Mary Band of Ktunaxa, Joe Pierre, and his version is just a fraction of what used to be told when time wasn't money and winters were long. Instead of skimming through the details, slow down and take the time needed to tease out the deep truths buried here. You may need to read it a second time. Read it as if you were sitting around a central hearth in a winter lodge, listening to a wrinkled but still bright-eyed elder, gesturing throughout the telling of this primal story.

The story of Naⱡmuqⱳin and Yawu?nik' teaches about the natural world as well as the cultural world, with names of places that go back to the beginnings of human occupation. In a way it is a love story, one that connects the Ktunaxa to their ancient lineage and the gifts of their heritage. Each time the story is told within their communities it adds a link to an unbroken chain of memory. See what you think about the connection between a water monster and the glacial lake floods.

⊕ ⊕ ⊕

Ktunaxa Creation Story as told by Joe Pierre[2]

The story of Naⱡmuqȼin and Yawu?nik' takes place "in the Beginning," the time of animals, before humans arrived. And at that time, Creator, Nupika, sent out word to all the living beings that he wanted them to come together for a meeting because he had something important to tell them, and he had something very important to ask them.

When all of the nasukin, the chiefs of all of the living beings of the world, came together, Nupika stood up in front of them and said, "Soon, very, very soon there will be 'Aqⱡsmakniǩ here on the earth. The 'Aqⱡsmakniǩ, human beings, are coming to the earth. And the question that I have for each and every single one of you is this: I want to find out what it is that you will do for the human beings when they come to the earth."

It was during this very long meeting, when all chiefs of the living beings told what they would do for the human beings, that two sisters—two little birds—went fishing at that place now known as Bonners Ferry and were swallowed by the giant water monster, Yawu?nik'. This giant water monster lived in the Kootenay River and the Columbia River, because at this time, when this story happens, the Kootenay River and the Columbia River were joined together in one big huge water system and the Yawu?nik' plied these waters. The Yawu?nik' had a giant appetite. He would eat any animal that came down to the water to drink, no matter how big or small. Even two little birds.

When the little birds' brother Yamakpaⱡ, the little red-headed wood-pecker [downy woodpecker], learned that they had been swallowed, he knew he had to do something. Humble enough to recognize the task was beyond him, he knew he needed help. He would ask Naⱡmuqȼin, the chief of all the land animals. Naⱡmuqȼin was so big that if he stood upright he would hit his head on the ceiling of the sky, and because of this he traveled around on his hands and knees. When Naⱡmuq¢in heard Yamakpaⱡ's story, he agreed to help. He said, "You know we should form a hunting party. We should hunt down that Yawu?nik' and kill him."

So word went out that a hunting party was being formed and one of the first animals to come along and join that hunting party is Skinku¢, the coyote. The group gets word that Yawu?nik' has been sighted up near ?akiskq'nuk, the area up by Invermere, British Columbia today, on the Columbia River. And so they go up there and sure enough, Yawu?nik' is in the river. So they start to chase him and Yawu?nik' starts to swim toward the south as hard and as fast as he can toward the Columbia River, then swims right into the Kootenay River because remember, at this time when this story happens, the Kootenay River and the Columbia River are joined together.

Animals on both sides of the river are chasing him, but they can't get close. Yawu?nik just keeps swimming as fast as he can. Other animals join and the chase continues. And Yawu?nik' keeps swimming from the Kootenay River back into the Columbia and now toward the north as fast and as hard as he can. At one point, the hunting party arrives to find the monster motionless. He is tired and needs to rest. Skinku¢, coyote, gets permission from the hunt chief Naⱡmuq¢in, to try to spear the water monster, but when he gets close enough to raise his spear, Yawu?nik' notices him and he starts to swim away. Although Skinku¢'s spear nicks the monster's fin, it isn't enough to stop him.

Yawu?nik' gets away and he starts swimming all the way around the circuit again. He leaves the Columbia River, swims right into the Kootenay River, and he keeps swimming toward the south all the way down to ?aqswaq, which is now Libby, Montana, turns toward the west and swims through Skinku¢ ?amakis, the land of the coyote, from northwestern Montana into northern Idaho, past ?aq'anqmi, that place where those two sisters went fishing. From there, he follows the river toward the north through ?a¢pu ?amakis, the land of the wolverine, past Yaqan Nu?kiy, which is Creston, into the west arm of the Kootenay Lake, Mi¢'qaqas ?amakis, the land of the chickadee, near Nelson, British Columbia, past ?aqyamⱡup, that place where you can see to the bottom of the water it's so clear, Kik'siⱡuk, Castlegar, where the Kootenay

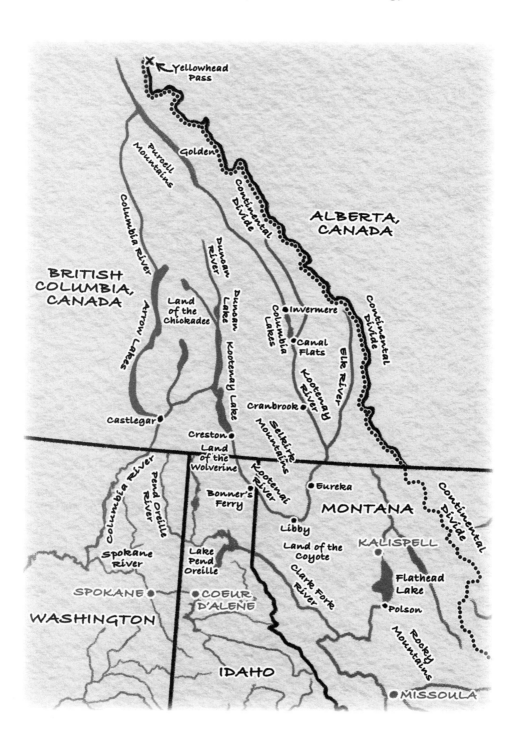

River flows into the Columbia River. Yawu?nik' turns toward the north and swims as hard and as fast as he can all the way up around the big bend of the Columbia and then back down toward the south and back into the Kootenay River. And the hunting party, they just continue to chase him and Yawu?nik' keeps swimming around and around in those two rivers. Around and around Yawu?nik' goes.

The hunters continue their chase around and around in those two rivers for days, and weeks, until one day, when they hear some laughter as they are chasing through the land of the chickadee. They stop and look around. Sitting up on the side of the mountain they see Kik'um, the wise old spirit, and he is laughing. "Kik'um," they say, "what are you laughing at?" And Kik'um says, "I'm laughing at you." For weeks he has been watching them run by every couple of days chasing that Yawu?nik. "You're never going to catch him," he tells them. "He's too big, he's too strong. That's what I'm laughing at."

He has a suggestion, though. "Naɬmuqǂin, you giant," he says, "why don't you use your size and your strength? Cut across the mountains. Go to that place where the two rivers join together and use your size and strength. Topple over the mountain there and cut those two rivers off and the next time Yawu?nik' comes swimming down from the north, you'll have him trapped."

Naɬmuqǂin recognizes a good idea when he hears one, and so, he cuts across the mountains to that place where the two rivers join together, while the rest of the hunting party continues chasing Yawu?nik' up toward the north. Naɬmuqǂin uses his size and his strength to topple over those two mountains, cutting those two rivers off from each other and forming the Columbia Lake.

Sure enough, just like Kik'um said, the next time Yawu?nik' comes swimming down from the north, he is trapped in the newly formed Columbia Lake. The honor of killing Yawu?nik' goes to Yamakpaɬ, the little red-headed woodpecker. When he kills the Yawu?nik', the giant Naɬmuqǂin, starts to tear the Yawu?nik' apart so the animals could eat. Naɬmuqǂin then scatters the bones and organs of the water monster in different directions. The rib bones of the Yawu?nik' turn into hoodoos, that can still be seen today. After Naɬmuqǂin has just about finished his work, he looks at his hands and he sees they are covered in blood. So he reaches down, picks up some grass and he wipes the blood off his hands. The blood and grass that fall right where Naɬmuqȼin is kneeling would be the beginnings of the Kootenai people.

And then the animals realize that they are the ones to fulfill the Nupika prophecy of the ʾAqɬsmaknik̓ coming to the earth. It's because of them that the human beings will be on the earth soon. This makes them very happy. They're so happy that they could do this that they start to celebrate. Naɬmuqȼin is so happy that he forgets himself, stands upright and hits his head on the ceiling of the sky. He hits so hard that he falls over and dies. Naɬmuqȼin's body forms the Rocky Mountains between Yakɬiki, Yellowhead Pass, to the north and Yellowstone to the south.[3]

When those ʾAqɬsmaknik̓ arrived, the Creator, Nupika, told them, "You have just lost a giant of the water and a giant of the land. It is now your responsibility to look after the water, to look after the land."

⊕ ⊕ ⊕

A Unique People

If you ask a traditional Kootenai where they came from, he or she will tell you their people began in the same places where they live today, only less confined. They would tell you that their ancestors since time immemorial are buried here. When linguists study the movements of people, they compare languages within one language family to assess differences and to analyze rates and direction of change. Oral histories contribute additional information about origins and migrations. Kootenai, though, have no other tribes with which to make these comparisons. They are a unique people, with a language like no other—what linguists call an isolate. Having no known linguistic relatives, they have long been surrounded by people who speak unrelated languages, especially those of the Salish and Blackfeet. Kootenai is a name of unknown derivation.

Names of tribes were generally given by their neighbors, based on some distinguishing characteristic. In Plains Indian sign language, one Blackfeet sign for the Kootenai meant "People-who-live-in-the-mountains." Others referred to them as "People of the White-Tail Deer," "Canoe People," "Water People," and "Fish Eaters." The people known as "Kootenai" don't know the meaning of that word, now definitive of them, spelled Kootenai in the United States and Kootenay in Canada, and Kutenai in anthropological literature. The people themselves, at least those in Canada, refer to themselves by the term Ktunaxa (pronounced k-too-nah-ha). Originally, they knew themselves as ʾAq̓smaknik̓, "the people." And before the ʾAq̓smaknik̓ were the animals, who helped the Creator make it possible for the human beings to live in this world.

⊕ ⊕ ⊕

Deep History[4]

The Kootenai and Columbia River circuit at the heart of this creation story might be interpreted as a simple telling of complex geological history dating back to the Late Pleistocene. According to the origin story, the Kootenay River once flowed into the Columbia at Columbia Lake, creating a circular system, before Chief animal, the giant Naⱡmuqȼin, dammed it up to catch the water monster. Today, the upper reaches of these rivers are a bit like interlocking Cs, or horseshoes.

In southeastern British Columbia, the great Kootenay River flows out of the Rockies north of Canada's Kootenay National Park, opposite the mountains from Banff, Alberta. From there it flows southward, generally within the landform known as the Rocky Mountain Trench, to its bend by Jennings, Montana, where it veers around the south end of the Purcell Mountains toward Bonners Ferry, Idaho, then turns back northward and parallels itself until it merges with the Duncan River from the north, and together they turn westward and flow into the Columbia near the town of Castlegar, B.C. The Columbia has done the opposite. It flows northward from Columbia Lake until its Big Bend around the north end of the Selkirk Mountains, where it arcs back southward on its long journey to the Pacific. A narrow, bermed landmass, just over a mile wide, now separates these rivers near the small community of Canal Flats, B.C. Within these flats are the crystal-clear springs that form the headwaters of the mighty Columbia River. Their source? The Kootenay River, now separated from the Columbia by a gravel berm.

Bird's-eye view of the Kootenai and Columbia Rivers, Rocky Mountain Trench, British Columbia. PHOTOGRAPH COURTESY OF THE GLENBOW WESTERN RESEARCH CENTRE, TAYLOR FAMILY LIBRARY, UNIVERSITY OF CALGARY.

Imagine back to the last major ice age, at the end of the Pleistocene, when immense sheets of ice extended down from Canada across the northernmost lands of the United States. On the east side of the Rockies, the Laurentide ice sheet was so massive that it turned the Missouri River back from its northeast course to Hudson's Bay and sent it eastward instead, along the south edge of the ice, toward the Mississippi. On the west side of the Continental Divide, the Cordilleran ice sheet was over a mile deep. It covered British

Mission Mountains; peaks on left were smoothed by the continental glacier. PHOTOGRAPH BY TAYLAR ROBBINS, *COURTESY OF DESTINATION MONTANA.*

Columbia and lapped over onto what became Washington, Idaho, and western Montana. So weighty was this ice that, when it retreated northward, it left behind ground-down mountaintops as evidence of where it had been. The Mission Mountains are one place where the work of this continental ice sheet is obvious. The rounded hills to the north of the terminal moraine just south of Polson are distinct from the jagged peaks of the south, beyond the reach of the ice sheet. In Glacier National Park, only the highest peaks escaped the ice.

As the climate started to warm some 20,000 years ago, ice and meltwater streamed along river corridors. Ice jammed up in places, creating dams. Lakes formed behind these ice lobe dams all along the southern edge of the thinning ice. Geologists postulate that the ice dam was lifted from its bed whenever enough meltwater accumulated to provide adequate buoyancy.[5] The result was that the glacial ice that dammed the Clark Fork drainage crept south as its frontal edge broke off, time and again, with each episode. One of the ice lobes extended into what is now Lake Pend Oreille, blocking the flow of meltwater from the Clark Fork River system and creating a lake as big as Lake Ontario, known as Glacial Lake Missoula. (Lake Ontario is thirty-six times larger than Flathead Lake today.) Other glacial lakes dotted the region as the ice melted, but none as massive as Lake Missoula.

The history and characteristics of Glacial Lake Missoula have been debated for a century, and details about the timing of flood events remained unrefined until the emergence of new dating techniques, which document a flood sequence between 18,000 and 14,000 years ago, with a later, smaller flood cycle that began around 13,300 years ago, and continued for nearly a thousand years.[6] The largest Glacial Lake Missoula flood was the first, with successive floods generally becoming less powerful through time. The first massive blast of meltwater out of the glacial lake is thought to have traveled to the Pacific as a 350-foot wall, the height of a thirty-story building, moving at least 65 miles per hour. In its aftermath, giant waves were trapped in time, as if frozen in mid-swell, when the new landscape settled. Eventually, after dozens of flood events, the source of the ice retreated far enough to the north that the waters of the Clark Fork system ran freely to the Pacific.

The melting moved northward. As the ice continued to thin, smaller dams formed and meltwater lakes accumulated in new places, including the upper Columbia basin. In what would become Kootenai Country, picture the southern half as islands above vast lakes and the northern half covered with ice, thinning, but very much in control of the landscape. Blocked by ice to the north and glacial sediment to the south, the water level of Glacial Lake Invermere eventually exceeded that of the surrounding terrain and was forced to flow out the south end and alter the landscape at what is now Canal Flats. At least for the period of the flood, the rivers flowed together. They created the system that allowed the water monster to circle round and round while avoiding its pursuers.

In a world where everything is sentient, it makes sense that the Columbia would have been confused about which way to flow, so minimal was the elevation difference between the two ends of the glacial lake.[7] It must have been tempting, as things settled down, for the Kootenai River to join the Columbia, but something kept it flowing to the southward instead.

In a world of geology and physics, the Kootenai River might have been kept from changing its course toward the Columbia by debris brought down and deposited during the flooding, blocking the Kootenai pathway toward the Columbia system. The Kootenai story shared here tells that a landform was knocked over to separate the channels in order to trap the water monster. In another version of the creation story, Naɬmuqʷin dammed up the end of the lake by breaking off a piece of mountain, and by solidifying it with his knees, he created the portage between the Kootenay and Columbia Rivers. Today, subsurface drainage from the Kootenai River feeds the springs that form the headwaters of the Columbia; in a sense, they still flow together.

Does the mythic Kootenai creation narrative tell about actual flooding events and geological processes that date to the terminal Pleistocene? More research is needed to solve the particulars of the geology, but the essence of what happened along the Columbia headwaters is clear. Massive lakes and a long sequence of floods shaped the landscape between Columbia Lake and the Flathead-Pend Oreille and Kootenai basins during the final millennia of the last ice age. Cataclysmic events, such as these, are the grist of myths. Perhaps Yawuʔnikʼ, water monster of the Kootenai creation story, represents the surging meltwater floods that came in waves, over and over, around and around. Metaphorically, only after the water monster was destroyed could habitable land be made ready for human occupancy. Land emerged where the Cordilleran ice had been. Chief animal Naɬmuqʷin's body became the homeland as the waters receded and the land settled into place. The ʾAqɬsmakniȼ, the Kootenai people, arriving from the spirit realm, have been there ever since.

The Kootenai, today, keep this history alive through continuing the traditions and telling their stories, even the ones that emerged from the mists of time. Maybe this history also explains why Kootenai chose their village sites to avoid man-eating giants who followed the big streams. Wisely, they "lived around little streams near the mountains."[8] The giants, in this case, were floods. The people had learned through experience not to set up their camps on the big rivers because of their potential to wipe out villages. The myth of the giants provided for a memorable story, one that would serve to teach one generation after the next where not to establish their camps.

People with such a deep and lasting connection to one place—the place where the giant Naⱡmuqǂin fell—have knowledge that others cannot fathom. The land is in their cells, as well as the stories, fed by thousands of generations of ancestors. I wonder about all the knowledge that has been lost over the last 200 years, and what it has cost us all. Mostly, I feel grateful to get a glimpse through this origin story into the deeply connected and interwoven reality that is the traditional Kootenai homeland. ✢

6

A BIG SURPRISE ON THE TRAIL
OF FATHER DE SMET

One of my primary areas of research has been focused on the records left behind by Jesuits of the Rocky Mountain Mission, particularly those of Father Pierre-Jean De Smet. Their writings, sketches, and maps are rife with observations of the Native people of the region. Some of my friends and family members might tell you that I am somewhat obsessed with this Belgian Jesuit.

At times I feel like De Smet reincarnate, so closely have our interests overlapped. We have worked with the same tribal communities and both been obsessed with the geography of the Rocky Mountains between the headwaters of the Missouri and Columbia Rivers. Motivated by different objectives—that is, I am not attempting a religious takeover of land and people—each of us has been drawn to exploring the routes of travel

Father Pierre-Jean De Smet at age forty-four in 1845.
PHOTOGRAPH COURTESY OF THE JESUIT ARCHIVES AND RESEARCH CENTER.

from one watershed into another. Tough trips haven't deterred us. Over a period of nearly three decades, this Jesuit-focused research has led me to Spokane, St. Louis, Montreal, and Rome, as well as to Leuven, Belgium, and even to De Smet's beautiful Flemish hometown of Dendermonde, to learn more about the Native peoples of Montana. In an effort to better understand life in the region before reservations, I have followed the old routes of travel, using his maps as guides. One of these trails led me to the story told here of the crosses De Smet left behind during a trip through Kootenai Country in 1845.[1]

Plantation of the cross on the tomb of the Blackfoot Chief Nicolas. SKETCH BY NICOLAS POINT, 1846. PHOTOGRAPH COURTESY OF THE JESUIT ARCHIVES AND RESEARCH CENTER.

A Big Surprise on the Trail of Father De Smet

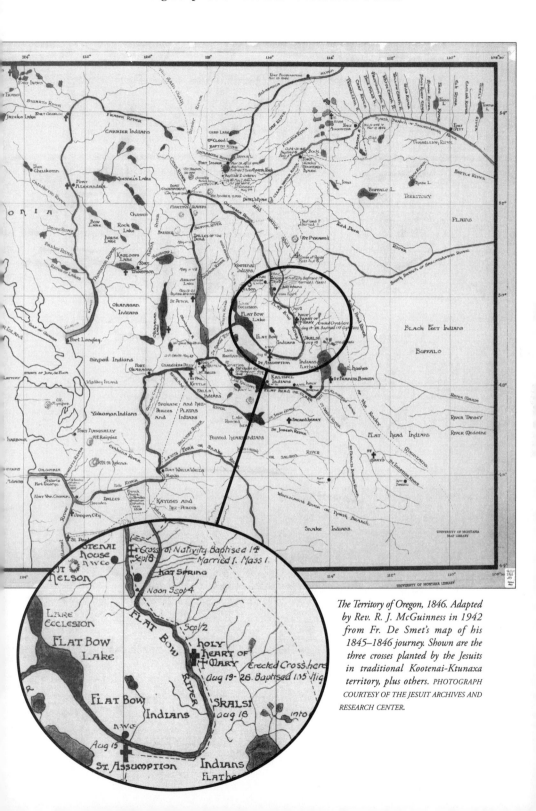

The Territory of Oregon, 1846. Adapted by Rev. R. J. McGuinness in 1942 from Fr. De Smet's map of his 1845–1846 journey. Shown are the three crosses planted by the Jesuits in traditional Kootenai-Ktunaxa territory, plus others. PHOTOGRAPH COURTESY OF THE JESUIT ARCHIVES AND RESEARCH CENTER.

⊕ ⊕ ⊕

Gonzaga University Archives, 2017

I was nearly at the end of my last day of research at Gonzaga when archivist David Kingma asked if I would like to see the research files accumulated by Father William Davis, S.J. A former history professor at Gonzaga, Father Davis, had been preparing a De Smet biography at the time of his death in 1971. "Sure," I told him. "I love benefiting from the efforts of others!"

Speeding through the collection, my eyes locked onto a photograph of three people—two Native men and one White priest—holding up an old cross, twice as tall as they were. I flipped it over, hoping to learn that this was one of the crosses erected by De Smet. Sure enough, the photograph was identified as the "Cross of the Nativity in the Columbia Valley, B.C." A second photo showed the pieces of the cross on the ground. These images had been sent to Fr. Davis by Fr. R. J. McGuinness, a Catholic priest from

Banff, Alberta. In 1939, Fr. McGuinness inquired among the local Shuswap band, formerly allied with the Columbia Lakes Ktunaxa, for information about the De Smet cross. Chief Louis Paul remembered the cross from his younger years and took Fr. McGuinness to the site, where they found evidence of this rough-hewn artifact on the ground nearly a century after its erection.[2] McGuinness marked the location on his map and had his picture taken with the chief.

Chief Louis Paul and Fr. R. J. McGuinness at the site of the Cross of the Nativity in the Columbia Valley, British Columbia, September 14, 1939. PHOTOGRAPH COURTESY OF THE JESUIT ARCHIVES AND RESEARCH CENTER.

I had long wondered about these crosses but had never been able to ascertain the particulars of their construction and how they were erected. The Jesuits "planted" crosses atop passes and in Native villages "to take possession, in the name of the Lord."[3] The only evidence prior to seeing these photographs were two sketches by Father Nicolas Point, who came to the region with Father De Smet in 1841. One scene illustrated "planting a cross" at a burial site and another showed a cross atop the Continental Divide. I never imagined that one of these crosses had survived.

Sketch by Fr. Nicolas Point; his caption reads, "The Cross of Peace on the summit of the Rocky Mountains at the source of the Columbia and Saskatchewan Rivers." PHOTOGRAPH COURTESY OF THE JESUIT ARCHIVES AND RESEARCH CENTER.

⊕ ⊕ ⊕

De Smet's Cross-Planting Travels through Kootenai Country

By the time Father De Smet arrived in the Tobacco Plains in August of 1845, he had already spent time with a band of Lower Kootenais, or Flatbows, in the area now known as Bonners Ferry, Idaho. The Flatbow community passed down the memory that while the Black Robe was there, he induced them to set up a large cross made of logs. De Smet reported that they erected the

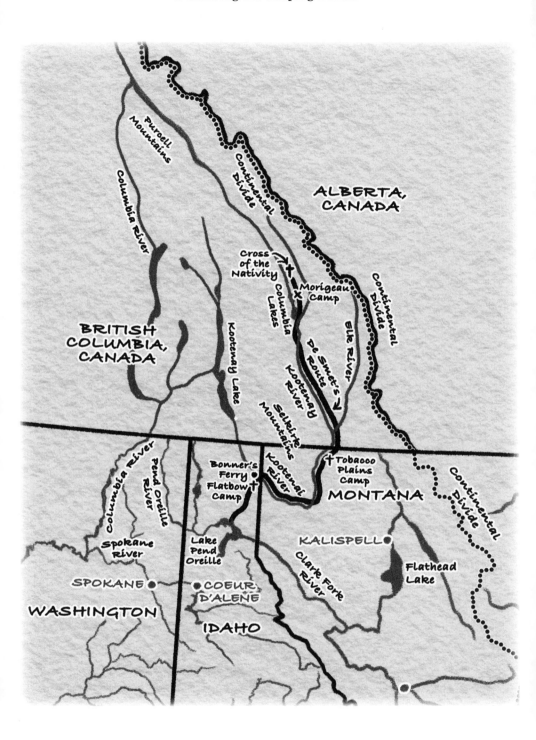

Cross of the Assumption 'on the shore of a lake,' to the cacophony of a ninety-gun salute.[4] The people remembered that the Black Robe stayed with them "but a short time," during which he offered them limited instructions in the Catholic faith. Then "he rode on, after promising to return," but he never did.[5] Missionaries did not settle among the Bonners Ferry Kootenai until the 1880s.

De Smet's next stop was to an Upper Kootenai village in the Tobacco Plains. His party had followed the Kootenai River eastward for some fifty miles to its big bend, where the Fisher River comes in from the south, generally following State Highway 37, then northward for another fifty miles to the Tobacco River, where they came upon a Kootenai camp of about thirty lodges. These people were no strangers to Catholicism. Métis and Iroquois believers came with the fur trade and married into the community. Their principal teacher was an Iroquois man who had been there for some thirty years, dating back to the time of David Thompson.[6] After spending five days in this camp, the Black Robe conducted mass, then baptized over 100 people, mostly children. After "a general salute from the camp," they raised a large cross to take "spiritual possession of this land."

Five days later, having traveled a little more than 100 miles along a traditional Kootenai trail, the De Smet party arrived on September 4 at the portage from the Kootenay (as it's spelled in Canada) River to the Columbia, and made their camp at the mouth of a creek on the east shore of Columbia Lake, where they soon had a visit from Francois Baptiste Morigeau and his large family of French-Canadians.[7] He was a free trapper with the Hudson's Bay Company, a hearty man in his fifties, and a devout Catholic. He strongly desired to have his marriage blessed and his children baptized. The missionary's group agreed to relocate to the Morigeau settlement a little to the north. They followed along the ancient east-side trail that crosscut the steep front range of the Rocky Mountains to the place between Columbia and Windermere Lakes, near where Fairmont Hot Springs Resort now dominates the valley.[8]

The Morigeaus weren't alone there, but the Native people with them were Salish-speaking Shuswap, not Ktunaxa (term used in Canada for Kootenais). This was traditional territory of the Akisqnuk (meaning "place of two lakes"), a band of Ktunaxa. The three Shuswap families were led by

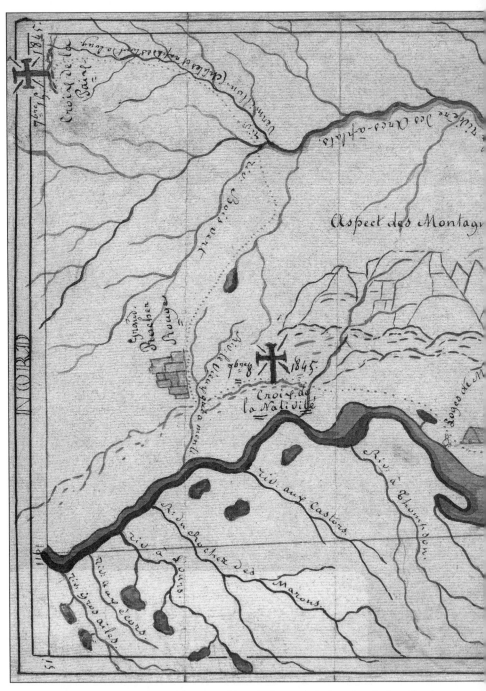

Carte des sources de la Colombie, or Map of the sources of the Columbia, 1847, by Pierre-Jean De Smet (from his 1845 travels). PHOTOGRAPH COURTESY OF THE JESUIT ARCHIVES AND RESEARCH CENTER.

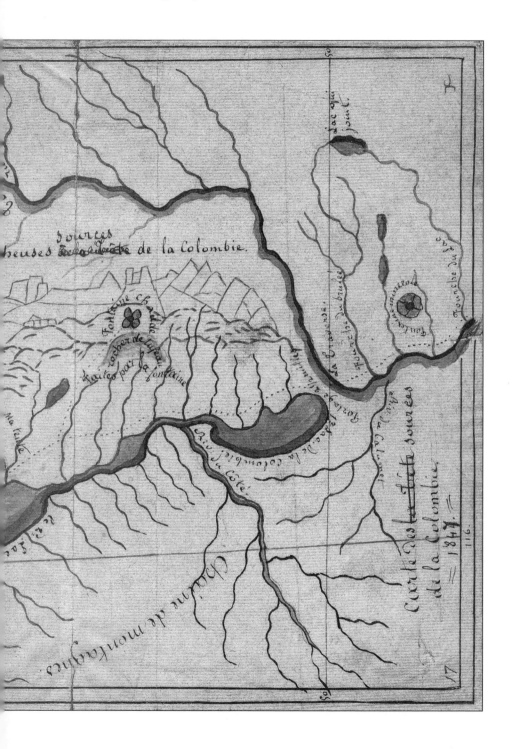

Chief Ken-pe-skut (commonly spelled Kinbasket), who had a trade relationship with Morigeau.[9]

De Smet thoroughly enjoyed himself during this visit. They ate well and shared many stories. The Jesuit was intrigued by the freedom of this Canadian, "solitary lord of these majestic mountains," who was able to go where he pleased, with his beaver trap and carbine, moving his "portable palace" of caribou and moose skin, without concern for anything but his day-to-day life. "Here no one disputes his right, and Polk and Peel, who are now contending for the possession of his dominions"—referring to the imminent boundary settlement between the U.S. and Canada—"are as unknown to our carbineer as the two greatest powers of the moon."[10]

The missionary conducted marriage rites for Francois and Isabella and baptized all the children of their little village. Then, in a final act before his departure, he and the Morigeaus erected a large cross, which the overconfident priest believed would, from that time forward, be called the Plain of the Nativity.[11]

⊕ ⊕ ⊕

In Search of the Cross of the Nativity, 2018

Since finding the photograph of the Cross of the Nativity, I had been determined to see if the old wooden cross was still there. Eighty years of weathering might have destroyed what McGuinness had seen lying on the ground in 1939. In May of 2018, bearing copies of the photos and notes from the Davis Collection along with De Smet's journal and maps, John Weaver, my partner in adventure, and I headed north into Canada from the Tobacco Plains on Highway 93 for some backroad explorations on the trail of the itinerant Jesuit cartographer.

The Ktunaxa world has been turned upside down since De Smet's time. The Kootenais lost the Tobacco Plains portion of their homeland on the U.S. side of the border through the Hellgate Treaty of 1855. Headquarters for the Tobacco Plains Ktunaxa First Nation, Aq̓it ʔa·knuq̓ɬi 'it sit on the north side of the Roosville border crossing, in Grasmere, B.C. Just to the north of the Tobacco Plains, in 1864, the Kootenay Gold Rush took hold on Wild Horse Creek, displacing the Ktunaxa and depleting the foods that had sustained them since the beginning of time. Historic Fort Steele is a reminder of those mining days. Where De Smet had seen "magnificent dark Alpine forests, where the sound of the axe has never resounded," we saw hillsides denuded of trees.

We pulled off the highway and found a lovely perch high above a lake to park the camper for the night. The loons were so talkative, it was hard to sleep. In the morning, about forty miles to the north of Fort Steele, we arrived at Canal Flats, a little town just off the highway. The Flats refer to the portage land where De Smet and other travelers crossed between the Kootenai and Columbia Rivers. The Canal refers to a failed method to move goods across the Flats.

Curious about what more we could learn about the Ktunaxa people in this area and any local history about De Smet, we stopped for breakfast at the little local café. This always works. The locals gather to compare notes of the day and are usually happy to share what they know about their home place with interested strangers. A couple of guys told us about the visitor center and the boardwalk out to the headwaters of the Columbia. "Don't leave without going out there!" they emphasized as we headed out the door.

Our first stop was the visitor center where the Ktunaxa creation story is told both visually—with a huge wall map—and through video. Before leaving we had a short visit with an

The author at the Columbia Discovery Centre in Canal Flats.
PHOTOGRAPH COURTESY OF THE AUTHOR.

employee of the Visitor's Bureau. When she learned we were following the travels of Father De Smet, she told us how they had planned to include the Jesuit in the large historically focused mural out front, but the local Ktunaxa vetoed his inclusion.

We needed to keep moving but agreed that we shouldn't miss the Columbia headwaters. We followed the turns indicated by our new friends at the café, then headed out the boardwalk partway to the surprising crystal springs. The name, Canal Flats, by no means does justice to this wondrous locale. I had passed by this spot on the highway on many previous occasions, with my attention focused on some destination in the national parks just up the road, but I can honestly say this is one of the most magnificent places I have ever visited. The luminescent waters, so clear that various animal tracks in the fine yellow gravels can readily be identified, the broad willow flats full of birdsong, and the sweet scents of new leaves and seeds emerging in May make this a place hard to pull away from. Something deep in my psyche felt fed there.

The headwater springs of the Columbia River at Canal Flats, British Columbia. PHOTOGRAPH COURTESY OF THE AUTHOR.

Back on Highway 93, we continued our journey northward along the west shore of Columbia Lake. The trail De Smet had followed was on the other side, where now only a hiking trail exists. Between the lakes, the highway crosses back to the east, where a vast expanse of green catches our eyes. The three golf courses of the Fairmont Hot Springs Resort now cover the valley on both sides of the road. The springs are the same ones that De Smet described as the temperature of fresh-drawn cow's milk.

I really wanted to know what the local Native people remembered about De Smet's visit. We stopped at the Akisqnuk First Nations Band office, situated close to where the Morigeau family camp had been in 1845. Nothing of that landscape remains. Everything has been sculpted to meet the needs and desires of our time. The biologist we spoke with suggested we try the Shuswap office in Windermere to learn more about the Black Robe. We thanked him and drove up to Invermere, near the outlet of the big Lake Windermere, the place the Ktunaxa call Kwataqnuk, like the CSKT resort in Polson.

As we pull into Invermere, I look around at the paved, fast-food world of this tourist town, and recall Father De Smet's naïve thoughts in 1845 about "the magic hand of civilized man" that he believed would transform this place into "a terrestrial paradise." He couldn't have been more wrong. The rich natural world has been nearly obliterated by sprawl. The haunting voice of Joni Mitchell floats through my mind, "They paved Paradise, put up a parking lot, Ooh, bop-bop-bop-bop."

We pull up to the nondescript administration building of the Shuswap First Nation on the main road to town from the highway. We enter and I explain to the receptionist about my interest in Father De Smet and the cross he erected near there. I ask if she knows anyone who might recall oral history about the time of his visit. She steps into the back offices and reemerges with a young woman. She and I do a double-take.

"Pauline?" I ask, seeing that she isn't quite sure about the connection. "I'm Sally Thompson, the anthropologist who organized the event for Kootenai elders at Flathead Lake a number of years ago. Remember?" She nods and smiles as she recalls her efforts to get Ktunaxa speakers from Canadian

Pauline Eugene and the author orienting to landmarks at the site of the cross. PHOTOGRAPH COURTESY OF THE AUTHOR.

bands to attend the gathering. I show her the photos and explain my interests. She walks us to one of the offices, offers coffee, and explains that she will have to ask one of the elders. John and I should make ourselves comfortable. For quite some time we hear laughter and engaged conversation from across the hall. Eventually she returns.

"I have some good news for you, and some even better!" she laughs. "First of all, I can take you to the location where the cross used to be, then I can take you to see what's left of it."

We pile into her rig, drive up on the high terrace above town, and follow a winding dirt road to the Shuswap Cemetery. With copies of photos from Gonzaga's archives in hand, we scope out some identifiable landmarks as we take in the expansive view of the upper Columbia basin. The gentle breeze through the trees seems like an old friend. Hoodoos on both sides of the valley and the peaks beyond provide a way for us to get our bearings relative to the photographs, as we try to figure where the cross had stood. Homing in, we eventually find fragments of weathered wood marking the spot. For most people this find might seem insignificant, but my satisfaction is equivalent to

The Cross of the Nativity in the Shuswap cemetery taken some years before the McGuinness visit in 1939. PHOTOGRAPH COURTESY OF THE ROYAL BC MUSEUM.

what gold miners experience when they see a large nugget in their pan. John seems nearly as enthusiastic.

"Okay. We need to keep moving," Pauline announces as she heads toward her car. Reluctantly, we climb back in and head toward town. Before we cross back over the highway, she pulls off and parks by a small painted, somewhat dilapidated, clapboard church. "Follow me," she says, as she pulls out the keys. The smell of mice hits my nose as soon as we enter the small chapel with its simple pews and handmade dais. Although the bright white paint accented with forest green looks new, the church hasn't been used for some time. Pauline again says, "Follow me," and we follow her into the back room. I don't notice it at first. I'm struck by the ancient organ and baptismal font crammed into the small space.

"Is this what you're looking for?" she asks, knowing that it is. She nods to the pew against the wall where we see, laid upon it, the stack of old beams that once were the "Cross of the Nativity." I'm flabbergasted. John laughs. When we set out on this trip, I never really thought this tangible evidence of the cross "planted" by De Smet and the Morigeaus in 1845 would still exist, but here it is. Three ends are carved, like the ones in the photograph we carry, and we can see four inch-wide holes in the center of the crossbeam, where it was attached to the upright beam. I notice one wooden bolt still in place and remember that Rev. McGuinness had sent one of these artifacts as a memento to Fr. Davis. Maybe McGuinness got the people to bring it in out of the weather when he saw it on the ground eighty years before.

Pauline seems to enjoy the discovery as well but needs to get back to work, and so do we.

As John and I head to our truck, we speak of the serendipity of the day.

"You know you would never have made that happen if you didn't happen to know Pauline before," John laughed. "You don't just walk in off the street, some random White woman, and get all of this to fall into place."

I know very well the truth of his words. Maybe ancestors escorted me along this old trail, with intentions unknown to me. It wouldn't be the first time. I'm delighted to be along for the ride. We head to the highway for the next leg of our De Smet trail adventure. Our plan is to hike up Cross River to White Man's Pass, to the location of another of his planted crosses.[12] I doubt we will find any remnants of that artifact, since Chief Louis Paul remembered only scattered remains on the ground over a century ago, when he was a child. It doesn't really matter. Maybe we will be able to line up the sketch of that cross with the landscape. To find the place where something occurred is almost as exciting as finding the object itself. Besides, when we reach the top, we will be looking across Banff National Park. You will get no complaints from me. ✢

Pieces of the Cross of the Nativity on a church pew in Invermere. PHOTOGRAPH BY SALLY THOMPSON.

PART III

BUFFALO COMMONS

A SUMMER LIKE NO OTHER

Researchers often assume that nothing new is left to discover from the historical record, and then something appears from someone's attic that sheds new light on old subjects—in this case, the peace treaty negotiated among bison-hunting tribes in 1855, known as the Judith River or Lame Bull Treaty. If it weren't for the letter reports and journals of two Indian agents for the U.S. government, Thomas Adams and William H. Tappan, the worst drought in the collective memory of local Native people up to that time might have been lost to history. I had read the official reports of both agents in years past, but only recently stumbled upon the digitized journals of Thomas Adams while working on this chapter.[1] The Adams journals add significant details to what turned out to be a grueling three-month trek suffered by the Indian delegations during the summer and fall of 1855 while en route to the peace council.

Two years earlier, Governor Isaac I. Stevens led his Pacific Railroad survey teams across what would eventually become Montana Territory but, at that time, was Nebraska Territory, east of the mountains, and Washington Territory, to the west.[2] Traveling east to west, Stevens ended the journey in Olympia, the newly established capital. The council on the bison plains would be the culminating event to follow Stevens' land-grabbing sweep back across Washington Territory in 1855.

The governor had done everything within his prodigious power to orchestrate the necessary elements for a peace agreement to be reached, but he hadn't imagined that a drought could derail the whole plan. From our vantage point, nearly 170 years later, it seems important to know of the dire conditions that affected travelers to the council to fully understand the negotiations and outcome of the treaty. See what you think.

Background

Thomas Adams was part of the railroad survey team. He served as a meteorologist, topographer, and assistant sketch artist before his assignment as agent to the Salish in early December 1854. He and a man named Fred Burr took up quarters at Cantonment Stevens, in present-day Corvallis, Montana, and settled in. Adams began to study the Salish language and to make himself useful as they waited for the treaty councils to reach them.

Adams "took a Wife" from among the Salish on January 21, 1855, according to a note in John Owen's journal.[3] The weather at the time was unusual. Like June in January, according to Owen, and it lasted through February.

As the spring progressed, Adams came to understand the difficult life the Salish had been

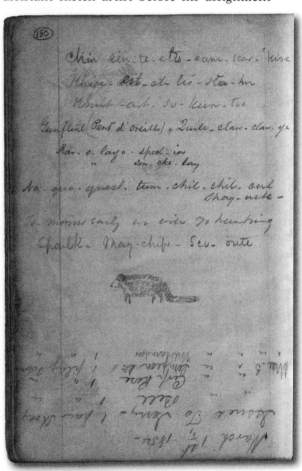

Thomas Adams' journal page showing translations for Salish words. PHOTOGRAPH COURTESY OF THE DEPARTMENT OF SPECIAL COLLECTIONS, PRINCETON UNIVERSITY LIBRARY, THOMAS ADAMS PAPERS, C1452, MANUSCRIPTS DIVISION.

experiencing for many years, caused by Blackfeet aggression. He had reason to wonder if Stevens could make his peace plan work. The previous spring, John Mullan reported that a preliminary council with the Blackfeet had been productive, and that they had promised not to steal horses that summer."[4] A month later, though, in April, they stole fifty horses from some White men and seven from an old Indian woman who was "put afoot" by the loss of her only horses.[5]

The Salish had a poor buffalo hunt that summer of 1854 and the Blackfeet had been "more than usually troublesome." Many Salish horses had been stolen and several of their men killed.[6] When the combined forces of Salish, Pend d'Oreille, and Kootenai hunters were returning from their winter hunt in the spring of 1855, a Kootenai chief was killed by a Blackfeet war party somewhere on the Blackfoot River. He and his companions had been hunting in the mountains. The Blackfeet "Waylaid him & shot him."[7] With so many troubles, the Salish were eager to attend the council if it could bring about an end to their troubles with the Blackfeet. Fighting had left too many of their lodges with only widows and children, and their enemies were getting bolder all the time.

En Route To Fort Benton

Twenty-four-year-old Thomas Adams, as Special Indian Agent for the Eastern District of Washington Territory under the authority of the governor of Washington Territory, Isaac I. Stevens, begins his journey to Fort Benton from the Bitterroot Valley on July 30, 1855. He leaves from Fort Owen, that summer morning, with six other White men, including William Tappan, sub-agent for the Nez Perce; William Craig and Ben Kyser, interpreters for the Nez Perce and Salish, respectively; John Owen, a trusted friend of the west-side tribes; and two of Governor Stevens' men, Ford and Hall, who will serve as hunters. Adams is responsible for getting the Salish to the council, and thirty-four-year-old Tappan is responsible for the Nez Perce delegation. The group plans to meet up along the trail with the Salish, led by Chief Victor, and a small contingent of Nez Perce, led by Spotted Eagle. They have no idea what they will have to endure over the next three months.

Above: Spotted Eagle, Nez Perce chief. PORTRAIT BY GUSTAV SOHON, COURTESY OF THE WASHINGTON STATE HISTORICAL SOCIETY.

Left: Thomas Adams' portrait of Victor, head chief of the Flatheads. PHOTOGRAPH COURTESY OF THE DEPARTMENT OF SPECIAL COLLECTIONS, PRINCETON UNIVERSITY LIBRARY, THOMAS ADAMS PAPERS, C1452, MANUSCRIPTS DIVISION.

The travelers are en route to a very unusual—and potentially risky—gathering of warring nations in lands dominated by the Blackfoot Confederacy. The governor's goal is to establish a formal peace agreement among all the buffalo-hunting tribes and between Indians and Whites that will allow for safe passage through these tribal lands. In addition, he wants to secure legal permission for roads to be built, including railroads. From Fort Owen, according to Adams' field journal, the group takes the Burnt Fork trail eastward to the valley of "Close Creek" (Rock Creek) and from there to Flint Creek, where they camp a short distance from Chief Victor's people on what would become the Mullan Road. For the next ten days they make steady progress heading toward the Hell Gate pass, except for their pause on August 5, because the Salish won't travel on the Sabbath, unless forced by necessity.

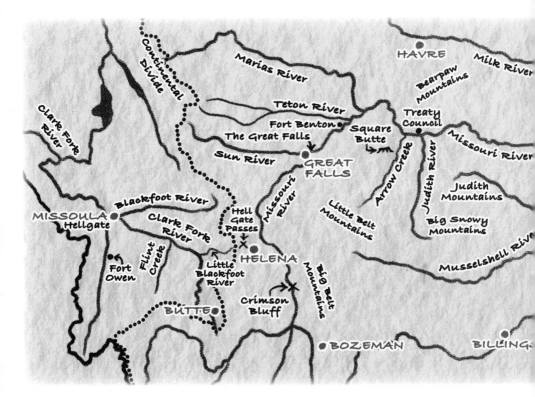

They camp together the following night and share fresh pronghorn, beaver, elk, and deer. They eat well all along the Clark Fork and Little Blackfoot Valleys. Adams records his surprise one late afternoon when hunters drive several pronghorn through camp. They kill two by arrows, and one they catch with a lasso.

Where the Waters Change Direction

On August 10, the travelers reach the Continental Divide and receive news from Governor Stevens' expressmen of an indefinite delay. The goods to supply the council are making very slow progress up the Missouri. Everything is thrown into limbo by extremely low water. Unable to give a precise time for holding the treaty, the governor recommends that "the Indians should go to Buffalo," and the agents should proceed to Fort Benton.[8]

The news is distressing due to the tenuousness of relationships. At this time, however, the travelers are unaware of the dire circumstances that await

them all. Conditions had been fine on the west side of the Continental Divide. But from this day until the council begins ten long weeks later, Adams and his companions will witness life on the buffalo plains without buffalo or adequate rain.

Tappan joins the Nez Perce for a side trip "to the Mountain from which is dug the red ochre" to gather a supply of the paint for trading.[9] Thomas Adams, whom the Salish call Pe-pah-hutsin [possibly spelled pxpaxcin, meaning "smart speaking"], is riding ahead with Chief Victor and a small group of his men, as they travel down the Prickly Pear.[10] They are startled by the rattling of snakes, which have been disturbed in the tall grass by their horses. One of the men, Hustamanee, fearlessly jumps off his horse and kills one, then grabs another as it tries to slither into its hole. He then cuts off the rattles and keeps them. The Salish have no fear of rattlesnakes, they tell Adams, because they "have a root, & some leaves that will cure the bite."[11]

On the night of August 12, before they head off in different directions, the Salish dress up and paint themselves and their horses, and parade around the agents' camp. This is the first time that Adams has seen Chief Victor "do anything of the sort." Later, they perform "a grand dance" and continue their celebration most of the night, filling the air with their singing. Adams paints a portrait of Victor with a red streak, side-to-side across his eyelids.

The government representatives intend to separate from the Flatheads the next day and proceed to Fort Benton, as arranged by the governor. Tappan, though, decides to travel with the Indians to the Musselshell River. As subagent to the Nez Perce, he knows that Spotted Eagle and his small group expect him to accompany them, so he chooses to ignore Stevens' directive. By the time Adams and Tappan meet again in September, they will meet as survivors of the worst summer in memory.

Thomas Adams' sketch of Fort Benton. PHOTOGRAPH COURTESY OF THE DEPARTMENT OF SPECIAL COLLECTIONS, PRINCETON UNIVERSITY LIBRARY, THOMAS ADAMS PAPERS, C1452, MANUSCRIPTS DIVISION.

Agent Adams Heads to Fort Benton

Adams and party meet up with the governor close to Fort Benton on August 18. These newcomers can feel the tension everywhere, especially "a coolness in feeling between our camp and the Fort," according to Adams. It is a time of uneasy waiting, when everyone wishes they could simply will the boats to move more quickly up the river. Men spend their days "writing, talking, and traveling from camp to the fort, and back again." In the evenings, they play backgammon in John Owen's lodge.

Commissioner Colonel Alfred Cumming, governor

Portrait of Alfred Cumming by Gustav Sohon, 1855. PHOTOGRAPH COURTESY OF THE WASHINGTON STATE HISTORICAL SOCIETY.

and Superintendent of Indian Affairs of Nebraska Territory, has not yet arrived. He has traveled from St. Louis to Fort Union on the American Fur Company supply boat. Then, at Fort Union, company employees have transferred the long-awaited goods onto two large mackinaws with sixty men to ensure that they make it up the river to Fort Benton.[12] From Fort Union, Colonel Cumming and Alexander Culbertson, chief factor at the fort, are proceeding overland toward Fort Benton, each in his own "conveyance."

Stevens, who has been packing a path about twenty yards long as he paces back and forth, can't wait any longer to learn the status of their critical situation. He rides out and intersects the two men on the Milk River. Things do not go well. Culbertson reports that animosity erupts between the commissioners over "who should take the precedence during the council, with Stevens finally yielding."[13]

Thomas Adams' sketch of one of the mackinaws. PHOTOGRAPH COURTESY OF THE DEPARTMENT OF SPECIAL COLLECTIONS, PRINCETON UNIVERSITY LIBRARY, THOMAS ADAMS PAPERS, C1452, MANUSCRIPTS DIVISION.

Tension between the two commissioners follows them to camp. Governor Stevens continues his pacing for hours every day. A few drops of rain fall during the afternoon of August 24, raising hopes around the camp, but the drought remains appalling. Provisions in camp are essentially nonexistent, and scarcely anything can be obtained at either Fort Benton or from nearby Fort Campbell.[14] Everyone is hungry and focused on the boats' arrival.

After experiencing the miserable conditions and tension of the government camp for a week, Adams is glad to learn that he will be sent with a message to invite the Crows to the council. With five pounds of sugar and only enough fresh beef for two meals, he sets out on August 27 in the company of interpreters Craig, Kyser, and "old Hugh Munro" to translate for the Blackfeet. They will have Delaware Jim (a Delaware Indian who is married into the Salish), and a Pend d'Oreille called Joseph to guide for them and translate the Crow language. Ford and Hall will go along as hunters. Adams is in capable hands.

Fort Campbell
was named in honor of Robert Campbell, a competitor
of the American Fur Company.

Nicolas Point's sketch of Fort Campbell. PHOTOGRAPH BY SALLY THOMPSON FROM WILDERNESS KINGDOM, INDIAN LIFE IN THE ROCKY MOUNTAINS: 1840–1847.

In Search of the Crow

On their first day out, the eight men begin to learn the extent of the drought and are shocked by what they see. Arrow Creek is dry. They set up camp by a little spring-fed creek. The brackish water is undrinkable by itself. Fortunately, they have gathered peppermint and brought sugar along, so they are able to make a pot of peppermint tea. The men aren't the only ones seeking this little oasis of grass and water. Mosquitoes are relentless. After unsaddling his horse at the end of this tiring and discouraging day, an exhausted Adams lies down on his blanket, only to have a rattlesnake crawl out from under it. To avoid further surprises, he and Craig move to a nearby hilltop, out of the grass.

The next day, traveling generally south-southeast, they can barely make out the "Square Butte" and the "Bear Tooth" through the smokey air. Then on August 29, they find a camp on a branch of the Judith River with water and wood, although grass remains a scarce commodity for their horses. Delaware Jim feeds the camp a scant meal available from a thin whitetail buck.

Thomas Adams' sketch of Square Butte and the Bear Tooth. PHOTOGRAPH COURTESY OF THE DEPARTMENT OF SPECIAL COLLECTIONS, PRINCETON UNIVERSITY LIBRARY, THOMAS ADAMS PAPERS, C1452, MANUSCRIPTS DIVISION.

Disturbing the Sleeping Buffalo

On August 30, a month after leaving Fort Owen, Adams and party cross the Judith River, which is low but running. The "grass is all burnt off in this section," so they head up a creek several miles and then cross into the "Muscleshell," where they find a small grassy tract that escaped the burn, and they camp. Adams is discouraged by what he sees. The prairie is so dry that any spark from a campfire can set it ablaze. That afternoon, they fight a strong wind, followed by a heavy shower of rain mixed with hail. They camp about ten miles south of a high round mountain, "which is the furthest eastern spur of the Rocky Mountains in this latitude." They call it "Finis Butte," or Last Butte.

The hunters do well at this camp and are able to provide enough deer meat for breakfast and some extra. Kyser traps a beaver to add to their fare. They set out on the same dusty trail they have been following to a Gros Ventre camp, but the rains of yesterday have obscured the route and they lose their way. The hunters manage to kill an elk and a grizzly bear. High winds blow again that evening, and the night is cloudy.

Finally arriving in the Gros Ventre camp, Adams meets with the leaders to explain the peace-making aims of the commissioners. One man responds that, on more than one occasion, they have "made peace with all the Nations . . . and that they had never been the first to break it," yet they assure him that they will guarantee the safety of any Indians attending the council and that they are willing to listen to the White chiefs. Adams is not convinced. He senses that they expect a "quid pro quo."

Two days later, the Adams group leaves in the company of two Gros Ventre representatives. The group proceeds through remarkably decimated land, where river water stands in pools. The hunters bring in a buffalo bull and an elk, but they provide little food. Every being is depleted by this extraordinary drought. The men are even less fortunate the following day.

On September 5, they have to spend the first part of the day in search of their wandering animals. With grass so scant, the horses break free of their tie lines whenever they can. The poor creatures are driven by hunger. The travelers are especially grateful when they arrive at Low Horn's camp of fifty-four lodges of Blackfeet where the people are flush with fresh buffalo meat. From them, Adams learns that a large camp of Flatheads, Nez Perce, and Snakes (Shoshone) are camped together on the Musselshell River, about two days travel away.

But they should expect terrible conditions the entire way—bone dry with scant grass. Cold rain falls again during the night. Adams is eager to reunite with the Salish and Agent Tappan, and to learn how they have fared since last they met.

The men stay in camp to meet formally with the headmen about the upcoming council at Fort Benton. Low Horn, speaking for his band of Blackfeet, guarantees the safety of the tribes who will come together for this important gathering, and a couple of their headmen consent to go with Agent Adams to inform the Crows. A few families who want to go to the Flathead camp will travel with them, as well.

Portrait by Gustav Sohon of In-hus-cay-stamy or Low Horn, Piegan chief, 1855. PHOTOGRAPH COURTESY OF THE WASHINGTON STATE HISTORICAL SOCIETY.

That afternoon, Adams takes advantage of an opportunity to see a buffalo "surround," a construction he describes as being of stones or wood, or whatever is available, made by Indians of this region, into which they drive buffalo. On this particular day, the Piegans have some difficulties with their drive, as reported by Adams.

> The Indians did not make the circle complete before the animals got wind of them, and started, then they had charged right after the Buffaloes, and ran them for miles. I cantered on slowly behind them, and saw them kill about twenty, the tongues of all of which were offered to me as I rode past; the Indian women performed the principal part of the butchering. It was an exciting picture as the ground came somewhat rolling, to see the different groups of Indians and Buffaloes, appearing and disappearing among the hills, and the main band lumbering off in the distance with the Indians dashing through, visible at intervals through breaks that would be made as a small band would be cut off.

The morning of September 7 dawns clear and bright, with a rime of heavy frost on the ground. Vanished are the smokey skies that have clouded their journey since leaving Fort Benton. The government party, with their Blackfeet companions, leave early and head southeast across rolling prairie to the Musselshell, aiming for the camp of the west-side tribes. They find the large camp of Salish, with some Blackfeet, farther down the river and join them there, despite the poor grass and pitiful "bowls" of still water where the river should be. The Nez Perce and Shoshone are camped separately.

Adams is delighted to see Chief Victor but distressed to hear his account of the twenty-two interminable days they have withstood.[15] Victor's people have not seen running water since they arrived on the Musselshell. They and their animals are suffering terribly. This entire time "they have seen but few Buffalo." Adams learns that they have scarcely had enough food for daily consumption, and certainly haven't had enough meat for the women to dry for winter stores. They are barely getting by.

Agent Tappan is not with this camp. The Salish had remained with Tappan and Spotted Eagle's contingent for about two weeks until August 27, when that group set out for the Yellowstone. They left the same day Adams and his group had headed south from Fort Benton with their message for the Crow.

From the Nez Perce camped below them, the Salish had learned that the Crow, with whom they had wintered, "had been afflicted with the measles during the past summer, that two hundred and sixty-seven had already died," eight of their headmen among them. Survivors have scattered in small bands "through the mountains of the Yellow Stone."[16]

The headmen in this camp are greatly discouraged. Their situation is dire regarding both the threat of measles and the unusual drought. They don't know which way to go. From Agent Adams' report of his travels, they know that much of the land to the north is "a vast waste of blackened prairies and mountains covered with ashes." Victor's people want to stay in close enough proximity to make it to Fort Benton when they are called, but they must find food. To keep their suffering horses alive, according to Adams, the Flathead peel the bark of the sweet (not the bitter) cottonwood trees to provide sustenance for their animals. Adams describes that the horse tenders "just threw the trees and the horses strip them of every vestige of bark."

The Salish leaders are weighed down by thoughts of the unimaginable. Their situation is akin to dogpaddling in a deep well until help arrives. Without some kind of intervention, in the form of steady rain to replenish springs for drinking water and grasses for their horses, and the appearance of bison or other animals to provide the food they so desperately need, they will not survive. They decide to continue their protracted pace down the "Bearded Fish," the name they call the Musselshell.[17] At their pace, it will take about fifteen days to reach the river's mouth. Perhaps they will have word from Governor Stevens by then.

Adams and his companions remain with the slowly moving Salish village for nearly a week, trying to decide what to do. Some days only "peppermint tea, and poor dried meat" is all they have for breakfast. On occasion the hunters manage to bring in "fat antelope." Now and then they score a buffalo, but these are rarely good eating, like the five poor old bulls Kyser and Craig kill on September 12. From the four oldest, they take only the tongues, and from the youngest they glean what little meat they can. The physical effort to butcher and transport the stringy meat left on these beasts is not worth the calories.

In total, these five old giants provide barely enough to quell the hungry stomachs of the Adams party.

On September 13, Adams, with Kyser, "a Flathead named Nine Pipes," and one of the hunters head to the Yellowstone. They hope to find the American Fur Company post, operated by Robert Meldrum, open for business. If they are lucky, they will find some Crow there, as well, with meat for trading. From them, Adams hopes to learn the whereabouts of their headmen to tell about the council. For two days his group travels along the river below the Bighorn River. They don't meet any Crow, but, thankfully, they do find grass, buffalo, and good water, the first they have seen for days. They relish the taste of juicy meat and marrow bones. The next day they are greatly disappointed to pass "two old burnt Trading Posts." Meldrum's Post seems to be no more and the Crow are nowhere in sight.

Reunion on the Yellowstone

Tappan and the Nez Perce, in the meantime, have moved to the Yellowstone but still find no buffalo. Their situation is dire. Like Adams, Agent Tappan decides to head to Meldrum's Post where he, too, hopes to get supplies and a guide to Fort Benton. He and the Nez Perce delegates who accompany him are sorely disappointed to find the fort abandoned.[18] They have taken a big risk to lead their scrawny horses all that way only to find the post abandoned. On the way back to their camp, they spot a group of people a few miles upriver. Thinking these are likely Crow, they are quite surprised to find Agent Adams and his Piegan companions instead. On the morning of September 15, the two parties meet and share the many discouraging experiences they have suffered since parting a month before.

All of these men, Indian and White, understand that they have few options. Chances are slim that they will be able to find any Crow in time to reach the council, and their "thin and weak" animals will be severely tested. The Salish will return to the Musselshell. The Nez Perce delegates decide to hurry back to their families while they still have horses able to make the journey. On September 16, Tappan and Adams head toward Fort Benton by way of the Salish camp on the Musselshell.

Adams' journal entry for September 18 reports, "Regular equinoctial storm last night," which continues furiously throughout the morning, while they have *absolutely nothing* to eat. They manage to stay dry by sleeping in an old war lodge. The evening before, one of the hunters wounded a bull elk, which got away. They go in search of him in the morning only to find that wolves have dispatched and nearly devoured him, but the men manage to scavenge enough for breakfast. Later in the day, the little group has occasion for a hearty celebration when the hunters succeed in bringing in the meat of a young buffalo cow. Maybe their luck is changing.

Adams and Tappan reach the Salish camp on September 20. Their layover is brief. Two days later, the agents, with Kyser, Ford, and Hall, set out for Fort Benton to update the Treaty Commission and to learn about the progress of the supply boats. They are barely able to make the journey without provisions and with horses too worn out to catch up with any buffalo.

Along the way, they meet up with a Gros Ventre camp of forty lodges who are also headed to Fort Benton. From them the agents learn the disturbing news that the Crow have killed two of their men and stolen fourteen horses. In retaliation, the Gros Ventre have killed four.[19] The fine balance required to consummate the treaty is teetering. Scarce resources escalate competition, and, these days, conditions are far worse than poor.

Coaxing their exhausted horses along, they travel only a few miles from where they started the day when they meet up with an express from Stevens. His message is that he is confident the council will begin by October 5. Tappan heads to the Yellowstone to inform the Nez Perce, and Adams returns to update Chief Victor on the news. In the Salish camp that night, he learns that some of their people, so destitute, have left for the Yellowstone in search of buffalo, while "the main party" with Chief Victor has continued down the Musselshell. With the news from Stevens, Victor sends word to the rest of his people to return. They arrive on the following day. Agent Adams is highly impressed by the loyalty and commitment shown by the Flatheads, given the circumstances. The date for the council is still two weeks away and food remains elusive.

Some of the men tell Adams that when the Blackfeet were in their camp, they stole several horses. The Salish found them hobbled, some distance away, and brought them back into camp. Later, a Piegan man approached the owner of one of the horses and asked for the return of "the piece of hair cord with which he had hobbled the stolen horse." Adams found the behavior "impudent," and was shocked to learn that the Salish "appreciated it as a good joke."[20]

Change of Venue

Caravan style, the Adams' party and the Salish progress slowly toward the Missouri River.[21] The agent sends a report to Stevens to make him aware of their dire situation. He explains that Chief Victor will not be able to lead his people all the way to Fort Benton. His animals, which still have to hunt buffalo and haul meat before returning home, are in too poor condition to make it farther than the mouth of the Judith River, some sixty miles away. They will just continue doing what they have been doing—existing on "small game, grass and water," and will relocate to attend the council when summoned.

The days are becoming unbearable for Agent Adams. They have wandered through these desiccated prairie lands far too long, and the consequences of extended deprivation are starting to affect him, both mentally and physically. With the council now in sight, he is dreaming of other places, where food is a given, along with good water. A bath would be welcome, as would some more familiar companionship. Each day on this trail seems a repeat of the dreary one before. Hoping to be relieved of duty as soon as he delivers his charges, he arranges with "Lo-lo, a Flathead boy," to escort him back to the Bitterroot.

At least the hunters in the Adams' camp are bringing in meat. They actually have excess. Then, on September 25, the four men camp too close to the Indian camp, and lose "every particle" of their meat "to Indian dogs." One of the Salish men provides them with breakfast, and another, Bear's Track, offers enough for their dinner. They proceed along, in sight of the Bear's Paws Mountains, through country with undrinkable water. Adams contemplates with wonder "that the Indians do not complain," and that, somehow, "the water they have been using for the last month does not make them sick," for he, himself, has been suffering.

On September 28, a "Cold, raw, disagreeable day," Adams notes that both wood and water are less available. They have no choice but to camp by "a pool of Strong water." The Salish, who have set up camp about 200 yards above them, spot "a small band of Buffaloes" and start after them. Just after Adams and his companions have unsaddled their horses and are about to settle in, and before they have a chance to get anything to drink from the pitiful pool, they see an old bull cantering toward the water. The men are under an old tree, about a hundred yards away from the tipi-sized pool. Frank Hall, their hunter, "wanted to see if he could kill him from camp, so blazed away, and gave him a mortal wound," but he didn't fall. They pursued "and had a good deal of sport with him, but to pay us, (in spite of our efforts,) he walks into our pool of water and after walking around in it enough to stir up all the mud . . . he laid down right in the center, and gave up the ghost." They are left with no meat, and no drinkable water for themselves or their animals.

The following day, September 29, Adams' group, including Lolo, readies to leave for Fort Benton, having received no updates about the council. The Salish, who will ploddingly continue toward the mouth of the Judith, send them off with "a few tongues and a little fresh Buffalo meat." The four men make good time that day, despite the poor condition of two of their horses. They stop for the night some four miles north of the "last Butte." Their camp is on the prairie, near water, but where the only wood is *"bois de vache"*—"cow wood"—otherwise known as buffalo chips. Light rain falls and the weather is turning cold.

On the morning of September 30—two full months after leaving the Bitterroot Valley—they head north and camp at a small spring at the foot of the Judith Mountains. Adams is feeling physically better than he has for a week. He notes in his journal that two days of good water "has stopped the diarrhea with which we have all suffered." That night, in a camp with good water and ample grass for their horses, they have wood to roast fat cow ribs for dinner. Things are looking up.

The next day is even better. Near the north end of the Judith Mountains, they find a stream of running water, surrounded by good grass. While the other men go hunting, the twenty-five-year-old agent chooses to stay behind to take a bath and do some washing for the first time since starting this journey.

Adams arrives at Fort Benton on October 3, with Tappan and the Nez Perce delegation right behind him. The report about Chief Victor's situation is a welcome relief rather than a problem for the commissioners. It solves their dilemma with the supply boats, which are already in the vicinity of the mouth of the Judith. Instead of having the supplies hauled so far overland, they will move the council site instead. Couriers are sent out to alert attendees of the change in venue. In just a few days, everyone around Fort Benton is packed up and ready to head to the new site, some 100 miles to the east.

A Great Gathering of Nations

The days between October 12 and 16 are full of excitement as the various tribal groups arrive for the long-awaited council on the broad floodplain just downstream from the Judith River, in a cottonwood grove on the north shore. The commissioners hold informal conferences with the Indians, "making the hostile tribes acquainted with each other by bringing the head men together, so that they will have the less to talk about at the time of holding the Treaty," according to Adams.

The "Grand Council" begins at noon on October 16. Reported numbers vary, but more than 3,000 Indians are in attendance, according to official reports, and at least 6,000 others are camped around the area. Many more would be there if they had met in August, as originally planned. Three important east-side bison hunting tribes are not there—the Crow, Cree, and Assiniboine. Although the latter group sends tobacco and their blessing, their absence matters. Few Nez Perce are able to get there, despite their good intentions. Attendees risked their very survival by keeping close enough to the Missouri to stay within "shouting range"

Chief Victor in 1864, wearing the medal and coat distributed as gifts to chiefs at the 1855 Lame Bull Treaty council. PHOTOGRAPH COURTESY OF THE UNIVERSITY OF MONTANA ARCHIVES.

of the commissioners. For them, the chance to have a legislated peace plan is worth it.

Although the council, to Adams' eye, lacks "pomp, or circumstance," without the presence of U.S. Army soldiers, he nonetheless experiences the "moral force of the Govt. of the United States, and of the white race," in this assembly. A day later, the treaty is signed.

The council is followed by the distribution of the long-awaited provisions: hard bread, bags of flour, sugar, and coffee. The commissioners' final act is to recognize the head chiefs with silver medals and military coats, after which this world-changing event, like a foggy scene from which White

Portrait of Lame Bull by Gustav Sohon, 1855. PHOTOGRAPH COURTESY OF THE WASHINGTON STATE HISTORICAL SOCIETY.

masses will eventually emerge, comes to an end.

Aftermath

Little of what was promised to the tribal nations came to pass and, despite the months of effort and expense put into this peace treaty, the tribes were soon back to fighting.[22] The commissioners had been naïve, at best, in thinking they could change this world with the flow of ink across paper. Lame Bull himself, the first leader to place his "X" on the paper, died in battle within a year of the treaty signing.

The Indians would regret this treaty every time a new road or railroad was plowed through their homelands. At the time of the treaty, all that country was Indian land. Within fifty years, Montana had gained statehood, two railroads crossed its boundaries, east to west, and tribal lands had been reduced to the reservations as we know them today. Bison on the open range were a thing of the past.

We are left to wonder about the ability of tribal leaders to consummate such important work in such short order, especially given their depleted state after the terrible preceding months. Did they have any idea what it would mean for roads to be carved through their lands? They certainly couldn't have imagined the hordes of miners that would soon arrive or "the Iron Horse"— trains—that would follow. The chiefs and headmen signed the treaty because they believed it would help them feed their families, and they signed despite knowing that they held little sway over their young men during these changing times. They couldn't promise peace any more than the commissioners could promise them access to a protected hunting ground for the next ninety-nine years.[23] After a summer like they had just weathered, they were ready to sign anything that would help them survive.

Postscript

Thomas Adams was not allowed to leave early. Instead, he was put to work copying documents, mapping topographical boundaries specified in the treaty, and helping to dismantle the camp when all was accomplished. He returned to the Bitterroot Valley and remained in the region for a number of years, trying to make a living primarily from raising cattle to sell on the emigrant road.[24] He was with Granville and James Stuart in May 1858 when they found indications of gold on a tributary of the upper Clark Fork. He spent that summer grazing cattle on Flint Creek. That fall he traveled to Salt Lake with John Owen and spent Christmas at Fort Owen before returning to the Deer Lodge area.

Adams was back in the Bitterroot in March of 1861 in an official capacity as census taker for the Indians. He distributed annuities to the Pend d'Oreille later in the month. He was serving as the substitute agent while John Owen was away. The first part of the summer of 1861 found him in the Bitterroot Valley, then he joined the Stuarts and others to prospect for gold at American Fork, later named Gold Creek. He also traveled back and forth from Fort Benton to conduct some trading.

Adams and his wife, "Louise," dissolved their union on March 2, 1862, by mutual consent, and she left. Two months later, Adams began boarding with the Stuarts, while they all focused on prospecting. In October, Adams learned that he had a son. According to Granville Stuart, Adams captured the little boy from a nearby Indian camp. Stuart reported the painful scene as Adams carted off his son. The little guy couldn't speak English and "was weeping bitterly for his Indian relatives."[25] The heartbroken child cried throughout the night. In the morning, Stuart convinced Adams to return the boy to his mother. Peace was restored as soon as the child was handed off to some Salish men on their way to meet up with the village.

By January 1864, mining must not have been paying the bills, so Adams, with a partner, picked up work making shingles for the mill at Fort Owen, completing the job in mid-February. Adams left the region that year and was farming in Maryland in 1866.[26] Serious searching in Ancestry.com failed to reveal any further evidence of his life after Montana. His legacy continues among the Salish people, through the little boy who stayed behind. ✢

8

THE STRANGE STORY OF HOW A
CROW CHIEF FOUND HIS WAY HOME

Joe Medicine Crow got a peculiar phone call in 1978, one that led to the reburial of a Crow chief who had died a century before.[1] The call was from a woman in Virginia, who had never been to Montana and, unless you count her strange visitations, had never met a Crow Indian. When renowned historian Dr. Medicine Crow told me this story, I wondered if the truly extraordinary tale had any corroborative evidence. Turns out, it does.

The switchboard operator for the tribe, Clara White Hip, received the first call from the woman who identified herself as Victoria Mauricio, a self-described medium. White Hip wasn't quite sure where to send the caller, so she started with the local office of the Bureau of Indian Affairs. Joe was working there at the time. He realized immediately this was no usual call when he heard her say, "Sir, I've been having dreams, dreams of a Crow Indian chief." This Indian had paid her many a visit over the prior three years. His first visit was announced through loud drumming, just as she was about to drop off to sleep. As reported in the *Billings Gazette*:

> She said she was almost asleep one night when the furniture started
> moving around her bedroom. She turned on the lights and saw that
> the room was full of Indians. She said she was scared because they
> were all singing and hollering and they had war paint on. Then one
> of the Indians raised his tomahawk and said, "Peace not war."[2]

The Strange Story of How a Crow Chief Found His Way Home

That was the beginning of Mauricio's relationship with the man she called Black Foot. He was well over six feet tall, with long black hair decorated with eagle feathers. He conveyed to her that she should remember the tomahawk.

Joe didn't recognize the name Black Foot as one of the Crow chiefs. He asked her if the man told her anything else that might be useful. Yes, he had. The dream visitor made clear to her that "he wants to go home," and that he kept saying "macheche." She asked Joe if he knew what that meant. He wasn't sure but would check around.

Joe soon learned that Black Foot was one name for their most famous chief, Awé Kúalawaachish, Sits in the Middle of the Land (1795–1877), whom the White people called Chief Blackfoot.[3] He was head chief at the Fort Laramie Treaty Council of 1868.

Mauricio had also discovered the identity of her visitor. Black Foot had reappeared to her and conveyed to her that she would learn more about him in a book about Plains Indians in the "room of many books." She went to a library where she found a book with a photograph of five Crow leaders taken by William Henry Jackson at Fort Parker in 1871. The one seated second from the left held the tomahawk the night visitor had shown her.[4] In the photo caption he was identified as Sits in the Middle of the Land, the "Chief of All Chiefs," of the Crow Nation, who died in 1877.

Crow chiefs at the Crow Agency in 1871: Poor Elk, Sits in the Middle of the Land (aka Black Foot),
Long Ears, He Shows His Face, and Old Onion. PHOTOGRAPH BY WILLIAM HENRY JACKSON, COURTESY OF THE
MONTANA HISTORICAL SOCIETY RESEARCH CENTER.

The oral history of his death had been passed down among the people by Plain Feather, who was born in the 1860s. He was a boy at the time of the Custer battle of 1876 and died in 1966, just three years shy of the first moon landing.[5]

Plain Feather in 1905, believed to have lived to more than 100 years old. PHOTOGRAPH COURTESY OF THE BILLINGS PUBLIC LIBRARY.

In the fall of 1877, Plain Feather was with his family in Chief Awé Kúalawaachish's hunting party on the Stinking Water (later renamed Shoshone River). They stopped in the area that later became Cody, Wyoming, where Plain Feather remembered there was a bridge at an old ford.[6] The party split up there. Awé Kúalawaachish wanted to go to a river to the south, about thirty miles away, where there were still some buffalo. Another hunt leader wanted to go up the Stinking Water to the mountains of the Yellowstone Park area, where they would hunt deer and bighorn sheep.[7] The storyteller's family went with the group going toward the park.

Plain Feather remembered that they soon heard terrible news. Two horseback riders galloped into their camp at the forks of the river, just above the narrow canyon where a dam would later be built.[8] These messengers told the group that their chief had died. His lungs were congested, and the medicine men couldn't do anything to help him. Both he and his wife took ill, and soon died. Tribal memory is that their sickness was pneumonia.

Plain Feather's people packed up their lodges and headed over to where the others were camped. They arrived the next morning. When they got there the bodies had been wrapped in robes and made ready for burial. Once everyone was assembled, the two were placed on a ledge in the cliff above the Greybull River and then covered up with rock slabs. Afterwards, the people mourned together. They told of the great things that the chief had done for his people. This place was close to Meeteetse, which means "meeting place" in Shoshone. That was the word that Black Foot kept repeating to Mauricio. "Macheche."

In the meantime, the fifty-two-year-old, English-born widow from Virginia continued talking with Clara White Hip. Mauricio wanted to know if the chief's grave had been disturbed. During his most recent visitation he had repeatedly conveyed the word "desecrating." White Hip didn't know; the Crow people had lost connection with the grave near Meeteetsee.

The psychic had news. Black Foot wanted her to travel to Crow Country where he would lead her to more information. White Hip helped make the arrangements, and Mauricio finally arrived in Montana on July 12, 1978. Soon after she settled in at the home of White Hip, she explained that she needed a Crow-speaking medicine man to help Black Foot convey his message. That request led Mauricio and White Hip to Francis Stewart, a fluent speaker of Crow, who listened to Mauricio's story. She assured them that she wanted no money for her services, "a gift from God." She just wanted to help Black Foot get back home.

Stewart agreed to assist them. With Mauricio's guidance, they held a séance. Communications came through to them from Black Foot, many in the form of images, including a pitchfork, an owl hooting in daylight, three distinctive rocks, and a branch that looked like a pointing finger. These clues, they believed, would lead them to the chief's grave because he wanted to come home.

Mauricio, having accomplished what she could as a medium between worlds, returned to Virginia following the séance. Others who had been present at the séance were convinced that they would be able to find the grave from the clues given. A group of them headed south on July 28. They stopped at a café in Meeteetsee for coffee and asked if anyone had information that could help them.

One woman told them to go to a ranch where Indian graves had been found. From there, they were referred elsewhere, then finally they were told to go to the *Pitchfork* Ranch. They could check off clue number one.

When they saw a large rock that Mauricio had described for them, they had their second clue. When they heard an owl hooting they knew they were in the right place. The sun soon set, and it became too dark to continue their search. They would have to return on another day.

Two weeks later, a larger group returned to the big rock. They called Mauricio. She told them to look for the highest ridge where they would see three unusual rocks and a big pine tree next to the opening of a cave. It was getting too dark to see their way around the ridge so, once again, they headed home without reaching their goal.

A third group set out on August 26, including some of Plain Feather's descendants and Bob Edgar, an archaeologist and historian from Cody, who would assist them if they found the graves. All signs led to that cave by the pine tree, just as the psychic had described it. The first thing one of the searchers saw as he entered was a big blue bead, like the one Mauricio had told them about after the chief had left one for her on her coffee table. Another of the searchers saw partly exposed bones and buffalo hide.

Edgar helped the Crow delegation remove the remains from the sandy fill of the cave. The bones were those of a single individual, a very tall man with heavily worn teeth, as would be expected for someone in his eighties. The search party never found the bones of the chief's wife. With the chief's bones they found beads of black, white, and blue. According to the archaeologist, all the beads were made before 1850.

The chief's remains were buried in full ceremony outside the Bureau of Indian Affairs office in Crow Agency on October 4, 1978, 101 years after his first burial. According to Mauricio, in her vision, Black Foot had specified both the date and location of burial. The community raised $200 to fly the woman, whose visions instigated all this, back for the occasion.

The grave is marked by a headstone with an epitaph dictated by the chief, himself, that reads, "He That Sits In The Middle Of The Land. Chief of all Chiefs of the Crow Nation. Founder of the Constitution and the Crow Reservation and the Four Corners." The reference to the constitution pertains to Black Foot's provision in the Fort Laramie Treaty that all decisions of the tribe should be made by the majority of the people rather than by only the chiefs. The Crow Tribe's constitution continues to operate by this directive. The "Four Corners" define Crow Country, using the metaphor of the four tipi poles that create the framework for each lodge.

Following this astonishing sequence of events, Mauricio returned to Virginia, where she died in 1996. As far as anybody knows, she stopped having her visions after the spirit was put to rest. Clara White Hip and Joe Medicine Crow, the two people who initially assisted Mauricio with her mission on behalf of the long-dead chief, outlived her by many years. Clara White Hip Nomee became the longest serving chairperson of the Crow Nation. She died in 2012. Joe Medicine Crow was awarded the Presidential Medal of Freedom by President Obama in 2009. The honored Crow historian died in 2016 at the age of 103.

Many Crow people celebrated the return of their chief, while others never accepted the results. They believe Sits in the Middle of the Land remains buried in a rocky ledge in the rugged Absaroka Mountains where he was placed long ago.

To any skeptical readers, I understand that using a medium to uncover a long-buried ancestor strains the bounds of empirical reasoning. Yet, until the story can be disproved, it seems worthy of consideration given the results that derived from Mauricio's visions. Those who were directly involved in this story believed it was true and were grateful to Mauricio for serving as a bridge between worlds that led to the return of their great chief. ✢

ABRAHAM MASLOW'S SURPRISING SUMMER AT SIKSIKA

During the summer of 1938, Abraham Maslow (1908-1970), a young psychology instructor at Brooklyn College in New York, traveled to the high plains of Alberta to conduct research among the Siksika Nation of the Blackfoot Confederacy. The surprising world he found there, fifty years after the last bison hunt, would, in a roundabout way, make him world-famous. What he learned from the Siksika was how to raise good people, which became the basis for his influential theory known today as Maslow's Hierarchy of Needs.

I was introduced to this information by Narcisse Blood and Ryan Heavy Head, colleagues from Red Crow Community College, Blood Reserve, Stand Off, Alberta, part of the Blackfoot Confederacy. They recovered the particulars of the story through interviews and archives, since nowhere in Maslow's published writings is there mention of his summer with the Siksika. Although the story took place on a reserve in Alberta, Maslow could have learned the same lessons among their Blackfeet relatives in Montana. It makes no difference to the people of the Blackfoot Confederacy which side of the Medicine Line they have been relegated to through treaty, for the four tribes share an original homeland, gifted to them by the Creator.

This story, like so many interesting tales, has been sprinkled with an ample dose of serendipity. Maslow, a Brooklynite through and through, hadn't

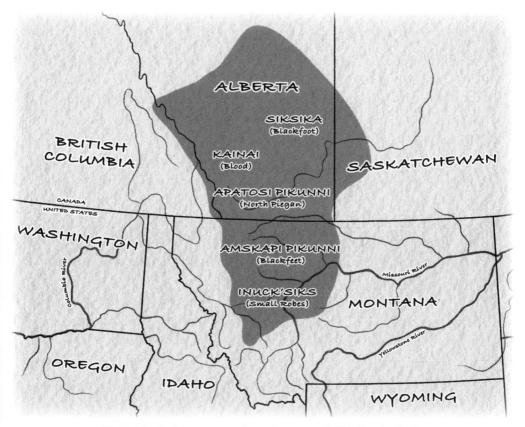

The Blackfoot Confederacy comprises four tribes spanning the U.S.-Canadian border.

planned to go to the middle of nowhere for the summer. As an eager graduate student, ready to launch his career, he believed he was ready to publish a
theory about how individuals came to their particular status in a community
based on several variables, including what he thought of as confidence in one's
sexuality. He had derived this theory from observation of rhesus monkeys and
then tested it on a sample of Brooklyn College coeds. (I am sorry to say I have
not seen this questionnaire. No doubt you have questions about his leap from
rhesus monkeys to coeds, as do I.) When he shared his research results at the
salon of the esteemed anthropologist Ruth Benedict, she cautioned him not
to publish prematurely. He needed a cross-cultural check on his theory before
he could justify any hard and fast conclusions about human behavior. She
facilitated his opportunity to work on the Siksika Reserve, where she already

had connections. Two of her graduate students were already planning to go there that summer. He would join them and take the opportunity to interview young people using the same questionnaire he used on the coeds.

That June, Maslow and his fellow researchers left the narrow, bustling streets of New York behind, and drove west across great expanses of far horizons. In Alberta, they followed the South Saskatchewan River to the Siksika Reserve where they stepped into a different world, a different time.

Their first task was to meet with tribal leaders to explain their projects and the interviews they intended to conduct. No record exists of exactly what was said during this initial meeting. English was the second language of these elders, and the abstract concepts and vocabulary of human behavioral theory was completely foreign to them. We can assume Maslow kept it simple and possibly vague. The meeting appeared to go well, and permission was granted for his project to begin.

This young researcher, truly a fish out of water, began his interviews with young women. He asked them the same questions he asked their contemporaries in New York, initially oblivious to the vast social chasm between the two. He found himself stymied by their reluctance to answer certain questions, particularly those about sexual activities, but he forged on.

Abraham Maslow (behind car) with anthropologists and an interpreter (in hat) on the Siksika Reserve. PHOTOGRAPH COURTESY OF GLENBOW WESTERN RESEARCH CENTRE, TAYLOR FAMILY LIBRARY, UNIVERSITY OF CALGARY.

Abraham Maslow on the Siksika Reserve. PHOTOGRAPH COURTESY OF GLENBOW WESTERN RESEARCH CENTRE, TAYLOR FAMILY LIBRARY, UNIVERSITY OF CALGARY.

Then one day, like a bad boy at school, he was called to a meeting with the authorities. These elders told him his questions made their young women uncomfortable. They would not allow him to continue with that research plan. He must change his subject or leave. He was set adrift without a rudder. Lacking the shield of his research agenda, Maslow unexpectedly became an open-minded observer of a very different way of life.

Although Maslow never published anything specifically about his field season among the Siksika, he prepared a draft manuscript entitled "Northern Blackfoot Culture and Personality."[1] The themes he chose to write about—leadership, parenting, competition, motivation, religion, and self-esteem—demonstrated ways in which the Siksika differed from the young psychologist's expectations.

A child with grandparent, Siksika Reserve. PHOTOGRAPH COURTESY OF GLENBOW WESTERN RESEARCH CENTRE, TAYLOR FAMILY LIBRARY, UNIVERSITY OF CALGARY.

Maslow was surprised, but also impressed, by the gentleness of leaders and the respectful ways they treated everyone in their community. The Siksika interacted lovingly with all the youngsters of their community, not just their own. The children were well-adjusted, rarely misbehaved, and took on responsibilities well beyond those of Euro-American children. They might have been considered spoiled by outsiders, so rarely were their desires denied. Discipline was applied, as necessary, but Maslow noticed that it was "never understood as involving the loss of love." These children grew up to be "secure," he wrote, "in the sense of feeling safe in an all-friendly world." Their behaviors were corrected gently—without shaming or threats—allowing everyone their dignity. The culture appeared designed to support all its people. Everyone knew their place within the whole, and each person had others to turn to for comfort and guidance through formalized relationships, family, friends, and spirit helpers. Relationships were what mattered, not just with people but with all living beings and the land itself. They lived in the place where Creator put them.

Competition was one of the themes Maslow had pursued in his prior work, so he looked for its expression in the Blackfoot world. Surprising to him, individuals showed little or no drive for power over others. What competition he witnessed was among young men striving to be the most generous in order to be recognized as good leaders. Wealth was measured by generosity. Material wealth, so important in Maslow's own world, was not a focus among the Siksika, so it was "not a source of potential conflict and social hostility." They had no pecking order of wealthy over poor.

Competition was most apparent in games and sports. All individuals sang and danced, but never in a show of talent. When Maslow asked who the best singer was—reflecting the competitive world of his own experience—his responders would look a little confused and reply that "all the young men were good." He came to believe that their general "lack of feelings of inferiority, envy and resentment of another's successes or superiorities" were because they did not experience other tribal members lording power over them. These findings were antithetical to what he had assumed based on his previous research.

One aspect of Siksika life that was new to Maslow was their use of humor. People grew up able to laugh at themselves and accept the circumstances of their lives, tragic as they might be. Formalized teasing, where a certain person, like an uncle, held community-dictated teasing rights with another, perhaps a nephew, served as a mechanism to help people remember appropriate behaviors and boundaries. Kind-hearted joking focused only on behaviors that could be changed or improved. "No man is laughed at for being a cripple, or for being homely, weak or sick," observed Maslow. Humiliation was not an instrument used by these people to control others. "Children are not humiliated by their parents as they are in our society," Maslow wrote. "Women are not humiliated by men. Inferior men are not humiliated by superior men, nor are the poor humiliated by the rich." Joking conveyed inclusion and acceptance.

Maslow noted that the Christian concepts of conscience and soul, often used as guilt-provoking mechanisms within church circles, were not present in Siksika society. Guilt was not a motivation applied by the Blackfoot. Instead, the typical individual within this secure world felt able to "reinstate himself in the good opinion of the society" through modifying his own behavior. The motivation to change stemmed from a desire to be in right relationship with the community rather than to save one's soul or to buy one's way into heaven. Their focus was on this day, on the one hand, and the future on Earth for the next generations, on the other. Siksika Chief Crowfoot, at the treaty signing in 1877, like a great philosopher of ancient Greece, described life as "the flash of a firefly in the night. The breath of the buffalo in the wintertime. It is as the little shadow that runs across the grass and loses itself in the sunset."

Blackfoot religion was functional, according to Maslow, rather than "morally obligatory or merely traditional." He had been told "there were no specific compulsions, taboos and demands imposed by it upon the whole group aside from . . . general ethical and personality demands," such as incest taboos. Theirs was an empirical world that included the spiritual realm. These were people still deeply connected to their Source. Their beliefs did not come from the realm of abstract thought, so they weren't apt to accept teachings that did not resonate, like Heaven and Hell. They weren't in need of redemption because they never fell from their original state of grace; they remained connected to their Creator and in right relationship to others. They had no reason to strive for Heaven, removed as it was from their beloved Mother Earth and lacking in buffalo, and the threat of Hell would never come from the spirit world they knew.

Maslow had landed in a different realm from his Brooklyn childhood, and what he experienced among the Siksika shook his understanding of human motivation to its core. There, he observed people generally free of self-doubt and notably less self-conscious than what he had observed among Euro-Americans. The well-adjusted, self-confident, generous Blackfoot people were motivated to earn the esteem of others more than they were driven to earn self-esteem. They did not strive to be like others or try to force others to be like them; differences did not threaten them. The larger structure of their society made room for a wider range of normal variation than the dominant European-derived society. No one was made to feel fundamentally flawed. He found that despite material poverty, secure individuals were the norm in their secure society. He came to understand that each Blackfoot person "was valued, welcome, protected, included, taught to give back, and provided the opportunity to become actualized." The good of the whole was best served by holding a space for each individual to grow, like a flower or a tree, without intervention toward some derived ideal. They honored the fundamental, original oneness of everyone as an essential part of the whole—and their entire cultural construct was built to support that understanding.

What Maslow witnessed in a Native community in the center of North America was a living demonstration that each person has a particular purpose in the integral workings of the community to which they belong. In the Blackfoot world, according to Pikunni psychologist Sidney Stone Brown, every individual's actualized journey is fundamental to the whole. And when a person is out of balance, a ceremony is held "to restore the person to his or her natural state, one of having the capacity to love and be loved."[2] In learning that their purpose is to provide for others, they become generous. Through giving back, Brown explains, an individual's purpose is activated, and the circle is completed as they become the person they were "spiritually meant to be." These beliefs are reflected in every aspect of Blackfoot culture and in the world around them.

Maslow returned to New York and his teaching position at Brooklyn College, enthusiastic about the new frame of reference for human potential and positive mental health he had learned among the Siksika. He came to see the point of life as "the harmonious development of one's character."[3]

In 1943 he published his Hierarchy of Needs theory in which he proposed that the full potential of individuals could best be achieved when their basic physiological needs are met in a secure, stable, and safe environment where they are loved. From this grounded place of nurtured belonging, people naturally grow to have self-esteem; they feel recognized and respected by their community, and they are free to become their best selves—to self-actualize. Maslow launched the field of humanistic psychology from what he learned, and the human potential movement grew from these beginnings.

Maslow's focus on self-actualization reflects a significant difference between Native communities and Euro-Americans. Where his model is linear and centers on individual fulfillment, indigenous perspectives are relational and tend to focus on the well-being of the community. Dr. Sidney Stone Brown explains that the Blackfoot worldview is more like the reflection of a tipi in water than the tipi itself. This inverted view, she explains, is like the spirit of a person. Instead of the material focus of Maslow's hierarchy of needs, the Blackfoot worldview places the emphasis on the immaterial.[4]

Dr. Cindy Blackstock, executive director of the First Nations Child and Family Caring Society of Canada, uses the tipi rather than the pyramid to better convey the model. And she flips the order of progression. "Self-actualization," she points out, "is at the base of the tipi, not at the top, and is the foundation on which community actualization is built." Individual success, in this world, comes from positively contributing to the community in a way that perpetuates the culture—"cultural perpetuity."[5] In this model, community actualization through healthy relationships ensures cultural continuity.

Maslow continued to learn and grow in his understanding of human behavior. Late in life, some thirty years after his summer at Siksika, he had come to understand that self-transcendence should be the goal, rather than stopping at self-actualization.[6] With this epiphany, he came closer to what the Siksika had shown him all those years before. It is each interwoven thread that makes a cloth whole. ✢

DISTURBING THE SLEEPING BUFFALO

I can't pass a rock like you
Without being mystified or hypnotized
I have heard stories of rocks and have known some rocks personally
They represent the world by their presence
Wisdom has no relationship to size
One time, perhaps many times, a man became a rock
Thinking that a fine way to gain immortality[1]

—Tauhindali, Wintu Tribe of California

⊕ ⊕ ⊕

One of the hardest things for non-Indians to wrap our heads around is the idea that rocks are sentient beings, that they have a will, and they participate in the lives around them. If we had grown up knowing rocks personally, like Wintu poet Tauhindali, we wouldn't question this perspective.

A friend of mine in Hawaii had a carved tiki stone call to him as he walked down the beach one day. "Take me home," he called. Hank was nonplussed as he identified the source of the voice. Seriously, Hank thought, this substantial boulder, sacred to native Hawaiians, wanted to be relocated? He lived a mile up a steep mountain and could see no way to manage it, even if he believed that a stone was talking to him. The stone persisted, so Hank leaned over and prepared to see if he could lift it. He almost fell over backwards when he strained to bear the weight only to find the stone had made itself weightless. When they got home, the tiki made it clear that "he" didn't want to go inside. Instead, he indicated where in the garden he wanted to be placed. He dropped to the ground with a thud, heaviness restored. Years later, the tiki asked to be taken inside where it has happily resided in the corner of the dining room ever since.

A Blackfeet friend once told me of a singing stone that was bothering a woman in Great Falls. It kept her awake at night. The woman contacted someone on the Blackfeet Reservation who understood that the stone wanted to be removed from the woman's garden and brought back to the creek bed that was its home. Relocation solved the problem.

Many rocks in Montana have been widely recognized by people who know what to look for. One such notable rock gained its reputation, long ago, when it resided on top of a steep hill just to the north of the Marias River along the Whoop-Up Trail between Fort Benton and old Fort Whoop-Up in Lethbridge, Alberta. In the 1880s, according to George Bird Grinnell, "as the soil about it was worn away by the wind and rain," this huge sandstone boulder moved slowly down the hill. Grinnell believed that it was the perceived ability to travel that made the stone so important to Native travelers.[2] He was unaware of a Siksika (North Blackfoot) story from the 1840s of a man traveling along the Narrow Ridge Trail who broke a taboo by eating rattlesnake meat. He died there and "his spirit became encased in this boulder and became a source of power to those who would feed him."[3] Blackfeet travelers along that trail would place offerings there. This medicine stone now sits near the entrance of the Museum of the Plains Indian in Browning.

Another storied rock in Montana created an obstacle known as Medicine Rock Hill along the old Mullan Road, just east of the Continental Divide. While non-Indian travelers dreaded the difficulties created by this huge stone, Native travelers had great respect for its power. One of Mullan's crew, John Strachan, described this "curious site" as a twenty-foot-high cone. The stone was surrounded by "pieces of cloth, bows, arrows, bears' claws and buffalo horns," which Strachan understood was a way the Indians could "prevent any disease or trouble."[4] The stone is no longer there; perhaps one of you knows what happened.

A glacial erratic from Hudson Bay at Snake Butte. PHOTOGRAPH BY ROD BENSON, USED WITH PERMISSION.

Powerful stones are strewn throughout the Northern Plains. These hefty boulders were left behind by the Laurentide Ice Sheet at the end of the Pleistocene, and they carry the energy of that monumental flow and ebb. In some cases, the power of these glacial boulders drew people to carve sacred images onto them. Snake Butte is one such place.[5]

Glacial striations in rock near Snake Butte. PHOTOGRAPH BY ROD BENSON, USED WITH PERMISSION.

Disturbing the Sleeping Buffalo

Although Snake Butte is a subtle landform from a distance, its power comes from much more than its elevation. This butte formed when magma from volcanic activity some 50 million years ago hardened underground and then later intruded. The strength of the columnar basalt is what holds these sediments above the lay of the land.[6] Atop this sacred place sit rocks that tell the glacial history of more recent times. When the Laurentide Ice Sheet pushed its way southward some 90,000 years ago, the surface rocks atop the butte were scraped by massive angular rocks carried by the ice, leaving impressive striations.[7] The powerful force dislodged huge chunks from Snake Butte and deposited them in an alignment several miles long, creating what geologists call the "Snake Butte Boulder Train." Not only did the glacier remove huge rocks from the butte, but it also left some behind. Boulders that originated to the far north, known as glacial erratics, like immigrants, found a home atop the butte and all over the prairie when the ice receded.

Boulders atop Snake Butte, left there by the receding glacier. PHOTOGRAPH BY ROD BENSON, USED WITH PERMISSION.

The best known of the glacial erratics is a massive boulder of gray granite known as the Sleeping Buffalo. When the continental glacier retreated from the area we Montanans call the High Line, an impressive, boulder-strewn ridge emerged as part of the post-glacial terrain along the southern edge of the Milk River, northeast of Malta, near Saco.[8] These boulders looked like a resting herd of bison overlooking Cree Crossing, one of the best fords across the river, used for thousands of years by Native travelers.

Sleeping Buffalo Rock. PHOTOGRAPH BY JUDY HOY, COURTESY OF THE MONTANA HISTORICAL SOCIETY RESEARCH CENTER.

Disturbing the Sleeping Buffalo

Former place of lead buffalo overlooking Cree Crossing. PHOTOGRAPH BY KIM LUGTHART, UM REGIONAL LEARNING PROJECT, COURTESY OF SALLY THOMPSON.

In the book *Land of the Nakoda*, published in 1942, Assiniboine storyteller First Boy (James Long) tells of the significance of the sleeping buffalo and how people made offerings of thanksgiving to the lead buffalo of the stone herd. People with buffalo medicine prayed there "for the welfare and prosperity of the people."[9]

One old story about the power of the sleeping buffalo tells of a man praying for help at that place because he and his wife were starving. Thunder beings appeared and used their power to send a few buffalo their way. The man, weak as he was, was able to kill one of the animals. The next day, the couple learned that their

"In the buffalo country is a rock which resembles a buffalo lying down."

Sketch of Indians and Sleeping Buffao Rock by Fire Bear (William Standing). PHOTOGRAPH BY SALLY THOMPSON, FROM **LAND OF NAKODA**, WORKS PROGRESS ADMINISTRATION WRITERS' PROJECT, FIRST EDITION.

people had managed to kill the other two. Those Assiniboine people were saved from starvation.

The A'Ainin (Gros Ventre) also had a relationship with these stone buffalo. One story of both fable and history from their oral tradition was told to a man named Spear by his grandmother, as reported in the September 16, 1937, *Great Falls Tribune*. This story, according to its teller, "dates to a time when the people had become greedy for buffalo robes."

⊕ ⊕ ⊕

It was a time of plenty, when living was too easy for the people. Now they knew that the buffalo had been placed on earth for the purpose of providing food, shelter, and all other necessities and that for these things he must be honored, but they were obsessed with a lust for killing and slaughtered the buffalo by the thousands . . .

Then there came a dream to a maiden of the tribe. In this dream the girl was told unless the slaughter of the buffalo was stopped the tribe and all others would hunger for many years for the taste of fat buffalo meat. The young woman went to the chief and told him of her dream. He laughed at her and continued with plans for a greater hunt than ever.

When the morning of the hunt dawned the young men appointed as scouts to locate the herds returned with word that there were no buffalo within a day's reach. The search widened and continued over a great distance for days and weeks and months. Supplies of dried meat became low, robes wore thin and tepees no longer kept out the wind, but still no buffalo were sighted. Never before had there been such a time for hunger and fear.

Then one evening a scout came to the village with word that a small herd of buffalo had been seen near the council hill at the crossing on Milk river, where the river turns to form the big bend. The most cunning hunters approached the place and saw quite plainly the herd of buffalo grazing on the slope of the hill. They waited until the animals had lain down and then crept closer for an attack. When the hunters were within arrow shot of the herd, they sprang up with a shout, meaning to startle the buffalo to their feet so they could more surely be killed. But before their eyes a strange happening took place. The buffalo began to look less and less like living creatures and more like boulders scattered on the hillside. The frightened hunters went closer until they could touch what had been flesh but was now stone. The leader of the herd was there and the cows and calves, but all were stone.

Awestricken, the hunters returned to the village and related the strange happening. A council was called, and it was remembered that a maiden of the tribe had dreamed a strange dream of the buffalo. She was brought before the chief medicine man and instructed to go to the place of the stone buffaloes and fast there until her dream was made clear.

After three days and three nights of fasting and prayer, the girl returned and told the people they had been punished for their cruelty and greediness and that henceforth, unless they killed only for the necessities of life, the buffalo and all other game would return no more to the hunting grounds.

This was many generations ago and thereafter the buffalo returned and became plentiful but the people remembered the time of hunger and killed only for meat and for skins to make their lodges and robes.

⊕ ⊕ ⊕

The earliest known observer history written about Sleeping Buffalo was by Granville Stuart in the 1860s. He wrote of how Native peoples often left offerings such as cloth, sage, meat, or tobacco on both rocks and trees. These "shrines" invoked "the aid of the Great Spirit." He was especially impressed by the Sleeping Buffalo and reported that the Blackfeet and River Crows treated this stone with great reverence. To make a long pilgrimage to the ridge was not uncommon. The offerings were a way to give thanks for the help received from this stone they considered to be sentient.[10] The tradition continued as long as the boulder remained in place. The earliest White settlers observed trade beads and pieces of cloth laid on the stone buffalo's back.

A second medicine rock, sometimes called "Big Medicine," had been laid to rest by the glacier on a hilltop along the Milk River, not far from Sleeping Buffalo ridge. This impressive, four-ton boulder was carved with numerous figures, including one human figure inside a circle.

Mattias Azure, a Cree elder who was born in the 1860s, remembered that he first saw the rock around 1870 when he came into this country from Canada with his parents and other Crees. He remembered that the sacred rock was kept covered with a buffalo skin lodge because of its supernatural powers. Azure never knew what the symbols meant. At one time, a low stone wall nearly surrounded the boulder in the midst of a huge tipi camp evidenced by stone circles. The stones had been used to hold down the lodge skins in that windy landscape.

Many tribes held these stones sacred—including Blackfeet, Chippewa, Gros Ventre, Crow, Northern Cheyenne, and Sioux—but that didn't matter to some local entrepreneurs.[11] After more than 12,000 years residing where the glacier had placed it, Sleeping Buffalo was separated from the herd in 1931, when members of Malta's Commercial Club decided to move the powerful lichen-covered boulder into town. Some reports claim that Big Medicine was also moved at that time or soon after. The Commercial Club's stated purpose for the relocation was preservation, and they figured it couldn't hurt to have the mysterious buffalo rock in the town's Tafton Park; in fact, it might be good for business. These two curios were brought into town where people might come to see them and spend some dollars while they were there. The boosters prepared a concrete pedestal to host the sacred rocks.

Troubles started to brew from the very start. Elders from the Gros Ventre and Assiniboine tribes later told stories of what happened once these boulders were moved to town, and news accounts documented the troubles. Townsfolk started hearing bellowing buffalo during the night and they wanted the troubling rocks removed.[12] Some people reported that the rocks would turn themselves around, aiming themselves toward where they came from. Assiniboine elder Leslie Fourstar reported that "one night, one of the city patrol heard a cow bellowing and wondered if it was coming from this rock. He got scared and told the other patrol, the police. And they came over and it bellowed again." The traditional people understood that the stones were doing what they could to go home, and it worked. In September of 1937, the people of Malta, with a truck and manpower provided by the Farm Security Administration, moved the mysterious stones out to the intersection of Old Highway 2 and the newly constructed American Legion's Plunge Road, where they could attract business to the hot spring.

The *Helena Independent-Record* ran an article on September 22, 1937, announcing that "the stone buffalo is back on his home range." (This would

The monument and medicine rocks on U.S. Highway 2 in the 1940s. PHOTOGRAPH COURTESY OF THE MONTANA HISTORICAL SOCIETY RESEARCH CENTER.

more correctly read "her" home range because buffalo herds are led by cows, not bulls.) The newspaper included a photograph of the new digs created for the "rudely carved . . . likeness of a sleeping buffalo." It had been placed on a cement slab in front of a monument built of glacial boulders. A plaque that would provide a brief historical sketch was in the works.

The *Independent-Record* article went on to tell how the sleeping buffalo was painted with red coloring when the first White men came to the area. In those days, while in the vicinity of the stone buffalo, according to legend, war parties could pass "unmolested by the enemy; women and children were safe from raiders and sacrifices left there were never disturbed by Indians of any tribe." After the medicine rocks were moved to Highway 2, the types of offerings left with the stones changed. Instead of the "bits of red calico, tobacco, beads, feathers and meat" reported by early observers, motorists started leaving pennies.[13]

Twenty-five years later, the Sleeping Buffalo was moved again when the state highway department relocated the highway two miles to the north. Travelers continued to make offerings at the new location. Tobacco, candy bars, pennies, whatever one might have to give, would be left along with prayers. The Big Medicine rock was left behind along the old highway. Stranded there, it became vulnerable to vandalism.

In the meantime, when new owners bought the Legion Plunge, they capitalized on the location by renaming their facility the Sleeping Buffalo Resort. In 1987, they petitioned the Montana Department of Transportation to build something to protect their namesake from damage. Soon, a wood and stone structure was in place to protect this unique rock being from the weather and from vandals. Tribal councils and elders from the three closest reservations supported the decision and, with the local historical societies, agreed that the site should be nominated to the National Register of Historic Places.

Chere Jiusto of the Montana Historical Society organized a gathering of elders at the plunge to listen to their thoughts about the best outcome for the sacred boulders. Their stories made clear that the Sleeping Buffalo remained a deeply ingrained spiritual tradition. They all remembered seeing it in place when they were young. Blackfeet spiritual leader John "Buster" Yellow Kidney, through interpreters, told how his grandfather used to take him to Cree Crossing and to visit the Sleeping Buffalo when he was a boy. He was told how the people "used to move there and they'd spent two-three days there, [conducting] nothing but ceremonies involving the buffalo."[14] Others, too, felt a deep and continuing relationship with Sleeping Buffalo despite its decades of dislocation. In the National Register nomination, Jiusto wrote that "the continued relationship and ceremonial use of the Sleeping Buffalo Rock by the traditional community is evidence of their perception that the rocks maintain their power, significance and meaning. . . . The integrity of the rock itself and its cultural link to the native peoples of the high plains remains unbroken."[15] Through the stones, cultural knowledge is remembered.

The tribes would have preferred that Sleeping Buffalo had never been moved, and that they could have continued to visit the herd atop the ridge as their ancestors had done since time immemorial. But that land was private and fenced, so they would not be able to visit. For most of those consulted, the location along the highway seemed like a good compromise. As part of the process, Big Medicine was moved from isolation and brought back together with the Sleeping Buffalo. Spiritual leaders from both Assiniboine and Gros Ventre communities came together there for a pipe ceremony, honoring the return. They prayed and made offerings to celebrate this positive outcome to an otherwise painful story.

The Sleeping Buffalo rocks in their shelter. PHOTOGRAPH BY CARLA HUNSLEY, COURTESY OF MONTANA'S MISSOURI COUNTRY.

Federal designation to the National Register was achieved in 1996. These sacred stones had "survived three forced migrations," in the words of cultural historian Joshua Horowitz.[16]

Other petroglyph boulders did not fare so well. They have been moved through the years to gardens and businesses for personal enjoyment. These include three boulders from Sleeping Buffalo's herd that were moved to the Legion's Plunge, according to Diane F. Smith, in her book, *The Sleeping Buffalo Rock and other petroglyph features in Phillips County Montana*, printed in 2007. Smith grew up in Saco, helping her parents who managed the plunge. She thought moving these stones from their home place was a desecration and, later in life, decided to do something about it. She found several young men from the Fort Belknap Reservation who wanted to help her return these stones to their rightful homes, and some of them found their way back to the open prairie.[17]

Hats off to Diane Smith, Chere Jiusto, and the tribal elders who helped protect these important pieces of Montana history. Whatever your belief system about rocks, perhaps the next time one catches your attention, you might just stop and sit a spell. You never know where the relationship might lead. ✦

Book cover for The Sleeping Buffalo Rock *by Diane F. Smith.* PHOTOGRAPH COURTESY OF TERRY LODMELL.

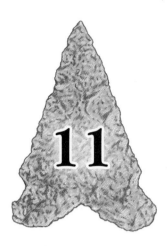

OLD MINDSETS DIE HARD[1]

When Governor Brian Schweitzer funded "Indian Education for All" in 2005, the state launched a unique effort to fully integrate the history, culture, and knowledge of Montana tribes across our school system. Achievement standards and textbooks began to change. The commitment of these funds had both enthusiastic supporters and vocal detractors. The former believed the more we know and understand about the First Peoples of Montana, the better our shared future will be. The latter thought the money would have been better spent elsewhere, and they resented the loss of time for teaching "the basics." Teachers and parents in some communities noted that they didn't have any Indians in their schools and argued they weren't given time to integrate the history, culture, and knowledge of the Irish or the Hmong, for example, so why focus on the Indians? The answer is because "Indian Education for All" is included in the Montana Constitution, leading the nation in recognizing the distinct and unique cultural heritage of American Indians.[2] By weaving these subjects throughout the curriculum, Montana educators provide a more balanced view of our shared history.

I had the privilege to assist teachers across the state in their efforts to make this Indian-Ed transition. Partnering with tribal educators, our team at the University of Montana's Regional Learning Project introduced the basics about tribal histories and explored ways for teachers to enhance content by incorporating well-researched, primary source materials. In the process,

I came to suspect that the most significant benefits to Montanans were ones we hadn't expected.

One interaction stays with me, probably because of the raw truth that emerged. At a mid-sized school district, my team and I had introduced Indian-focused content to teachers and administrators before separating into grade groups to discuss ways to integrate the material into their classrooms. I went with the high school group and began by inviting them to share how they were feeling about the workshop so far. One teacher said, "My students love Indian history, but whenever I venture into a more contemporary topic, it's like a haze fills the room and we can't really move forward. The haze is too thick."

I asked if she could give an example because I wasn't really following what she was saying. "It's about racism," one of her colleagues blurted from across the circle. He went on to say that many of their students carry deeply rooted racism toward Indians. This fact will be no surprise to Indians of Montana, but it might be for other citizens.

Euro-Americans sentimentalize Indians and tend to trap them in the past. This phenomenon is so ingrained as to be hard to see. Imagine a book called "Ten Little Caucasians." Inside you find little White children not wearing blue jeans and t-shirts but dressed as pilgrims. Or imagine "Caucasian Head Mountain," with some stereotypical quality Indians associate with the appearance of White men, such as a beard. Many book publishers are only beginning to understand how such images perpetuate stereotypes and keep us all trapped in the past, blindered by cultural biases.

A story that ran in the *Montana Standard* in 2007 jumped out at me as an example of how unconscious biases about Native people continue among non-Indians. The story confirmed the importance of Montana's commitment to Indian Education for All. See what you think.

The *Standard* reported on an effort led by the Dillon-area U.S. Bureau of Land Management office, working with the Madison Valley History Association, to locate the site of what the headline declared a "Trapper-Indian Battle." Following leads from the detailed journal of Osborne Russell, they knew that in 1835 a group of trappers, including Jim Bridger, came upon a tipi containing the bodies of nine smallpox-bloated Blackfeet.

Old Mindsets Die Hard

The trappers knew that a Blackfeet camp must be nearby. Bridger encouraged them to travel wide of the camp, leaving it undisturbed. They didn't follow his advice. As you read Russell's account of what happened the next morning, imagine you are one of the people in the camp—a mother, a child, or perhaps the man in charge of their safety—and experience this "battle" from a different point of view than that of the trappers.

> The next morning (June 4) as we were passing over the ridge around this place we discovered the Village about three miles above us on the river. We immediately drove into this Kanyon with the Camp and prepared for battle. Our leader was no military commander therefore no orders were given after the company property was secured. About 15 men mounted horses and started for the Village in order to commence a skirmish. . . .
>
> While our men were approaching the village, I took a telescope and ascended the highest point of rock which over hung the camp to view the maneuver. They rode within a short distance of the edge of the bench, then dismounted and crept to the edge and opened a fire on the Village which was the first the Indians knew of our being in the country.

They fired, unprovoked and indiscriminately, upon the sleeping camp of suffering, pox-infected Blackfeet men, women, and children.

When is an event a massacre and when is it a battle? What makes a confrontation a skirmish instead of a slaughter? How would the description change if this had been a story of fifteen Blackfeet firing into a camp of sleeping, miserably sick trappers? Perspective is everything.

Osborne Russell and Jim Bridger knew to beware of Blackfeet—many a trapper lost his life to members of this tribe. When this "battle" occurred, on the Upper Madison River, the Blackfeet had been at war with America for thirty years, ever since Meriwether Lewis and Reubin Field had killed two of their young men on the Two Medicine River.

Trappers and traders had immediately followed Lewis and Clark into the country, including some of the men from the Corps of Discovery, leading to a situation where American economic interests came into direct conflict with the lifeway of the Blackfeet. Anthropologist Linda Juneau (who is Pikunni) explains that for people whose most sacred ceremonial object is the Beaver Bundle, trappers were not welcome. Beaver were revered for their ability to create their own worlds of expanded wetlands. According to Narcisse Blood (who was Kainai), the Blackfeet were warlike during these years simply because they were protecting their lands. Some of their young men took their anger beyond the boundaries of their own territories and attacked American trappers as far south as Fort Hall, Idaho.

The BLM research team informed the Blackfeet Nation about the investigation of this historic event, and the *Montana Standard* article notes that some tribal members visited the location. Although no interviews were included and no tribal representatives were named, the article mentions their somber countenance. In contrast, one of the amateur historians noted that this battle wasn't as noteworthy as the Little Big Horn, but, for their area, "it's as good as it gets."

Thankfully, fifteen years after the Madison Valley History Association and the BLM set out to relocate the site, much progress has been made in Montana toward less bias and greater understanding of this history. The BLM has since conducted appropriate consultation with the Blackfeet Nation about this 1835 tragedy and has plans for collaborative work at the site.

When the BLM historians create an interpretive sign at the site of this massacre, they can help Montanans understand this historic event by placing it in full context and by telling the story from both points of view. For far too long we have deprived ourselves of the opportunity to move forward together— as distinct cultures with distinct histories—by only telling one perspective of our shared past. Through a more thorough inclusion of both perspectives, we create great potential for our shared future. If you don't see yourself as part of the past, how can you see yourself as part of the future? With funding and implementation of Indian Education for All, Montana took a big leap toward healing. ✢

History Day in Jordan

I get a call one October day from the superintendent of schools in Garfield County asking if I would like to give a talk for their history day in late February. Jordan, where the event will take place, is a long way from Missoula—400.7 miles, to be exact. As part of the Humanities Montana Speakers Bureau, I have the opportunity to see all parts of the state, and so I decide, then and there, that I would enjoy seeing the Jordan area. "Sure," I tell her, and put the event on my calendar. I will get back to the details after the first of the year.

In mid-January, I begin to think about my topic for the Jordan presentation. Realizing I have not received much information about their expectations, I decide to call the superintendent to learn more. I wonder about the audience, the location, their available technology, and whether they have any particular requests regarding the topic. "Well," she says, "the whole county comes out for the event, so we hold it in the gym at the elementary school." Imagining rows of bleachers filled with squirming children and the echo of my voice reverberating off the walls, I feel the impacts of dread take hold of my gut. I try to set my discomfort aside and focus on the anticipated audience. My mind is slowly realizing that those who will gather include elementary students, an audience I have never addressed. High school students are the youngest minds I have ever attempted to engage in one of my presentations. I need more information before I panic.

"What is the target audience?" I ask.

"Why don't you aim for 2nd grade," she replies, with no hint of humor. She assures me that whatever history topic I find appropriate for that age group will be fine, reminding me that parents and grandparents from throughout the county will also attend, along with the rest of the school.

Knowing that to cancel at this late date would leave them in a bind, I quell my unease and hope some creative idea will manifest to address this curveball. In the meantime, I should reserve a car. I've already booked a flight on Big Sky Air, the wonderful commuter airline that served Montana from 1978 to 2008. I will fly to Miles City late in the afternoon of the preceding day, rent a car, and drive to Jordan. I was surprised, however, to find no rental car company in Miles City listed on the internet. Not knowing what else to do, I call a car dealership, hoping they can direct me. Good call, it turns out, because they are the only place in town where I can acquire a rental. They will leave the car, keys in the ignition, parked behind the airport. This kind of trust is one of the things I love about Montana. Okay! At least my travel arrangements are in place.

I need to get back to work at editing interviews with tribal elders for a film project, so I'll have to think later about a topic for Jordan. One of the interviews is with Alice Finley, a woman of the Kalispel Tribe (relatives of Montana's Pend d'Oreille Tribe), based in far northeastern Washington along the Pend Oreille River before it flows into the Columbia. I listen to this eighty-year-old talk about how things were done when her grandparents were alive and realize I can create a presentation about how things were done long ago in Montana. What a relief. I have my topic selected and, with great enthusiasm, I go through transcripts of interviews with tribal elders from Montana in search of additional insights into past life in the plains and mountains where we now live. With the help of my staff at the University of Montana, I pull together clips from these interviews focused on how people acquired, prepared, and stored food before refrigeration; how they communicated before phones; kept warm before furnaces; and traveled before cars. I begin to look forward to my trip.

The weather in eastern Montana is terrible in late February, but I remain unaware of that issue in the days before my departure. I have an old flip phone and it isn't equipped with a weather app. In fact, the term "app" has yet to emerge in the popular culture. Snow has melted in Missoula and the first buttercups of the year have already been sighted. On the appointed day, I catch a ride to the airport, climb aboard, and crouch my way down the short aisle of the nineteen-passenger, twin-engine, Beechcraft turboprop fixed-wing airplane, happy to find myself seated next to an old friend. We visit our way across the western half of the state, with stops in Bozeman and Billings. As we begin to taxi for take-off on the third leg, dusk already beginning to color the sky, the pilot informs us that heavy snow to the east might result in a direct flight to Glendive, rather than stopping in Miles City. I plead with the weather gods to let us land, and they listen. Around 6 P.M. the pilot manages to land in the historic town of Miles City at the confluence of the Powder and Yellowstone Rivers. But I can't see the cottonwoods along the rivers or the site of the famous annual bucking horse sale, or anything else, actually. Not only has night fallen, but heavy snow fills the air.

I'm faced with a decision. Should I wait to drive in the morning light, or should I get to Jordan before the snow gets any deeper and eventually freezes on the highway? My presentation is at 9 A.M. All things considered; the latter option seems the wisest. I brave my way into the stormy night, snow on my eyelashes, and walk around to the back of the terminal where I see, as promised, a big Buick parked and waiting, keys inside. I toss my bag in the trunk, back out of the parking spot and find my way to Montana Highway 59, grateful for blacktop instead of ice and snow on the road. The going is slow in the dark, as I make my way through the open rangeland toward Jordan. The only named place along the eighty-mile stretch between the two towns is Cohagen, an unincorporated community whose population, at that time, hovers around 200. As I make my way, the wind challenges my ability to keep the car on the road. Most Montanans have had at least a couple of experiences like this, and the terrifying details stay with us, especially the way the snowflakes come right at you, making it hard not to focus on them instead of the road. What should have been not much more than an hour-long trip takes more than three. Rarely have I been so grateful to collapse into a clean bed after prying my fingers from the wheel and fighting my way through the blizzard into the motel.

The snow stopped sometime in the night, but as the sun wakes the day, its spawn lies deep and blindingly white as far as my eye can see. I make my way through unplowed streets to the school where the superintendent greets me.

"We'll have a smaller crowd than expected," she reports. Most of the roads are impassable, so it will just be the town kids. She is disappointed, and so am I, as we head to the gymnasium.

I hook my computer up to the projector they have provided, greet the assembly of eighty or ninety people, and share clips that later become a half-hour video called "Long Ago in Montana," distributed by the state Office of Public Instruction to all Montana elementary schools on DVD and later made available on YouTube, through The Montana Experience: Stories from Big Sky Country.[1]

What I remember now, some fifteen years later, is the attentiveness of the students and the astute questions they asked. Since many of them came from farms and ranches, they had fewer layers of obscurity to travel through between the past and their current circumstances than urban kids. Helping raise food was what they did, and sometimes they were challenged to get from one place to another, even that very day. Communications were often interrupted when lines went down in the wind, and their own grandparents had memories not dissimilar to those shared by the tribal elders they had just watched on the screen. They seemed unusually grounded. Their rich connection to the land and to the other beings that share this place with us heightened my awareness of what urban children are missing. As much as we benefit from technology and the opportunities of modern life, I can't help but reflect on what we may be losing as the old ways fade from memory.

I would have liked to stay longer or to have returned when the snow melted and spring emerged, but I never did. Thank you, Jordan, Montana. You were the reason I produced this video that introduced thousands of Montana students to the way life was lived long before we were born. ✛

PART IV
CLARK FORK BASIN

CLARK FORK JOURNEY, WINTER 1859

Have you ever tried winter camping in the wilderness? If so, did you do it with GPS and high-tech, lightweight gear? What if, instead, you had no such amenities available but, like Jesuit missionary Pierre-Jean De Smet, you had wool, canvas, and leather, and "the road" is an unmaintained trail through thick woods bordering a rapid-filled river. Impassable during winter except by the heartiest snowshoers, the thoroughfare is "opened" for travel by the first horses able to trudge through the wet, spring snow. If it weren't for my discovery of De Smet's field journal documenting this Clark Fork trek, I wouldn't be able to tell you of this historic journey along snowy trails in 1859, five years before Montana became a territory, and all the threads that came together through my encounter with the contents of his journal.

The discovery came about when I walked into the Special Collections section of the Pius XII Memorial Library at Saint Louis University in 2006 and asked the archivist if they happened to have any Rocky Mountain mission material. I assumed they wouldn't, since the university had transferred their collection to the Jesuit Archives some years before. Imagine my surprise when the archivist asked his assistant, "What about that box that came in recently?" The next thing I know I am reaching into an unprocessed box and lay my hands on a bound field journal with lizard-skin cover, penned (actually penciled) by De Smet. Looking through these handwritten pages, I realize that the content of this journal is focused on a round-trip journey from Fort Vancouver

Father De Smet with tribal delegates, Portland, Oregon, 1859. PHOTOGRAPH COURTESY OF THE UNIVERSITY OF WASHINGTON LIBRARIES.

to St. Ignatius Mission in the winter of 1858-1859, connected to a well-known photograph of the famed Jesuit, posed with a group of Indian men, usually entitled "Father De Smet and the Indian Chiefs." General William Harney had appointed Father De Smet as an official agent of the U.S. Army to go into the mountains to find fugitives from the Plateau War and convince them to concede that the war was over, that the White world was too big for the Indians to continue their fight. The journal fills in some important blanks in the story behind the photograph.

For a researcher like me, the discovery of this only known field journal of Father De Smet is astonishing, and to have it focus on the area where I live is even more amazing. Of special interest to Montanans is the account of the landscape, trail conditions, and weather along the Clark Fork River during the winter and snowy spring, along with glimpses into village life during the cold months.

Written in French, I could only thumb with care through the journal at the time, but I soon had a scanned, digitized version for translation. As I read through the entries, I realized that De Smet's story parallels one by John Owen, trader and Flathead Indian agent at the time. Their overlapping stories paint a picture not shared in their official accounts, revealing a glimpse into their complicated relationship and their conflicting sense of responsibilities.[1] An added bonus came with the details provided about Chief Kamiakin, one of the few tribal leaders who managed to escape punishment for his role in the recently concluded Plateau War. This war was actually a series of separate conflicts that erupted between the U.S. government and several tribes of northern Idaho and eastern Washington and Oregon after the 1855 Walla Walla Treaty was signed.

Backdrop

Father De Smet has been away from the Rocky Mountain Mission for twelve years, since the fall of 1846. Fifty-seven years old, he is eager to see his old friends again, unconcerned that he will undertake an arduous journey that would challenge most thirty-year-olds under twenty-first-century conditions. To get there from St. Louis, the famous Jesuit travels first to New York, part of the way by train, to meet up with General Harney at Army Headquarters. From New York, the two men travel by ship down the Eastern Seaboard to Panama, then by train across the Isthmus of Panama, then board another ship to San Francisco, and then up the Columbia River to Fort Vancouver. Most people would be exhausted and want a good rest before proceeding on. Not Father De Smet.

The Journey Begins

From Fort Vancouver, across the Columbia River from present-day Portland, Oregon, De Smet sets out in late October for the mountains, "some 800 miles distant." Due to some delays at Fort Walla Walla, he doesn't make it to Sacred Heart Mission among the Coeur d'Alene people until November 21. He expects to stay just a short while before heading on to the new location of St. Ignatius Mission (established in 1854), north of present-day Missoula. Instead, because weather conditions make mountain travel impossible, he remains at the mission for nearly three months, during which time he writes letters, tracks the weather, sketches, and visits. The Indians tell him he will have to wait until February for conditions to improve.

In mid-February, as predicted, changed weather conditions allow for travel. Heavy rain at the end of January had been followed by a severe frost, making it possible to cross the mountains on snowshoes. De Smet would finally be able to proceed into the country of the Salish, the tribe with whom he has the longest and strongest relationship. En route he will visit "Kamiakan's little camp" somewhere on "the Kalispel or Clark's river."[2] Kamiakin and his kin of the Palouse and Yakama nations, are among the few leaders who escaped after the recent war. While other chiefs signed Colonel Wright's agreements with terms of surrender, Kamiakin sent word that he would not disgrace the memory of "all the fighting chiefs . . . by surrendering to a hated race." Instead, with his "few remaining horses," he and his family would "journey to find a different people."[3] The other chiefs were hanged, using John Mullan's wagon as a platform.

Into the Mountains

An eager De Smet leaves Sacred Heart on February 18, 1859. A detailed picture emerges from the field journal, in addition to his letter reports and other records.[4] From the mission he descends the Coeur d'Alene River by canoe, crosses the ice-covered Lake Coeur d'Alene, then heads overland, by horseback, to Lake Pend Oreille, "the great Kalispel Lake," arriving at the "Bay of the Coeur d'Alenes" at the south end ten days later. Indians provide "barges"— large, dugout canoes—to transport the party's gear to an Indian camp near the "Bay of the Pend d'Oreille" at the far northeastern shore, near what is now the little town of Denton, Idaho. It takes four days.

From the lake, they begin their ascent of the Clark Fork by "frail, bark canoes." De Smet fails to mention how they manage getting through "The Cabinet," a narrow gorge of fast-flowing water. They get stopped once they reach "Thompson's river," where the falls and rapids, along with ice, snow, rain, and wind, force them onto shore. The rest of the journey is by snowshoe, then horseback. All along the route, De Smet employs his cartographic skills. In total, he documents thirty-four rapids and waterfalls along the Clark Fork in the course of seventy miles.[5] He maps every one, noting the Salish name for each of these locations.

Above: *Map showing the return trip route, April 1859.*

Left: *Cabinet Gorge on the Clark Fork River.* PHOTOGRAPH BY ROSS HALL, COURTESY OF WATER ARCHIVES.

Below: *Thompson Falls circa 1908.* PHOTOGRAPH BY CHAUNCEY E. WOODWORTH, COURTESY OF THE UNIVERSITY OF MONTANA ARCHIVES.

On their third day of travel, near some rapids where he hears the song of a "small bird," his party finds a camp of Kalispels (Lower Pend d'Oreille, who call themselves Qlipsé). They are tucked into the edge of the woods at the mouth of a river his guides call the "Inkotel," now known as the Bull River. Despite food shortages near the end of winter, the Kalispels graciously offer housing and share their "small rations and tiny provisions."[6] De Smet notes that this major tributary is "navigable by Indian canoe." All along the route, he encounters small winter camps on the rivers and lakeshores, where the people hunt, trap, and fish.

A brief and seemingly ordinary note in his journal tells that he "met with Kamiakin and Schloom," his brother. The priest provides more details in a letter, telling of the family's heart-wrenching situation and "the poverty, and misery" of their children. He finds that Kamiakin, "the once powerful chieftain, who possessed thousands of horses, and a large number of cattle," has lost everything, and is "reduced to abject poverty."[7] Despite their circumstances, these families greet him warmly. Schloom is almost blind and only able to travel short distances. His health is so bad that De Smet is unclear

Sketch of the Kalispel "camp at the Inkotel River" by Pierre-Jean De Smet from his field journal. PHOTOGRAPH COURTESY OF THE SAINT LOUIS UNIVERSITY ARCHIVES.

Portrait of Kamiakin in 1855 by Gustav Sohon. PHOTOGRAPH
COURTESY OF WASHINGTON STATE HISTORICAL SOCIETY.

Portrait of Skeloon ("Schloom") in 1855 by Gustav Sohon.
PHOTOGRAPH COURTESY OF WASHINGTON STATE HISTORICAL SOCIETY.

whether he will live through the end of summer. Kamiakin and Schloom
will think over what Father De Smet tells them of General Harney's order for
them to travel to Vancouver where they can officially surrender.[8]

Saying his good-byes, De Smet once again heads up the Clark Fork.
He mentions horses but not where they got them. Had Kamiakin provided
mounts for the tired Black Robe from his remnant herd? Wherever they came
from, the horses afford welcome transportation across Thompson's Prairie
and over some twenty miles of "terrible rocks" (now known as Bad Rock).

That night they camp at "Horse Prairie" (now called Plains), where the
trail to the Flathead and Jocko Valleys leaves the river. It transects Camas
Prairie, where De Smet reports losing his cross but makes no note of its
description. He may have traveled with a simple wooden cross rather
than one of the ornate crucifixes that appear in some of his portraits.
On March 11, the missionary finds himself in view of the remarkable sight

Above: Sketch of St. Ignatius Mission by Pierre-Jean De Smet. PHOTOGRAPH COURTESY OF THE SAINT LOUIS UNIVERSITY ARCHIVES.

Left: Portrait of Chief Alexander in 1855 by Gustav Sohon. PHOTOGRAPH COURTESY OF WASHINGTON STATE HISTORICAL SOCIETY.

of St. Ignatius Mission. He is thrilled to be greeted there by his old friend, Alexander, the Pend d'Oreille chief.

One might think that De Smet would allow himself some downtime upon completing this grueling trip from Sacred Heart Mission (not to mention the preceding months traveling by sea from New York, and then up the Columbia). Instead, the very next day he heads north to visit a village of Kootenai at the north end of Flathead Lake.

Enter John Owen

During this time, an entry in John Owen's journal tells that he sees De Smet at St. Ignatius Mission on March 16, 1859. That might have been when Owen tells De Smet he has orders from the Superintendent of Indian Affairs to escort a delegation of chiefs from each tribe of the "upper country" to meet with him in Salem, Oregon. The two men appear to have parallel assignments. Somehow this seems fitting. Although De Smet is nearly two decades older, the two men are remarkably similar. Both are short and stocky, built like bulls, and know the trails of the Old Oregon Country better than almost any other non-Indian. Each has lived in the heart of the Bitterroot Valley, and they share many of the same friends, Indian and White. Both are affable, well-read, and generally enjoyed by others. However, in this case, instead of finding a way to combine forces, they remain aloof toward each other. Something is amiss, as their journals will reveal.

The Jesuit heads south to visit his Salish friends in the Bitterroot Valley. En route, he and his guides camp at what is now the top of Evaro Hill, which he calls "the horse run," meaning a racetrack, noting that many battles had occurred there. The following day he arrives at the Hellgate Ronde, where people from various tribes are returning from their winter buffalo hunt.[9] De Smet is delighted to come upon five lodges of Salish and notes their joy at seeing him after so many years. He spends only one day visiting the Salish community in the Bitterroot before returning to the Missoula Valley. Perhaps the sight of this failed mission of St. Mary's—first and dearest to De Smet— now under the jurisdiction of John Owen's trading center, is too depressing for him to want to linger. For more than three weeks, between March 23 and April 16, De Smet's diary is bare.

John Owen has traveled to St. Ignatius because he is ready to head west but finds that he is "too Early for the road & Shall be detained here Some 12 days."[10] He decides to move to the Flathead River, across from the Jocko, to wait. His March 30 entry tells that he "laid over Waiting for the Revd Father De Smet and Mr Ogden to come up." (Mr. Ogden is Michael Ogden, son of De Smet's old friend Peter Skene Ogden and his Salish wife, Julia.) The road is still not open for travel and won't be "practicable," apparently, for another two weeks. Around April 10, Owen and his camp begin to slowly move down the trail to provide better forage for his animals. They arrive at Horse Plain four days later. Snow still covers the ground in the valley during this "unheard of Spring," but horses find dried grasses on the wind-swept slopes nearby. On April 17, a Sunday, they stay put, while waiting for somebody to work at opening the road. A group of Kalispels, camping nearby, are as anxious as Owen to travel but they are unable to pack the road because "their horses but recently from Buffaloe are too low in flesh to break Snow."

Dueling Escorts Heading Down the Clark Fork

De Smet and Ogden arrive at Horse Plain on April 18, having left the Hellgate valley two days before. The priest resumes his daily journal entries. This is when the story gets really interesting, with all that simmers beneath the surface. The Jesuit and the Indian agent must have interacted while camping in the same valley, but neither mentions the other. Michael Ogden switches camps and begins to travel with Owen, with whom he has traveled before.[11] Despite being business competitors, they also are friends.

Only Owen, Ogden, and François Saixa, an interpreter who has worked for both De Smet and Owen through the years, are known to be in the Owen party. No one else is mentioned. Their group tends to keep a day or so ahead of De Smet's unspecified party. The two accounts, in addition to De Smet's trip up the river just two months earlier,

John Owen. PHOTOGRAPH FROM THE JOURNALS AND LETTERS OF MAJOR JOHN OWEN, DUNBAR AND PHILIPS.

provide unusual documentation of winter travel through these wild lands before the time of engineered roads. It took Owen five days and De Smet six to travel between Horse Prairie and Lake Pend Oreille. Today, if you are following State Highway 200 between Plains, Montana, and Clark Fork, Idaho, you could cover the distance of eighty-four miles in about an hour and a half.

Father Pierre-Jean De Smet. PHOTOGRAPH COURTESY OF THE MARQUETTE UNIVERSITY ARCHIVES.

April 19
Owen *and Ogden move to Thompson's River.*

De Smet: *We camped at the base of rough rocks; about 15 miles journey.*

April 20
Owen: *Made a short drive of four hours & campd on a small branch in the timber.*

De Smet: *5 horses escaped and they set out in the direction of the mission. It took nearly 11 hours to bring them back. We left [soon after] and met with Kamiakin.* [Thompson Prairie]

April 21
Owen: *Made a nother short drive below the uteswomen* [Vermillion River] *some snow to day but trail open we are now as far as horses have been this year from this to the lake we expect trouble.*

150

De Smet: *baptisms, then–Crossed the Thompson River Prairie. Camped at the Skylkum, about 15 miles. Baptized Kakriyue as Marie– about 60 years in age. We left camp after allowing the horses to have a long rest. Pine wood was clear and strong. We took the mountain side route that extends a great distance. We traveled through a mile of strong water and deep snow. Camp at the Kumolosee Point. About 20 miles.*

April 22

Owen: *Made an early move to the jokutel Snow deep but from there to partridge encampment had to use snow shoes   mr ogden & francois ahead leading the strongest horses the loose animals driven immediately after them to open the trail 12 hrs.*

De Smet: *Long horse hunt–4 horses missing. Depart. Crossed the Vermillion River; deep snow. Torrents and waterholes. Trekked through snow. We camped in a little place uncovered [by snow]. About 15 miles.*[12]

April 23

Owen: *From our camp on bulls head creek to the cabinet but little trouble but over the cabinet mt. For some 8 miles we found the snow 3 feet deep & in places a full fathom we camp on the mts face in view of the lake out 12 hrs & came into camp very tired all hands.*

De Smet: *Trekked through snow and strong woods for about 10 miles. We arrived at the river, diverted by snow. Camped in the snow. About 15 miles.*

April 24

Owen: *Easter sunday made a short march to the lake & halted for the day.*

De Smet: *Mass and communion [in the morning]. Trekked through snow and forests. Passed through torrents. Arrived at the Clark River or Pend d'Oreille. Welcomed the long road of the river. Passed through the mountain of the cabinet and camped after 25 miles. Horses rested in . . .*

April 25

Owen: *Made another short drive to & over pack river which we found rising.*

De Smet: *Depart. Passed through a beautiful forest of fat cedars. Arrived at the Pend d'Oreille–about 12 miles. Festival of the Bear*

⊕ ⊕ ⊕

The diarists' brief entries reveal little of the stress they endure from difficult travel conditions, or from their interpersonal challenges. "Trekked through snow and forests" and "Passed through torrents" are phrases that barely allude to the difficulties. Father De Smet provides a more detailed account in a letter, where he admits to "great misery and danger . . . due to high river water and heavy snow." Travel required clearing fallen trees, while traveling mid-slope through snow as deep as eight feet. All along the way, day after day, the missionary and his horse fell frequently. He reports that he escaped fairly unscathed, except for "moderate contusions and scratches, a torn hat, inconvenience, torn pants, and a shredded cassock."[13]

To the Spokane Plains and Fort Walla Walla

Travel conditions improve greatly once they reach Lake Pend Oreille. The two groups travel independently from there to Antoine Plant's Ferry on the Spokane River, with Owen's party arriving on April 28 and leaving for supplies at Fort Colville before De Smet's party arrives. While waiting several days for "the chiefs," De Smet records the distances they have traveled, baptisms of children, and names of the five tribal representatives heading to Fort Vancouver. They are Alexander Tomglagkerzine, the Man Who Only Takes Horses; Victor Alamoken, or the Happy Man; Adolphe Kwikkwidpape, or Red Feather; François Saixa, or the Iroquois; and Denis Zeneimtretze, or the Wood Robe. Presumably these men are with Owen's party, who will return to Spokane Prairie after a week. De Smet meets with Spokane Chief Garry while he is there. "Spokan Garry" had led an unusual life. Schooled by Anglicans at the Red River settlement in Canada as a child, Garry had been trained as a lay minister. By the time he meets Father De Smet, however, he has left that life behind. Father De Smet has a favor to ask of Garry. When the priest met with Kamiakin in April, the exiled chief agreed to attend the council with General Harney "if he had a horse to ride, his own not being in a condition to undertake a long journey."[14] De Smet had none to lend him, but perhaps Garry could help? The Spokane leader agrees to send a horse to Kamiakin along with an invitation from De Smet to accompany the other chiefs to Walla Walla and on to Vancouver.

Both groups start out again on May 7. De Smet's record tells that he travels along the Spokane River through "Beautiful prairies and forests," followed by the brief entry—"Kamiakin followed us." Owen notes only that his party "moved camp & crossd Spokan river" and that "the Revd Father De Smet is traveling." For reasons unknown, that phrase about De Smet is the last entry in Owen's journal.[15] Poof. He stops writing. We lose him as a source until after his arrival in Vancouver, when he writes a flurry of letters in self-defense about troubles that ensue.

De Smet arrives at Fort Walla Walla on May 13, where he meets with army officials. The very next day, with no explanation provided, he is aboard a wagon heading west. His immediate destination is the confluence of the Walla Walla River and the Columbia, where he will board the brand-new *Colonel Wright*, the first steamboat launched above The Dalles. The disgruntled priest arrives at Fort Vancouver on May 18, but not as he imagined. He is not escorting warriors who fled into exile, as he hoped he would be. Apparently, he is not escorting anyone.

The Long-Awaited Meeting with General Harney

The story of what happened at Fort Walla Walla and also in Vancouver remains veiled behind a cloak of mystery. We know from an Owen letter sent on the morning of May 28 that the tribal delegates are with him in Vancouver, all except for Kamiakin. These men meet that day with General Harney. According to his records, seven tribal delegates attend. They include:

- **Alexander** (*Templogketzin*, or the Man without a Horse), (Pend d'Oreille)

- **Adolphe** (*Kwilkwilskepo*, or Red Feather), (Salish)

- **Victor,** (*Alameken*, or the Happy Man), (Kalispel)

- **Denis** (*Zilenametietze*, or the Thunder's Robe), (Colville)

- **Andre** (*Uteesh*), (Coeur d'Alene)[16]

- **Bonaventure** (*Similkai*) (Coeur d'Alene)

- **Garry** (*Insula*, or Crested Head), (Spokane)[17]

Much to General Harney's disappointment, no doubt, none of the attending delegates have participated in the recent war. Although the Coeur d'Alenes and Spokanes had been major actors, the three delegates sent to represent them had not been among the participants. The Palouse and Yakama nations, principal drivers in the conflict, are not represented at the table.

One success of the council is that the four delegates from the Coeur d'Alene, Colville, and Spokane express their desire to participate in a treaty so they can secure land for their people, like their Salish and Pend d'Oreille allies. With so many Whites flooding into the area, they need protection.

Upon conclusion of the council, General Harney prepares passports for each of the delegates to secure their safe travels through the territory.

> I give this letter to Garry to show that I recognize him as a chief of the Spokanes. Garry is a good man and I believe in his desire to be friendly to the whites. His people have acted badly, but I now forget the past, and only require them to listen to what Garry tells them from me.
>
> I recommend Garry and his people who listen to him, to the friendship and good will of all white men.[18]

Sometime after the meeting with the general, De Smet spends three weeks touring the delegates around Oregon and Washington Territories. Of those who attended the meeting with General Harney, only Garry did not travel with the group. We are left to speculate as to the reasons why. Following the tour, the group returns to Fort Vancouver, where, according to Father De Smet, "all the chiefs received presents from the general and superintendent and returned to their own country contented and happy and well determined to keep at peace with the whites."[19]

154

Left: Spokane chief Garry, 1861. PHOTOGRAPH COURTESY OF THE LIBRARY OF CONGRESS, LC-USZC4-11449.

Below: Three of Chief Garry's men, 1861. PHOTOGRAPH COURTESY OF THE LIBRARY OF CONGRESS, LC-USZC4-11449.

The famous photograph taken in a Portland studio is carried by newspapers far and wide. De Smet, by this time, is a Belgian-American icon and the caption that accompanies the photograph implies that he brought peace to the region through his influence on these tribal leaders. However, all seven men who appear in the photograph are known as fast friends to the White man. They are dedicated Catholics, having been baptized by the Jesuits at missions originally established in their homelands in the 1840s under the leadership of Father De Smet. Most, if not all, are his old friends. They are not the "renegades" who escaped punishment after the war.

An 1899 letter and copy of the photograph, published in the February 12, 1939, *Spokesman-Review*, explains that the photograph was arranged for by a local jeweler and soon-to-be mayor, Collier Robbins, who had invited the delegation to dine with him. Collier, in his letter, reports that General Harney had sent Father De Smet into the mountains with a "message to the Indians that they must surrender one of the principal chiefs of the hostiles to him unconditionally at Vancouver and, un-less they did so, he had troops enough to exterminate every one of them." It seems unlikely that De Smet would have used such threatening language to motivate tribal leaders who had always been friendly to the United States. Kamiakin and Garry were already well aware of the wrath of General Harney. Collier went on to say that the chiefs chose to go to Vancouver despite their fear that they would "be either hung or shot," and claimed that, when they arrived, "they were placed in a stockade and surrounded by a guard of soldiers." Upon conclusion of their meeting, according to Collier, General Harney instructed Father De Smet to take the delegates "to Portland and Salem in order to convince them of the power of the whites."[20]

What Became of Kamiakin?

De Smet addresses Kamiakin's disappearance in a report on May 25.[21] The frustrated Jesuit explains that the deputation of chiefs was delayed at Walla Walla by Major Owen while he waited for a response from the Superintendent of Indian Affairs at Salem to a letter he had sent from the Spokane Prairie. De Smet claims to have had daily conversations with Kamiakin during the six days of travel until they reached Walla Walla.

Once they arrived, Kamiakin camped with the other Indian leaders and, presumably, was still there when De Smet left for Vancouver.

De Smet held Owen responsible for his failure to bring Kamiakin and other escapees to General Harney for their official surrender, but a good paper trail of what really happened has never surfaced. Only one cryptic explanation for Kamiakin's disappearance is offered in a postscript by Brevet Major P. Lugenbeel, Captain of the 9th Infantry to Lieutenant John Mullan at the Colville Depot, dated July 13, 1859, noting that "the Indians all say, that Kamiakin was scared away from Walla Walla by Timothy and other Nez Perce chiefs."[22] This account may overlap with one provided by John Owen claiming that Kamiakin heard rumors that the Whites planned to hang him.[23]

According to his friend A. J. Splawn, Kamiakin "went to a friend, a fur trader whom he called Wap-chien, living in Kootenai, B.C.," where the chief without a country remained for about a year. He and his family spent the next two years on the buffalo plains with the Crow Tribe. By then, Splawn explains, "his wife was homesick and he was weary of being a wanderer in a strange land." They returned to the land of the Palouse, his father's people, crossing the Bitterroots by way of the new Mullan Road. He and his wife settled on Rock Lake, about forty miles southwest of present-day Spokane, where they enjoyed a quiet life on a little farm, near relatives. Kamiakin died in 1877 at an age of about seventy-six years.[24]

Owen and De Smet

During the years following his troubling journey to Fort Vancouver, John Owen returned to Fort Owen just as the White world was making its presence felt. Ratification of the 1855 Hellgate Treaty opened lands for non-Indian settlement throughout western Montana, except for reserved lands in the Flathead and Bitterroot Valleys.[25] Construction of the Mullan Road through the mountains was soon followed by the establishment of Hell Gate and then Missoula. The road connected the intermountain basins of western Montana and northern Idaho with a much wider world. Months before the conditional Bitterroot Reservation was illegally opened to White settlement in 1872, John Owen, at the age of fifty-three, was committed to a hospital in Helena. His troubles were not from alcoholism as some would claim.

More likely, he had what we would now refer to as early onset dementia. After six years in the care facility, the territorial government sent him to Philadelphia where he could be cared for by relatives and removed from Montana's tax burden. He died in 1889, the year Montana became the forty-first state, when he was seventy years old.

Father De Smet never fully recovered from the events of 1859. Following his time in Vancouver, he made his way back to his base of operations at St. Louis University. Although he continued to serve the Jesuits as well as the U.S. government in the role of peacemaker, he was hounded by poor health for the rest of his life. He died from kidney failure in 1873 at the age of seventy-two.

Postscript

As a result of their 1881 treaty, the Spokane Tribe officially ceded all but a small fraction of their original ancestral lands. They lost the heart of their homeland around Spokane Falls. Spokan Garry continued to farm the lands he had nurtured for nearly two decades in what is now the city of Spokane until 1883, when a German immigrant used devious means to lay claim to Garry's farm. Chief Garry, so important as a peacemaker through the challenging transitional years in the interior Northwest, spent his last decade in the wooded hills of Indian Creek, made available to him through the kindness of a settler, while trying to regain ownership of his farm through the legal system. A December 1891 judgment went against him, with no compensation for his losses. He died a month later of lung congestion at the age of eighty. ✢

14

DEER LODGE IS IN WARM SPRINGS

What? Deer Lodge is in Warm Springs? Maybe it would be more accurate to say that the Deer's Lodge, not Deer Lodge, is in Warm Springs. This unusual name refers to a cone-shaped geological feature, about forty feet high, created by minerals that percolate from underground, building the mound as they accumulate. The mound has been an important landmark in its namesake valley since time immemorial. The appellation comes from the Shoshone, who called it It-soo-ke-en-car-ne—the "lodge of the white-tailed deer." Herds of deer were commonly seen licking minerals near the base of this lodge-shaped accretion. The Salish word for it, momo'o, refers to the steam that looked like smoke emerging from a lodge. Only a dim memory remains of this special place in the region's history.

Imagine entering the valley from the headwaters of Silver Bow Creek or Warm Springs Creek, before railroads, ranchers, the mining industry, and the interstate highway changed everything. You would have seen a magnificent, verdant valley adorned with ribbons of cottonwood- and willow-lined streams, flowing from mountains to the north and south toward the Columbia-seeking river that bisected the length of the valley. Since the early nineteenth century, fur traders, missionaries, and survey teams traversed the valley along trails long used by Salish, Pend d'Oreille, and other bison-hunting tribes on their journeys to and from the plains. In those days, before trees were planted and buildings erected, and before the Anaconda stack commanded the skyline,

Deer Lodge is in Warm Springs

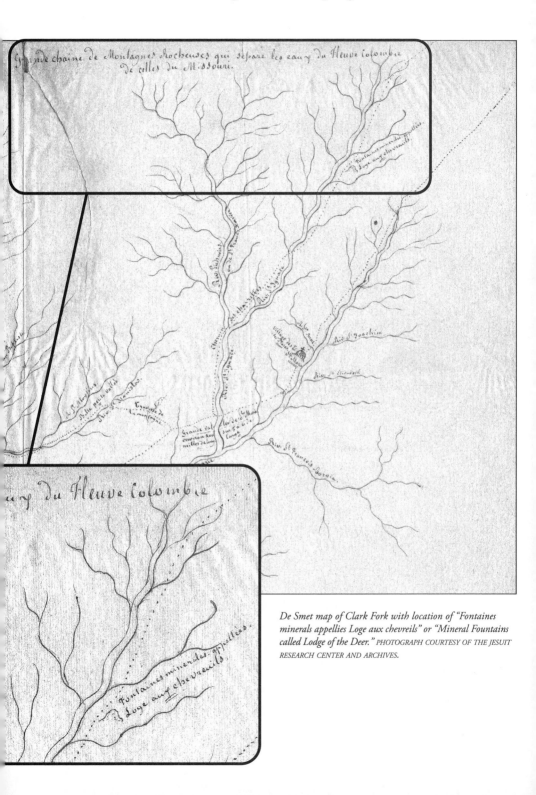

Grande chaine de Montagnes Rocheuses qui sépare les eaux du Fleuve Colombie
De celles du Missouri.

ay du Fleuve Colombie

Fontaines minerdes appellies
Loge aux chevreuils

De Smet map of Clark Fork with location of "Fontaines minerals appellies Loge aux chevreils" or "Mineral Fountains called Lodge of the Deer." PHOTOGRAPH COURTESY OF THE JESUIT RESEARCH CENTER AND ARCHIVES.

the Deer Lodge was visible for miles in all directions. You might wonder why you have never seen it.

For the Salish, this valley was one of the significant areas on their annual seasonal rounds. What this valley was, back then, is now hard to see, given what the smelter's toxins have done to the land and water. When fur trader Warren Ferris passed through the valley in September 1831, he described a land of great abundance. On that trip, about eight miles below what is now Mill Creek Pass from the Big Hole, he met with a camp of 100 Pend d'Oreille lodges on their way to buffalo grounds. This mobile village, comprising some 600 to 800 people, traveled with 3,000 horses.[1]

In January 1854, John Mullan reported the upper valley to be "a great resort for the Indians west of the mountains at all season, and especially when returning from the buffalo hunt." They would recuperate, resting their horses and their own weary bodies. The rich and abundant grasses found there helped to restore the animals. They would remain several weeks.[2] Mullan went on to explain that the mild winters were the reason for its attractiveness. The valley had very little snow even during "the severest winters."

The abundance of food in this area—including deer, elk, sheep, pronghorn, and even bison, in addition to plant foods, and rich grasses for horses—allowed for huge gatherings of allied western tribes. A large camping area near Anaconda that the Indians used to call "Big Flat," or *qua oyah*, was well used. This area is now covered by the 5,000-acre Opportunity Ponds, located just above the confluence of Warm Springs and Silver Bow Creeks. As remembered by Salish elder Eneas Granjo in the 1940s, the people camped around the creeks, hunting, digging bitterroot, and gathering kinnikinnick, depending on the season. In midsummer, currants and gooseberries were especially plentiful. Elders remembered that everything was bigger there, especially the kinnikinnick.

In late August 1854, Elijah Wilson, a White boy who lived many years with the Shoshone, estimated that 6,000 people were congregated in the Deer Lodge Valley. They gathered there every three years, for trading and socializing.[3] In the colder months, the people would soak in the hot springs, called *inhihidwa*.[4] Until the early 1870s, they would set up their tipis among the trees around the twelve pools at what eventually would be commercially developed as Gregson Mineral Springs, now known as Fairmont.

It is possible that the warm waters of *momo'o* were not used by the Salish. No written record has been found to document that use, but the two pools at the Deer's Lodge were enjoyed by non-Native travelers, at least until 1867. According to Granville Stuart, as reported in an 1869 article in the *New Northwest*, they were too hot for soaking, but this had not long been the case. Alongside reports of the murder of rancher and fur trader Malcolm Clarke by Blackfeet, the impacts of massive fires, and an account of a weekend fishing excursion to Lost Creek by "six gentlemen" who, in one day, "brought in Five Hundred and Twenty-Six Trout, some weighing three pounds," Stuart noted the temperature in the larger pool was 113 F. and the smaller was 122 F., "so hot as to prevent bathing." He had learned from others that the temperatures had increased in just two years by 15 or 20 degrees; before that the pools had been pleasantly warm for baths.[5]

In 1877, Warm Springs State Hospital was built next to this important landmark and the pools were once again used for soaking. Eventually, a path was constructed to the top of the mound where a cupola was built to provide shade and a viewpoint. The juxtaposition of the Deer's Lodge and the state hospital is the reason why most Montanans have never caught a glimpse of the valley's defining feature. The buildings and large maple trees tend to screen it from view.

Adding more confusion to this story, not only is the Deer's Lodge in Warm Springs, but the town of Deer Lodge is in Powell County. Originally, it was in Deer Lodge County, created in 1864 when Montana became a territory. The huge county ran from the headwaters of the Clark Fork all the way to the Canadian border. In 1901, this enormous and awkward space was divided, leaving the Deer's Lodge at Warm Springs within a much smaller Deer Lodge County, while the town of Deer Lodge became part of the newly created Powell County.

Next time you are driving through the Deer Lodge Valley, try to imagine the bottomlands covered with native bunch grass, with serviceberries and wild plums growing along the creeks, bitterroots on the dry hills, and kinnikinnick spread along the ground in the more wooded uplands. Imagine streams so full of trout that you could catch your evening meal faster than the time it would take to drive through a McDonald's for a Happy Meal. Imagine after a long day gathering berries you could soak your tired bones in one of the many places available along Warm Springs Creek. When you reach the east side of the state hospital, look back to catch a glimpse of the cupola atop the Deer's Lodge. While you pause, you might acknowledge the Salish who ceded these lands in 1855 and made them available for the rest of us to enjoy. ✢

Gustav Sohon lithograph of the "Hot spring mound of the 'Deer Lodge' prairie," 1860. PHOTOGRAPH COURTESY *OF EASTERN WASHINGTON UNIVERSITY LIBRARIES.*

15

WEST SIDE BISON

Long ago, on the plain of the Cold Spring on the south side of the Missoula Valley, some Salish people were camped during the Bitterroot Moon. The women and children were digging that important root, the first to be ready after winter released its hold. Some of the men were lounging around, soaking up the sun on that beautiful day. Suddenly, one of them saw what looked like five buffalo bulls on the slope of what was then called Hell's Gate Mountain, and what is now called Mount Sentinel. People sprang into action. All able-bodied men jumped on their horses and went in pursuit. But rather than buffalo, they found footprints of men. They had been tricked by enemies who had posed as bison. While the Salish men were out of their camp, a party of Blackfeet warriors killed the old people, women and children who had been left in camp, probably settling some old score.[1]

A tipi camp near the Cold Spring area, Mount Sentinel in the background, 1860. PHOTOGRAPH COURTESY OF THE UNIVERSITY OF MONTANA ARCHIVES.

This tragic story of the Cold Spring camp, told to fur trader Angus McDonald by an "old Flathead chief," invites a question about bison in the Missoula Valley. What were the presumed bison doing on Mount Sentinel? After all, didn't bison occupy the short-grass prairie, the Great Plains ecoregion between the 98th Meridian and the Rocky Mountain fringe, more than 100 miles from the Missoula Valley? To me, the story makes no sense unless the sight of bison was not surprising to the small group of Salish encamped there.

Corroborative evidence for bison in the Clark Fork basin (which encompasses the Missoula Valley) exists in the form of a map created by the artist George Catlin, along with archaeological remains. These sources confirm that, in fact, bison were sometimes seen in these valleys on the west side of the Rocky Mountains. Catlin created his map of the United States based on evidence gathered during a trip up the Missouri in 1832, along with subsequent research, in which he included the distribution of the American bison, shown by stippling.

Although his stipples largely conform to the Great Plains region, exceptions occur in several locations along the Continental Divide. The Clark Fork basin is one of these exceptions. It's plausible. Why would bison care which direction the water flowed, as long as they could follow grass-covered landscapes? Even today, bison in the hills and valleys of the CSKT Bison Range thrive on those grasses.

The archaeological record and homesteader history confirm Catlin's findings. Bison remains have been discovered west of the divide in river basins that are accessible through low passes. These were the same trails followed by people, like the trail from the Big Hole Valley into the Warm Springs area via Mill Creek; the Pipestone Pass trail from the Jefferson into the Silver Bow basin; the trail across Champion Pass from the Boulder River into the Deer Lodge Valley; and trails over the old Hell Gate passes into the Little Blackfoot basin.

Scores of abandoned campsites found throughout the upper Clark Fork basin produced evidence of bison butchering and cooking. Associated artifacts extend back into time for thousands of years. West of Butte near the town of Ramsay, one bison kill site, now buried under Interstate 90, was used over a period of more than a thousand years.[2]

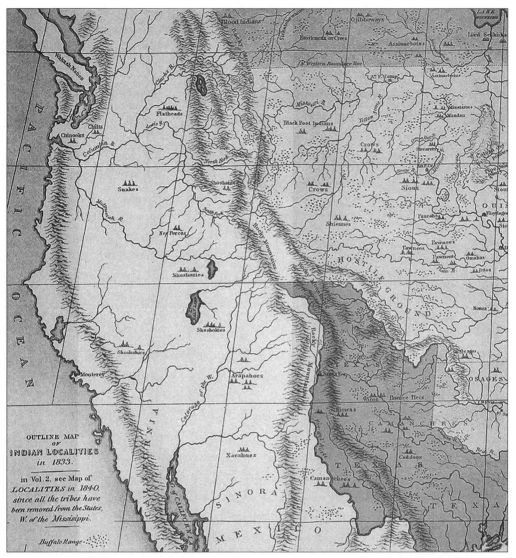

A section of an 1841 map of the West by George Catlin. Stippling indicates where bison roamed.

Archaeological evidence of bison extends all the way into the Missoula Valley and up the Bitterroot Valley. A site by a spring at the old Zaugg farm at West Riverside (near the confluence of the Blackfoot and Clark Fork Rivers) was a large campsite as evidenced by bighorn sheep and bison remains alongside hundreds of stone tools of jasper, quartzite, and basalt.

In addition, Mr. Zaugg reported finding "a double-headed hammerstone with a hole through the center for a handle."[3] The presence of corner-notched dart and arrow points at the site suggests multiple occupations by Salish people during the last 3,000 years.

Two connected mid-basin valleys, Flint Creek and Rock Creek, have produced particularly rich evidence of bison, both in the form of archaeological remains and in stories carried by homesteader families. The Gilles family remembers that it was common for early settlers in Upper Rock Creek to find bison skulls.[4]

Pat McDonald's family homesteaded along Flint Creek, close to Philipsburg. Pat grew up on the heels of his grandfather and carried a rich reservoir of memories about the transitional time, when the area shifted from Indian to White. When thinking about evidence of bison, he remembered a place on Sluice Gulch (Upper Rock Creek) where the bank would collapse and expose buffalo bones. Through the years, he found the remains of four or five individuals there, based on the number of skulls.[5]

The Conn family homesteaded on Willow Creek in 1893. Grandson John was born early in the twentieth century on Flint Creek. He remembered Salish people coming through in summertime to camp by the warm spring across the road from his place. Through the years, he found extensive evidence of a large camp that had been used, off and on, for some 5,000 years. Bones found there were identified as elk, deer, and bison.[6]

Farther down Flint Creek, near the town of Hall, evidence of bison came from archaeological sites. Excavation of campsites, found in protected spots along tributary creeks, revealed the cooked remains of bison, along with antelope, deer, elk, cottontail, and grouse. In addition to projectile points that date back some seven or eight millennia, an early settler found a clay smoking pipe and an old cartridge case among other archaeological remains, indicating use right up through the late nineteenth century.[7] The presence of numerous bison skulls provides evidence that the killing took place locally. Skulls are too heavy to pack back from across the mountains, except, perhaps, on some rare and special occasion.

What happened to the Flint Creek bison? Although the area is rich in archaeological evidence, no living bison were observed in these valleys by the time the first White settlers arrived. Carl H. Siria may have stumbled onto the explanation when he served as a forest ranger on the Bonita District (encompassing the Rock Creek drainage) in the 1930s. He reported on the remains of more than 100 buffalo found near Little Hogback Creek, some ten miles up Rock Creek.[8] No evidence of human involvement was found; there were no arrow points, no jump site, no butchering. Curious about this peculiar prevalence of bison remains in the area and, in particular, wondering why so many animals were found in one spot, he asked around. Eventually he heard a story that answered his questions.

> As to origin of so many in one spot, the story is that many years ago, probably before the white man came, a large herd of buffalo either drifted or were driven by the Indians from the buffalo country east of the Continental Divide to the open prairie country in the Deerlodge and Flint Creek Valleys. These buffalo were harassed by the Indians and most of them killed. The last remaining remnant of the herd took refuge in the rough country along Rock Creek. They were trapped by the deep snow in the little basin below Hogback Creek and all perished.

Salish oral history differs a bit from that of Ranger Siria. The bison of Flint Creek were like an important food and supply cache for them. They tried to keep them in the Upper Rock Creek area instead of Flint Creek because there the buffalo would be less accessible to Blackfeet raiders.

The last of the Flint Creek Valley buffalo are believed to have died in Upper Rock Creek during the winter of 1846-1847.[9] During that horrific winter, not only that one small bison herd died, but also deer, antelope, and elk, and many of the cattle, pigs, and horses of the Bitterroot Salish. In the Columbia River country, 500 horses got trapped in a little valley where they had sought shelter. There they died, all huddled together, "frozen fast where they tried to paw and stand, with little to be seen of them in the deep icy snow."[10]

The story told by the old chief to Angus McDonald about what appeared to be bison on Mount Sentinel seems to make sense, after all. The story happened long ago, and back then, small herds of bison found their way into the valleys of the Salish homeland. ✢

16

SOMEBODY'S DAUGHTER
An Early Missoula Story

Discovery

On December 11, 1950—a day when the city of Missoula was announcing its snow removal schedule, President Truman was pondering what to do in Korea as the Chinese worked their way south, and the Harlem Globetrotters were in town to play the University of Montana Grizzlies—a bulldozer operator was leveling a terrace of the river to make room for a new Safeway store. His blade hit an old wooden crate. On the next sweep he hit it again, but this time he could see bones. He stopped, climbed down from his perch, scraped dirt away from the crude box, and found himself "face to face with a skeleton."[1]

The *Missoulian* reported on the following day that the distressed equipment operator, Dale Newhoff, called the county sheriff who, in turn, called the coroner, who examined the site on West Broadway, just west of St. Patrick Hospital. The article reported that the coroner found the skeleton of a child alongside "Indian relics" in the rotted remains of a "plain board box," four and a half feet long and one and a half feet wide, almost six feet deep, below undisturbed soil. He concluded the child had died a natural death, since he found no marks to indicate foul play. He believed the child was Indian, based on the objects recovered from the site, including a purse, in which "several Indian beads" were found, "deteriorated leather which slightly resembled

170

moccasins" found near the feet, and rotted leather found near the skull. The sheriff, based on "the state of deterioration of the body and coffin," estimated that the burial had been in place "for more than fifty years."[2] The coroner, in his report, estimated the burial had been "in the ground since about 1850 or 1860." Since the death occurred so long ago, he anticipated that the child would be reburied in the Missoula cemetery.

Carling Malouf, an anthropologist from the university, was called to view the nearly complete skeleton and the objects recovered from the site, including a small "white man's purse," found with some white beads, along with various scraps of leather. Based on these items and the child's shovel-shaped incisors, (a trait commonly associated with Native Americans that rarely occurs in European populations), Professor Malouf concurred with the coroner's determination that this child was American Indian.[3] Although gender is difficult to determine from a young skeleton, he assumed the child was a girl, based on the presence of the purse.

Six decades later, I would be tasked with resolving the mystery of this child's identity. Somehow it seemed fitting since I was born into this world just twenty days after her remains were discovered. Throughout those years, her remains would be kept in a drawer in the anthropology department at the University of Montana, not the City Cemetery, as the coroner supposed.

Who Might This Child Have Been?

Professor Malouf's inquiries on the Flathead Reservation about the grave went unanswered, and no records of the burial were found in the local archives. A *Missoulian* headline on December 19 announced "Skeleton Found Here Possibly Child of Indian Fishermen." An interview with Joseph Allard of Ronan provided a tribal perspective on the case.[4] He proposed that the child might have been with "tribesmen who came to the Missoula area to fish for salmon" (the term they used for bull trout). Back in the years before Missoula got established, he told the reporter, the Indians would gather in the area when the fish came up the river to spawn.[5] For bull trout, this would be late August to early November. The source of the information was Mr. Allard's grandmother, "a full-blooded Indian." She was born around 1820, just a decade after fur traders came into the area. She married one of them in 1836. These were years blurred by warfare and disease, when bison were still plentiful. During her long life, the world she knew in childhood was completely transformed—nearly erased—by Euro-Americans. She died in 1904. According to Allard, Missoula's Indian name always had been *En-theigh-EE*, meaning "salmon waters" (Nɫʔay), and one favorite place to fish was "on the river at the point where the Northern Pacific bridge in Missoula now crosses the stream." In today's terms, this would be referred to as the NP's Bitterroot spur line, the stretch that runs a block west of the burial location. Conditions were good there, where "the riffles in the river at this point were very wide and the water was shallow."

Thinking about who might have been the family of this little girl, he noted that there were always visitors from the north and west during these "fishing occasions," presumably referring to the Kootenai to the north, and the Nez Perce to the west. These tribes and the Salish had intermarried with fur trappers and traders from France and Scotland since they first arrived in the area, early in the nineteenth century. Mr. Allard pointed out that having boards used to build the casket meant that this burial happened after Whites were in the area. To have boards, they needed a sawmill. The first one in the valley was built by David Pattee in 1860.

Mr. Allard's recollections brought this child's world to life. These bones and belongings weren't just remnants of the past, but of a family. This was someone's child, placed in a casket of rough pine boards and buried on a terrace of the Clark Fork River, where Missoula now stands. Nothing marked the grave, at least not decades later when her remains were found. Who was this child and what was the context of her short life?

Resurrection, 2012

Christmas of 1950 came and went and the *Missoulian* moved on to other news stories. The child's remains became part of the teaching collection of the university's anthropology department but were otherwise forgotten. Fast forward forty years, when federal legislation—the Native American Graves Protection and Repatriation Act of 1990 (NAGPRA)—required public institutions, including the University of Montana, to assess their collections for remains of Native Americans to be repatriated. Leap ahead another twenty years to the day when attorneys for the Confederated Salish and Kootenai Tribes sat down with University of Montana administrators and representatives of the anthropology department to remind them of their legal responsibility to review their collections under NAGPRA regulations. They carried with them a tall stack of documents detailing all of the burials investigated by UM archaeologists back when burials were desecrated for the purpose of "study," as if the humanity of these Native people was somehow less than that of people buried in official cemeteries with headstones telling who they were. Tribal representatives demanded to know what had become of these human remains and burial objects.

This is where my story and that of this little girl came together. I was contracted to review the collections and bring UM into compliance with the requirements of NAGPRA. Over the next several months, working with Bethany Campbell, curator of collections, we identified the remains of more than sixty individuals as Native American and designated them for repatriation. Many of these remains had been removed from locations in western Montana and therefore would be repatriated through the Confederated Salish and Kootenai Tribes.

Most the cases we dealt with were straightforward in that the remains were clearly Native American and would be repatriated; not so for this young girl. Although this child was reported as "Indian" by all those involved in the original discovery, physical anthropologists at the university were unable to substantiate the designation through their biometrical assessment. They could not corroborate Professor Malouf's claim of shovel incisors since the single incisor that remained in the collection was badly broken. They concluded that she was seven or eight years old and that her remains showed no evidence of Native American ancestry. Acknowledging that children have fewer indicators of ethnicity than adults, they concluded that this child was more likely to have been White. In their opinion, too little evidence existed to justify repatriating her remains.

Of the various objects recovered from the grave, the manufactured purse seemed to hold the most promise for expanding our understanding of who this child might have been. What remained of the little bag was limited to the stamped copper alloy frame and deteriorated leather. Too little remained to be able to ascertain original size and shape, or decoration. The bag was designed

Coin purse found with burial.
PHOTOGRAPH BY ROSELYN CAMPBELL WITH UNIVERSITY OF
MONTANA NAGPRA PROJECT, COURTESY OF SALLY THOMPSON.

to be carried by a chain or strap, but no chain was recovered from the burial site. The clasp was hinged and worked as a lever. Later versions of similar bags were available in mail order catalogues for ten cents.

Where and when might the purse have been acquired? The 1850–1860 Fort Owen ledger documents the variety of objects available for purchase in the local area.[6] Clothing and accessories included shirts, leggings, blankets, hats, children's shoes, handkerchiefs of cotton or silk, rings, and ear bobs, but no purses. Commercially manufactured purses may have been available at the Worden & Co. store established in the town of Hellgate in 1860, and subsequently moved to Missoula, but these records are not available. The first mail-order catalogue was published in 1872, and catalogue use became common by the early 1880s, making a much wider variety of products available to isolated regions. From the various lines of evidence, this purse was most likely acquired by the 1880s, and no earlier than 1860.

Back in 1950, the equipment operator's report of "a pocketbook full of white beads" was misleading.[7] In reality, too much of the finished leather bag had disintegrated to say whether the beads had been in the purse or beaded onto the purse. As the bottom half of the bag disintegrated, the beads would have become detached. Unfortunately, only one pink "seed bead" remained in the collection six decades later. Close examination of what remained of the leather revealed tiny holes within a circular area along with a small length of two-ply cotton thread, suggesting that the front of the bag had a circular beaded medallion attached subsequent to manufacture. Indian women were known to scavenge cast-off manufactured purses and then to modify them with their own beadwork.[8] Two such examples are present in UM's Ethnographic Collection.

Although this little purse might have been buried with an Indian child, the UM team suggested that the manufactured purse was just as likely to have been buried with a White child. More research into the era of Missoula's founding would be required to get better evidence of who this child might have been. Perhaps her burial pre-dated the presence of White children in the valley.

The World in which She Lived and Died

Had the burial been that of a White man in the 1870s, the trail would have been littered with breadcrumbs, but for this little girl the path was nearly bare. If we knew the timing of the burial, we could determine if it pre-dated the presence or absence of Euro-American children in the valley. Early journals and reports, trading post accounts, patent records, deed books, Government Land Office maps, and "Bird's Eye View" city maps provide the fine-scale evidence to sift through these early years of Missoula. The burial was found close to the Clark Fork River before that part of Missoula was developed. Although the river was named for William Clark, fur trader David Thompson called it "the Great Saleesh Road," a testimony to long use of the route by Native peoples. The same general route became known as the Military Road—the Mullan Road—completed in 1862, seven years after the treaty signing between the local tribes and the United States. Missoula was established along this corridor in 1865, one of several towns emerging in the new Montana Territory as remote outposts between Fort Walla Walla and Fort Benton. The road had been a major travel corridor between the Columbia and Missouri Rivers for thousands of years before Meriwether Lewis passed through, and Native travel continued here until the decimation of the bison in the early 1880s, and even later, after Missoula was well-established.

In the 1850s, the five valleys that converge at Missoula were inhabited by Indians with a small scattering of White men. Some of the latter had Indian wives and mixed-blood children. No White women or White children lived in these parts. Since the late 1840s, Euro-American men had traded livestock and goods between the Missoula and Bitterroot Valleys and the Emigrant Road from Fort Hall, to the south. These men were not full-time residents but instead established short-term camps in the "Hell Gate Ronde," now known as Grass Valley, located about five miles west of the burial location. According to Thomas Harris, an employee at Fort Owen, by 1860 "the frontier was really vanishing." That year he visited Mullan's camp at Grass Valley and reported that he had "the pleasure of seeing seven white women and a baby." Although these women were transients associated with the road crew, by the end of the following year a number of White women had settled with their husbands in Grass Valley, and more would settle in the Missoula area after 1865."[9] Although numerous children of mixed ancestry were growing up within the local tribal communities, no known Euro-American children lived in the valley at the time of Missoula's founding.[10]

As reported in 1940 by early Missoula historian Will Cave, "the white population of the town when first begun was somewhat less than two score," and grew slowly until after the discovery of gold in Cedar Creek, near Superior, in October 1869.[11]

Granville Stuart sketch of the Missoula Mills, Christmas Day, 1865, from The Montana Frontier, 1852–1864, *published in 1925. PHOTOGRAPH BY SALLY THOMPSON.*

East Front Street, Missoula, circa 1875. PHOTOGRAPH COURTESY OF THE UNIVERSITY OF MONTANA ARCHIVES.

The parcel of land from which the burial was retrieved was granted to the Northern Pacific Railroad by the U.S. government in 1864, just before the Missoula Mills became established, and remained in the company's possession until 1888. The parcels immediately to the east and northeast of the burial location were sold by W. T. McCormick in December 1872 to Father Palladino, a Jesuit priest, who described it as being a good distance from the center of town.[12] Father Palladino transferred the property to the Sisters of Providence who, in the spring of 1873, opened "Providence of the Sacred Heart," the first hospital, asylum, and Catholic school in Missoula.[13] The treeless streets that bordered their property were dusty and dirt packed. The hospital was later named St. Patrick, an institution that continues today at the same location.

Would this girl, whose skeleton remained for sixty-three years in a drawer in Social Sciences at UM, have attended school? Missoula's first school was established in the summer of 1869 with fifteen students, both Euro-American and children of mixed ancestry. As the city grew, the Sisters of Providence opened a Catholic school in 1873 and also provided care for orphans. The school was located about a half-block from the burial site and, at the time of its founding, was the only building in the immediate area at the northwest edge of town. By 1877, three buildings were added at the west edge of the hospital block, across from the burial location.

The school initially served only two orphan girls. Unfortunately, the chronicles of the Sisters of Providence provide no details about them. By 1877, increasing numbers of both students and orphans required the Sisters to expand their space, with an addition of separate quarters for each of the three groups of children they served—girl and boy students (thirty-five to forty children in 1882) and orphan girls. These buildings were situated to the west of the hospital. In 1882, increasing demand for the hospital and asylum space required them to build an addition to the original building.[14]

Taking into account the extent of buildings and the large number of people associated with the complex, it seems unlikely that someone would have buried a child in the adjacent vacant lot after the mid-1870s, unless it was the Sisters themselves, given their extensive presence. Could they have buried an orphan child in the open field west of their hospital?

An incident recounted in the chronicles of Sacred Heart Academy, 1900–1901, documents just such a case, where a child was buried in secret, at sundown, on a winter evening. For several weeks prior to the death of little four-year-old Cecilia Burmingham, sickness spread through the school. The Sisters sequestered the ill in one building, and one of the nuns cared for them there, with as many as ten patients at a time.

> A little baby of four years old succumbed. Happily no one outside knew about it. Her little body was buried, without knowledge to anyone, on Saturday night at sunset. We had had her baptized at the beginning of the sickness. It is one more angel in Heaven, and no one knows yet about her disappearance. Her mother had died at St. Patrick Hospital a few months before, and her father never bothered with her at all.[15]

The story of Cecilia Burmingham's secret burial raised the possibility of a similar action earlier in the history of the school, but no other incident was recorded in their detailed chronicles. The Sisters of Providence recorded the first deaths of students at their school in 1884:

For the first time since the establishment of this mission, that, is, in the space of twelve years, we had the sadness of seeing one of our students die . . . a young girl of 14 years. . . . In the month of February, she was taken with inflammatory rheumatism. She then got better, and was already convalescing, when chorea (St. Vitus's Dance), seized her and carried her to her tomb in very few days. The young girl was Protestant, as were her parents, with this difference however, that she wanted to become Catholic. . . .

Another little girl of four years was also baptized, unknown to her mother who strongly opposed it. The little one had been brought to the hospital around 5 o'clock in the evening, and at 6 o'clock of the same evening, her pure and beautiful soul was in the breast of the One who said, "Let the little children come unto me."[16]

The Sisters of Providence appear not to have been responsible for the burial of the little girl whose remains were disturbed in 1950.

The original St. Patrick Hospital and Sacred Heart Academy, 1874. PHOTOGRAPH COURTESY OF THE PROVIDENCE ARCHIVES.

Will Cave reported that Missoula had grown "to something under 250 individuals" by 1872. He speculated that more Indians than Whites were "in and around the town" during the first ten years. "At no time was there an entire absence of Indian tepees," he wrote, noting that forty to sixty tepees were often in sight.

During the 1870s and into the 1880s, the Salish were split. Chief Charlo's band remained based in the Bitterroot Valley, while others had moved to the Jocko Valley on the Flathead Reservation. Missoula was commonly visited by members of both groups and also by the Pend d'Oreille, Kootenai, and Nez Perce. This pattern of occupation is widely documented in newspapers and other written sources and in tribal oral histories.

One semi-residential group of Indians stayed around the mouth of Rattlesnake Creek, about a mile east of the Safeway site burial location. As reported in the *Missoulian* on September 26, 1948:

> The Garden City's first shack town, according to old timers, was scattered along the west side of Rattlesnake creek prior to 1870. Nondescript shanties, some of them partially walled with cowhides, were occupied by Indians who lived on change they could garner loading freight and by trading ponies, hunting and fishing.
>
> As the city expanded to the banks of the Rattlesnake, the occupants of "shanty town" moved to "the island," an area south of East Front Street, and between Mt. Jumbo's southeast end and the river.[17]

These were difficult times for the people who had called this area home since time immemorial. In March 1880, after two years of unsuccessful bison hunts, "Indians" were observed scavenging meat in Missoula, as reported in the *Missoulian* on March 19, 1880: "A number of Indians made a stake last week by bringing in the hides of frozen cattle, and an enterprising squaw was observed dragging home a piece of veal which had succumbed to the rigors of winter."

Women were cutting hides off cows that froze to death in order to acquire what they needed to keep themselves and their families warm and for trading for food. A month later, on April 9, the *Missoulian* reported "numerous Indian parties" in town, returning from hunting buffalo, "and either their animals are too poor to pack provisions or they did not get any." This unraveling world was the one the little girl had been born and buried into. She was somebody's daughter.

Traditionally, the Salish, Kootenai, and other tribes of the area west of the Continental Divide buried their dead in shallow pits or natural concavities on rocky slopes where they could be well covered and protected by rocks, or in sandy deposits where they could be buried more deeply. Coffins were introduced along with the establishment of Catholic missions in the area in the 1840s. Evidence is unavailable to document precisely when coffin burials replaced more traditional methods throughout the area and away from the missions, but a nearby sawmill would have been requisite. Prior to 1860, the closest sawmill was located near Fort Owen at what is now Stevensville, more than thirty miles away.

In his discussion of the Safeway site burial, Carling Malouf found that by the 1860s coffins were coming into use by the Indians.[18] A *Missoulian* reporter observed an Indian burial at the north edge of town in February 1880, in which a coffin was employed.[19]

> Instead of placing the body in the coffin at the lodge, it was wrapped in a blanket, tied securely, and fastened to a lodge-pole, men at each end of it carrying the corpse to the receptacle on the hill. Here it was deposited in the coffin—a box prepared for the occasion—snugly packed in, whence it was lowered into the grave with lariats.

Unfortunately, Missoula County didn't start recording deaths until 1895. Prior to the establishment of the first formal cemeteries in Missoula, most non-Native people were buried in an area at the base of Mount Jumbo, east of Rattlesnake Creek.[20] A Catholic cemetery began in 1874. Most Protestants continued to be buried in the Mount Jumbo burial ground until the city established the first official cemetery in December 1884, although some were buried in family plots around the valley. Chinese residents continued to be buried in that area at the base of Mount Jumbo for some years following the establishment of the city cemetery.[21]

Examined in the context of Missoula history, the lone burial uncovered at the old Safeway site probably dates to the period between 1865, when both lumber and commercial goods became locally available, and 1884, when the city was beginning to surround the site. The Sisters of Providence complex of hospital, asylum, and school expanded into adjacent parcels of land in 1882. The Northern Pacific Railroad was completed in 1883, with tracks running east-west, four blocks to the north of the burial location. A spur line was constructed a few years later just to the west of the burial location, through the favorite fishing spot remembered by Joseph Allard's grandmother. Based on this timeframe, we were unable to date the burial to an era before White children arrived.

Still Not Enough

The research threads seemed to lead to a stalemate. The UM team continued to hold the opinion that none of the evidence proved that the child was Indian. The only things left to investigate were the leather scraps buried with the child. I didn't have much confidence that they would be very informative but had run out of other options. The very fact of their presence was important though, because Native people of the area buried their loved ones with objects of importance to them, and we might be able to learn more about the nature of these belongings. In contrast, it was rare for White people to include objects with the body.

Of the remaining objects found with the burial, the one that held the most potential for shedding light on cultural identity was the roughly cross-shaped piece of rawhide. Upon close examination, this artifact had been a pouch created by folding and securing the four arms inward, in the manner of a *parfleche*.[22] All three intact edges had been hand-punched to create holes for lacing, and old creases verified the folds.

This was a small but common type of women's pouch. Such pouches have not been forgotten by the local tribal communities. They carried essentials and were worn attached to a belt. Two narrow fragments of rawhide found with the burial may have been from the belt. In traditional life, children

Right: *Sketch showing the pattern of hand-punched holes in the rawhide pouch.* PHOTOGRAPH COURTESY OF SALLY THOMPSON.

Below: *The rawhide pouch found with the child at the burial site.* PHOTOGRAPH BY ROSELYN CAMPBELL WITH THE UNIVERSITY OF MONTANA NAGPRA PROJECT, COURTESY OF SALLY THOMPSON.

Right: *Sketch showing the pattern of hand-punched holes in the rawhide pouch.* PHOTOGRAPH COURTESY OF SALLY THOMPSON.

Below: *The rawhide pouch found with the child at the burial site.* PHOTOGRAPH BY ROSELYN CAMPBELL WITH THE UNIVERSITY OF MONTANA NAGPRA PROJECT, COURTESY OF SALLY THOMPSON.

were taught to make whatever the adults made, but they made them a reduced size to better suit their needs.

One last scrap of leather, dried out and curled into a hard cylinder, had potential to shed more light on the case, despite its distorted state. I needed to create a pattern of what the object had looked like before it curled up, to reveal the original shape. The solution was to sketch one side, then carefully roll it over while continuing to sketch the entire form. The results revealed the leather object to have been symmetrical and parallel-sided, with one square end and one rounded. Both long parallel sides had been hand-punched for stitching. The stitching appeared to continue all the way around the torn tapered end as well. This little scrap proved to be part of the "deteriorated leather which slightly resembled moccasins [found] near the skeleton's feet" as reported in

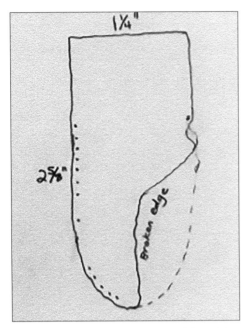

Above: Sketch showing the original form of the curled-up leather. PHOTOGRAPH COURTESY OF SALLY THOMPSON.

Right: This curled-up leather found near the feet, enlarged to show detail, is part of a moccasin. PHOTOGRAPH BY ROSELYN CAMPBELL WITH THE UNIVERSITY OF MONTANA NAGPRA PROJECT, COURTESY OF SALLY THOMPSON.

the *Missoulian* back in December 1950. Moccasin design is distinct from one tribal culture to another, and this little scrap could help us infer cultural affiliation.

A trip to UM's archives revealed that only two types of three-piece moccasins (with a separate tongue) are found in North America, one of which, importantly, is a Kootenai "center seam" type of moccasin, with the other being from the eastern part of the continent.[23] The dried-out tongue from the burial was a perfect match to the Kootenai example in George White's *Craft Manual of North American Indian Footwear,* and its size was appropriate for a child.[24] This evidence would be an important clue to cultural identity only if other explanations could be ruled out. Could the tongue have come from a commercially made shoe rather than a moccasin?

A review of shoe styles from the mid-to-late nineteenth century found two types to be common, either ankle-height, with long tongues, or "Mary-Jane's," without tongues. Moccasins were the normal footwear for most people, Indian or White, during the fur trade era in the Northern Rockies, and leather objects made by Indians were often used by White men, as needed. These trends changed with the arrival of commercial stores and Euro-American women in the 1860s. Granville Stuart wrote in his diary on July 23, 1862, about the changes coming with civilization.

> Certainly we are approaching civilization or rather civilization is coming to us. All the men are shaving nowadays and most of them indulge in an occasional hair cut. The blue flannel shirt with a black necktie has taken the place of the elaborately beaded buckskin one. The white men wear shoes instead of moccasins and most of us have selected some other day than Sunday for wash day.[25]

The recollections of a girl who attended school at the settlement of Hellgate in the 1870s help bring some local perspective. Emma Minesinger remembered that her family, the only non-White family at the school in the year of 1873, was unable to purchase shoes, no matter how badly she wanted them. "Brass-toed ones were the mode of the day, and proud, indeed, was the possessor of a pair," she remembered. Instead, she was sent to school in "a pair of new moccasins and red flannel leggings" made by her Indian mother.[26] Emma remembered that her family made "gloves, moccasins, and suits" from buckskin, which "was sewed with deer sinews."

By contrast, the first White women to settle in the region distinguished themselves from the "primitive" ways of the local Indian women by wearing clothing of cloth, not hide; wearing shoes, not moccasins; eating with utensils of metal, not wood and horn; and teaching their daughters to embroider, not to bead. It was the women's job to "civilize" their men and their children.[27]

Besides moccasins, no evidence of the child's clothing remained. Although remnants of buckskin had been recovered from the burial location, none were present in the collection. Indian girls' dresses at that time were either calico or buckskin. No evidence of cotton cloth was found. Indian girls learned to tan hides as soon as they could handle this heavy work, generally around the age of eight to ten, with help from their mothers. The scraps of hide could have been what remained of her dress or a robe used to cover her.

Going Home

Ultimately, it was clear to me, as the NAGPRA specialist for the University of Montana, that the remains of this little girl, who had been lovingly buried in a coffin with her favorite purse, pouch, and belt, and wearing Kootenai three-piece moccasins, were culturally affiliated with members of the Confederated Salish and Kootenai Tribes of the Flathead Reservation. This was an Indian burial. It mattered not whether her father might have been a White man, her mother was surely Indian. The need to declare ethnicity based on physi-cal evidence is connected to the ideology of White people, which categorizes human beings by race, ethnicity, and blood quantum. Yet cultural heritage is what makes us who we are. These were never issues for Native people before the arrival of colonizers. The descendants of men of Iroquois and French heritage who married into the Salish and Kootenai tribes were considered "full-bloods." What mattered was how they identified, what they believed about the world, and their community. Colonization has changed all that.

On the evidence of the rawhide pouch and the scrap of moccasin found in this little girl's grave, her people wanted her to come home. Each bone was carefully wrapped and packed in heavy cardboard for transport. The remains were reburied in a quiet ceremony of ancient words at the Kootenai cemetery in Dayton, Montana, near the shore of Flathead Lake on September 18, 2012. I still carry the weight of this sad story, knowing how this difficult process of claiming the remains of displaced ancestors is another nail in the coffin of all that has been lost and all that has been taken. ✢

17

ANDREW GARCIA AND
THE PLACE WHERE IT HAPPENED

M any Montanans have read *Tough Trip Through Paradise,* Andrew Garcia's amazing narrative of a journey with his Nez Perce wife In-who-lise (White Feather) from the Musselshell River to the Big Hole Valley and on to the Bitterroot in 1878. This was one year after the Battle of the Big Hole between the Nez Perce and the U.S. Army. The couple almost didn't make their destination. Readers will remember how, while in the Upper Rock Creek country southwest of Philipsburg on the last leg of their journey, a striped blanket and some foolish behavior almost cost Garcia his life.

Tough Trip is more than a great read. The story continues beyond the 1870s and beyond the lifetime of Andrew Garcia,

Andrew Garcia. PHOTOGRAPH COURTESY OF KELLY GARCIA.

187

who became a mysterious historical icon. I stepped into the story in 1999, through an encounter with Buss Hess, an old miner on Upper Rock Creek. When Buss was a boy, he got to tag along with Andrew Garcia, then in his late seventies, when this larger-than-life character returned to the scene of his hair-raising experience. Garcia returned to McKay Gulch to get clear about the lay of the land so he could write an accurate description in his manuscript. Nearly seven decades later, when Buss was in his late seventies, he shared his story with me. In this way, a link was made that helps keep Garcia's story alive, and also the story of Buss Hess, whose grandfather came to Montana not long after Garcia.[1]

This story revolves around events that began on a summer night in 1878, after Garcia and In-who-lise survived a trip along an almost impassable trail in the Sapphire Mountains. They were lost. That night they suffered through an intense thunderstorm. In the morning, Garcia discovered that their horses had pulled their pickets and were nowhere to be seen. Tracking his horses led him to a wagon trail into a gulch where he could see two cabins. He decided to walk over there to ask about the best way to get across the Sapphires to the Bitterroot Valley.[2]

No one was inside the cabin, but fresh tracks led to a placer mine where two men were working in the bottom of a cut. No doubt, Garcia asked himself a hundred times why on earth he did what he did next, best told in his own words.

> Like all bonafide squaw men of that time, I usually wore buck-skin clothes from toes to chin. But after this heavy rain, to keep my pants from getting wet in the long grass and brush, I had wrapped an Injun blanket of rainbow colors around me, fasten-ing it at the waist with my cartridge belt. Silently crawling on the bank of the cut, I lay there like a savage with deadly hatred gleaming in my eyes, as I look at these two white men. Now like the bad Injun bucks and old squaws in the buffalo camps did whenever they see a white man, I hissed to myself 'Souie-app-e A-O [White men yes]'. In-who-lise says they are all bad. She hates them. There is only one good white man and that is I, all the rest

are evil and bad. Coming to my senses I remember it was not long ago when I was a white man myself. Then I yearn to hear the voices of them men, to talk with them. . . . But first I would fool them. Like the fool I was, just to show off, I stepped out on the edge of the bank above them, where they could see me well and not fifty feet away from them. I raised the Injun blanket up over my shoulders, and up over the lower part of my face. Assuming a dramatic pose, straight as a ramrod with my broad brimmed hat pulled down so they could not see the rest of my face, I stood as erect as a statue, gazing sternly down at them, with my rifle resting in the hollow of my arm.

As would be expected, the first man to see this looming presence was so shocked that he dropped his gold pan and yelled to his partner, "Get Bill, Injuns, Injuns!" Then they ran across the gulch "like startled deer." At first, Garcia "roared with laughter, seeing them legging it for their lives in their heavy gum boots." Soon, though, he recognized how foolish he had been and decided to hightail it out of there himself.

He went in search of his horses, all the while unaware of the true magnitude of his troubles. Not so long before, three miners had been killed by some Nez Perce men, right there, in McKay Gulch, named for one of the men who died. Close to where the blanketed fool pulled his stunt, the lone survivor of that incident, "Nez Perce" Jones, was working his claim. Given these circumstances, the miners assumed the worst about the bold "Injun."

The Nez Perce men who murdered the miners were from White Bird's band.[3] They, along with some people from Joseph's band, had escaped the Battle of the Bear Paw Mountains, wintered with Sitting Bull's people in Canada, and were returning to the Wallowa Valley of their homeland. This fascinating journey is documented in *Yellow Wolf: His Own Story*, as told to historian L. V. McWhorter. When these displaced Nez Perce met with hostility along their journey, they responded in kind. The Nez Perce understood that these miners who declined to help them couldn't be trusted and had the power to call in the military. The Nez Perce felt they had no choice but to kill them, to save themselves. Besides, like In-who-lise, these Nez Perce had no love for White men.

189

From left to right, interpreter Thomas Hart, Yellow Wolf, and historian L. V. McWhorter, October 1908. PHOTOGRAPH IN POSSESSION OF THE AUTHOR.

When Garcia returned to camp, he failed to tell In-who-Lise what he had done. He had a plan and hoped she would never know what a fool he had been. He would change from his "Injun rig and innocently . . . ride over the ridge and ask them [the miners] about the trail." Before he managed to finish dressing and get out of the tepee, their dogs sounded an alarm. In-who-lise peered out to see armed White men—*Suyapos*—on horseback. "Then the flap was thrown violently back," and Garcia found himself "looking into the rifle muzzles of several half-drunken white men," who said to him, "Come out of there, you and them buck Injuns, and be sure you don't try any monkey work." These miners, including the brother of John Hays, who had been killed the year before, were out for revenge. They expected to find a bunch of Indians who were returning to the scene of their crime in search of the miners' gold. Surprised to find only Garcia and In-who-lise, they decided they would take them to a cabin and tie them up, while they went for the sheriff in Deer Lodge.

Whatever prayers Garcia had spoken were miraculously answered that day when he recognized two members of the impromptu posse. He had helped them out at Fort Ellis in 1876. After substantial prompting, they finally recognized him and vouched for his story. Garcia's life was spared, and the miners told the travelers how to find the trail into the Bitterroot Valley. They should follow down the creek until they came to the Salish buffalo trail, which they did, thankful to have survived this dramatic misunderstanding.[4]

⊕ ⊕ ⊕

As soon as the snow was gone from the high country in June 1999, I drove up the West Fork with my daughter Ingrid to spend the day with our friend Buss. He had offered to take us up to the old mining claim where he met Andrew Garcia. We arrived and transferred our gear into Buss' pick-up truck and jumped in. He talked while he drove, telling us about that summer when he was a kid. He remembered that Garcia talked about an Indian woman who had died from being dragged by a horse and that she was "buried up there somewhere with gold." The old miner remembered how he followed Garcia around like a puppy dog, or that's how I pictured it. Buss idolized this long-haired, bearded reminder of earlier days. I can't remember now if he described him in a long back coat, like old-time sheriffs wore, or in buckskins. For the boy, telling us how Garcia "held himself upright," this larger-than-life visitor was something out of the Old West. We had a temporary delay when we found the forest road blocked by treefall. "No problem," Buss said, "I've got my chain saw in the back. You can't travel these roads without one."

Buss removed the downfall and climbed back into the truck, and we continued up the steep, rough two-track road. He explained that this visit with Garcia happened because Buss' dad spent summers working the claim. From Buss' memories, I would

Buss Hess. PHOTOGRAPH COURTESY OF BECKY HESS METESH.

have thought that Garcia had spent the whole summer with Buss and his dad. I recently learned that Garcia's visit was brief.[5] He came with some Forest Service personnel from the Big Hole, which he had also revisited. When they came to McKay Gulch, Buss was with his uncle and some family friends. Buss' dad was already dead.

I didn't know this at the time, but Buss was an orphan. He lost his mother Cecil Hinthorn Hess when he was a baby. The family was living in Superior at the time.

Andrew Garcia at his cabin. PHOTOGRAPH COURTESY OF KELLY GARCIA.

(Ironically, the Garcia family was also living on the lower Clark Fork, at Rivulet on Fish Creek, and the two families might have crossed paths.) When Cecil went into labor, the family traveled by train to the Missoula depot where Cecil was transferred to an ambulance for the trip to the hospital. Buss became known as "the ambulance baby" because of the place he made his entrance that day, March 10, 1922. Nine months later, Cecil died of peritonitis.[6] She was only sixteen.[7]

Widowed Ray and motherless baby "Buss" returned to Upper Rock Creek to live with Ray's sister. The 1930 census lists Ray as a widowed farmer living on Ross' Fork in a rented house with his eight-year-old son. Ray helped his sister's family with ranch work and worked that old claim on McKay Gulch. Life must have been bleak beyond hope for Ray, in the middle of the Great Depression. The forty-year-old ranch hand hung himself in the woods a week

Buss Hess as a baby with his grandparents, T. R. and Rebecca Hess, 1922. PHOTOGRAPH COURTESY OF BECKY HESS METESH.

before Christmas in December 1933, when Buss was eleven years old. As reported in the *Great Falls Tribune*, the day before, he had asked a rancher friend if he could borrow a gun. When the rancher told Buss' dad he had no gun to give him, Ray said, "All right then, lend me a rope. I want to catch my horse." He used that rope to take his life.[8]

Buss parked the truck and we walked over to see the old placer pits. While he got himself reoriented, Ingrid and I walked around those wooded slopes and imagined the stories from the 1870s. We found an area by a large rock littered with flakes of Eyebrow Chert. This local material was widely used by the Salish and Pend d'Oreille to manufacture their arrow points, scrapers, and knives before metal became available to them in the 1820s. The spot would have been an excellent lookout.

Buss showed us where John Hays' cabin had stood and re-created the story for us, as he had learned it. Then he walked us down to a spot about fifty yards below the cabin where, years before, he and his dad had found a big old lodge-pole pine that had markings etched into its bark. He couldn't show us these glyphs because they no longer existed. Some years before, he had cut down the tree and put the marked section in an old outhouse to protect it. Instead, a hole developed in the roof that leaked right onto the bark and destroyed it. He drew us a simple sketch showing three tipi forms and two intersecting lines, with two bullet holes in the larger of the two. Then he told us the explanation as he remembered learning it from Andrew Garcia.

The summer when Garcia visited the Gulch, Buss was excited to show him the tree and to ask if he knew what the glyphs meant. According to Buss, the old mountain man explained it to have been a message showing that three tipis were down the creek from where the trail crossed it. He wasn't sure of the meaning of the cartridge shells stuck in two holes in the wood.

Perhaps this bark map showed the same trail that the miners described to Garcia when he and In-who-lise were heading back to the Bitterroot.[9] When the Nez Perce came through in 1878, they traveled in separate groups and would leave messages to help them reconvene.

At one time, these forests and prairies were probably littered with messages, but most of them have gone with the wind. Buss deeply regretted his decision to cut down the tree and lose its treasure. In this case, although the tree was gone, its history had been recorded. Buss had no idea that Garcia had photographed the glyphs and left a record about the circumstances.

The "message tree" near Rock Creek, 1935. PHOTOGRAPH BY ANDREW GARCIA, COURTESY OF THE MONTANA HISTORICAL SOCIETY RESEARCH CENTER.

The photograph appears in L. V. McWhorter's book, *Hear Me, My Chiefs! Nez Perce Legend and History*, along with a detailed caption provided by Garcia based on the translation provided by In-who-lise during their tough trip.

The caption in McWhorter's book attributes the marks in the bark to "fugitive Nez Perces who had returned from Canada." According to Garcia, the message conveyed that "three tepees of us have gone and will wait for you up the creek. Look for us at the place where the trail crosses the creek." Garcia photographed the tree on July 12, 1935, presumably during the time of his visit with Buss and his uncle, making Buss thirteen years old at the time. Garcia donated the image to the Montana Historical Society in 1942. A note with the photograph indicates that a Nez Perce Indian was buried at the foot of the tree. If Buss knew about that, he didn't say anything.

Thinking back over this story, I recognize that a suite of special circumstances had come together to preserve this bit of Montana history. If Andrew Garcia had never met historian L. V. McWhorter in Missoula in 1928, he probably never would have written *Tough Trip*. If he hadn't written his book, he wouldn't be known today, as evidenced by his brief obituary in the *Lethbridge* (Alberta) *Herald* where he is remembered simply as a mule skinner.[10] If I hadn't had the opportunity to visit with Buss Hess about local history, I never would have learned about Garcia's return, or about Buss' tough life. The "ambulance baby" died in 2011 at the age of eighty-nine. His stories live on. ✢

THE GIFT OF A PARK

This chapter interweaves the story of one visionary family with one piece of ground as it transitions from a seasonal Salish home to a park at the edge of a growing populace to a beloved place of refuge surrounded by neighborhoods. This is a story of the competing values that have shaped parks in towns throughout Montana, and nationwide, beginning in the late nineteenth century and continuing right up to the present. Today, with virtually no other undisturbed land within the city limits of Missoula, we can recognize the rare foresight behind this gift.

"A Lasting Monument"

On May 30, 1909, on page 27 of a multi-page spread in the *Missoula* section of the hefty *Sunday Missoulian*, citizens could peruse photos and read about "Greenough Park, a lasting monument to kindly, public-spirited generosity."[1] This nature park along Rattlesnake Creek had been given to the city in 1902 by Thomas L. and Tennie E. Greenough and had become one of the highlights of the growing town.

The Greenoughs had been thinking about creating a park for quite some time. Their home and manicured grounds on Rattlesnake Creek occupied an enviable position between downtown Missoula and the woodlands along the creek that became the park. The well-heeled couple, who had lived on that property in Missoula's new East Side neighborhood since 1884, were concerned about changes occurring just upstream of their home. As Mr. Greenough told the *Anaconda Standard* in January 1902, "I have seen campers come in here and pitch their tents and go right out and cut down some of the finest trees there."[2] To save it from being ruined, he and Mrs. Greenough set out to protect this beautiful refuge. They thought it should become a city park. Once the city added "a neat fence around the land," and developed walks and driveways through it, Thomas reasoned, the park would provide a "delightful place to spend afternoons." Between the lines of his commentary lay Thomas's insight that a park enjoyed by Missoula families and their visitors would be less appealing to the vagrants who were becoming all too common on these grounds adjacent to the Greenough home.

Tennie Greenough had her own version of the story behind the park's creation. She remembered one hot summer day, around the turn of the century, when she observed a group of visitors from Butte enjoying a cool place to spend the afternoon in the woods along Rattlesnake Creek. In that moment, she realized the importance of that shady refuge, and from that understanding launched the idea of the city park.[3]

The Greenoughs

The Greenoughs arrived in Missoula in 1882. Thomas had been born in Iowa in 1851, and, five years later, Tennessee "Tennie" Epperson entered the world in Cumberland, Tennessee. When they were children, each of their families acquired a farm in Kansas Territory. Both of their fathers fought in the Civil War. They married in Dakota Territory on Christmas Day, 1879, on her twenty-third birthday. Thomas was twenty-eight years old and had spent the previous decade exploring career options in the railroad and mining industries. He was a man with promise, and she was a remarkably capable woman.

The 1880 census shows them living as boarders with his parents in a mining town near Rapid City. Although Thomas was listed as a miner, he did contract construction work during those years, "sinking shafts and running tunnels."[4] When the short-lived placer mining frenzy gave way to hardrock mining, the Greenoughs abandoned their efforts. They would seek their fortunes elsewhere.

History tells us that Thomas was an energetic and innovative man, known for his "strong personality" and a "keen business judgment," along with a great capacity for hard work. "He was never fully contented," according to one colleague, "unless he was struggling under responsibilities involving large sums of money and a brushing against the keen wits of other men."[5]

Although no written record tells about Tennie's life at that time, later evidence makes clear that they were a team—true partners. We can assume Tennie contributed to their plan to move to Montana Territory. Driving a wagon with a team of mules, Thomas, Tennie, and their toddler, Estelle, landed in Miles City on March 16, 1882. An age-old, bison-hunting lifeway was coming to an end as the Greenoughs drove their team across Montana. They traveled westward through short-grass plains, virtually empty of buffalo. That was the year when many tribes had their last successful hunts. As they traveled across Montana, Thomas negotiated contracts with the Northern Pacific Railroad to furnish ties. From Miles City, the young family stopped in Bozeman, Helena, and Deer Lodge, before settling in Missoula in July.

During the summer of 1883, Thomas was taking timber out of the Rattlesnake Mountains and sending the ties down Rattlesnake Creek to a landing near the bottom, for use on the nearly completed Northern Pacific track. Both he and Tennie fell in love with the beautiful spot on the lower creek between Mount Jumbo and Indian Hill (later known as Waterworks Hill), in a place that had long seen tipi lodges, not square houses. Just that spring, a feast had been hosted by Indians on Rattlesnake Creek to honor the passing of Paristie, a wealthy Nez Perce leader who lived in the Bitterroot. The chief's belongings and eighty head of horses were given away to his friends. Many Salish were reported to be in attendance.[6]

According to oral history of the Salish people, their relationship to this place dates back to time immemorial. After the last of the Pleistocene ice had melted and Glacial Lake Missoula emptied, Salish people came to the lower Rattlesnake Valley for the bitterroot harvest in April and the bull trout run and serviceberries in June. At the beginning of the twenty-first century, despite the nearby train tracks and the interstate highway, people still enjoy the abundance of life in this area, where bitterroots still blanket Waterworks Hill and the spray of white across Jumbo's hillsides in the spring holds the promise of serviceberries and chokecherries. At the juncture of Rattlesnake

Sketch by Thomas Adams of entering Hellgate Canyon from the west, January 9, 1854. PHOTOGRAPH COURTESY OF PRINCETON UNIVERSITY LIBRARY.

Creek with the Clark Fork River, anglers still cast from the gravel bar at the mouth of the creek, giving testament to the rich fishing opportunities that have always characterized that location.

In 1884, the year their first son, Leo, was born, the Greenoughs took profits from Thomas' lucrative timber contracts to purchase their Rattlesnake property and build their first home, just north of the Northern Pacific tracks. Back then, the arrival of the train was a welcome sight. It brought visitors and the mail, connecting the town with the rest of the country. The Greenoughs saw it as an asset, not a noisy and smelly bother.

Theirs wasn't the first home in that area on the north side of the new tracks, but few had expanded into this part of the rapidly growing town. Tipis were still more common than permanent dwellings in the Rattlesnake Valley.

1884 bird's-eye view of Missoula shows lower Rattlesnake as a wooded area and tipis by the railroad berm. PHOTO-GRAPH COURTESY OF THE LIBRARY OF CONGRESS, G4254.M6A3 1884. W4.

A *Missoulian* article in October 1884 complained about the continuing presence of "the Indians." Townspeople were accustomed to seeing Salish, Pend d'Oreille, and Kootenai people in and about town, but the presence of about thirty Blackfeet lodges camped in the neighborhood was an entirely different matter. "While no white man fears for his personal safety," according to the article, "there is a feeling that a strange Indian in a strange land

will not hesitate to break into a cabin or drive off a good horse if he finds the opportunity."[7] The Blackfeet had come on a fishing and hunting expedition. They had just suffered through what is remembered as "Starvation Winter," when hundreds of their people had starved to death. Survivors were seeking refuge and food. The Salish weren't doing much better. Old hunting, fishing, and gathering grounds like the Rattlesnake Valley continued to provide sustenance in lean times.

Indians camped along Rattlesnake Creek. PHOTOGRAPH BY MORTON J. ELROD, COURTESY OF THE UNIVERSITY OF MONTANA ARCHIVES.

The Greenoughs weren't deterred by the continuing presence of Indians. They focused on their growing family and opportunities in mining, timber, and real estate in this town on the cusp of modernity. As their fortunes grew, so did the family. Their son Harry was born in 1886, followed by John in 1887, the same year Tennie contracted for the building of a boarding house a few blocks toward town from their home. Thomas was not the only entrepreneur in the family. The boarding house was just one of many real estate ventures Tennie initiated during the next four decades.[8] She gave birth to two more children, as well: Ruth in 1889 and Edith in 1892.

Their neighborhood was growing, alongside their family. By 1890, the city directory listed seventy residences in the lower Rattlesnake area, generally to the east of the Greenoughs. Most of these were little houses occupied by working-class families, many of whom worked for the railroad. Indians continued to camp alongside the creek.

A decade before the Greenoughs were acquiring lands to donate for a park, they had already grown exceedingly wealthy through their investments. In 1897, they had their original home on the banks of Rattlesnake Creek moved from the site they so loved to make way for their lavish, A. J. Gibson-designed, twenty-two-room Victorian mansion. As an indication of their wealth, Tennie spent nearly $2,000 on light fixtures for their home.

Above: Greenough Home on Rattlesnake Creek, circa 1890. PHOTOGRAPH COURTESY OF THE UNIVERSITY OF
MONTANA ARCHIVES.

Below: The July 24, 1911, Missoulian *touted Tennie and Thomas Greenough for their generous gift of a park.
This is the only known photograph of Tennie available from public archives.* PHOTOGRAPH COURTESY OF THE
UNIVERSITY OF MONTANA ARCHIVES.

Neither Thomas nor Tennie came from money, yet some decades later
they were gifting the city of Missoula with a substantial park along a beautiful
creek right near the heart of town. It would seem that the synergistic vision of
the Greenoughs brought about the park. Despite the vagaries of this particular
history, one fact is clear—both Tennie and Thomas had loved the location
from the time they first arrived.

The Park

At its weekly meeting on September 5, 1902, the Missoula City Council discussed the pros and cons of accepting the donation of 8.2 acres along Rattlesnake Creek for a city park. The Greenoughs wanted this remarkable place to be "set aside as a natural area for the enjoyment of the public" and wanted the city to accept responsibility for its preservation. In his presentation to the council, Thomas encouraged the councilmen to accept this gift of land forever as a park "to which the people of Missoula may during the heated days of summer, the beautiful days of autumn and the balmy days of spring find a comfortable, romantic and poetic retreat." He hoped the assembled councilmen would appreciate the spirit behind the offer, assuring them it is "entirely devoid of any selfish motive or ulterior purpose."[9] The park proposal, by full vote, was accepted.

The perspective the Greenoughs had gained from nearly two decades on that land provided the inspiration to catalyze the vision behind the park. In the transfer documents, they described the park as a place to which citizens and visitors "may have free and uninterrupted access for the purposes of a pleasure resort." The city, in accepting the gift, was bound to "improve, maintain and forever preserve the said property." If the city failed to maintain and use the "land and premises for a public park and park purposes," the title would "immediately revert to the donors or "their heirs or assigns." The same consequence would result if the city for any reason allowed the sale of "any spirituous, vinous, malt or other intoxicating liquors" to occur within the park.[10]

The Anaconda Standard, in a splashy photo-filled spread on September 5, 1902, reported that "Missoula no doubt will have one of the finest city parks in the state."[11] The visionary process had been complicated, and it took quite some time for "this magnificent gift" to come together. The Greenoughs had originally hoped "that the city itself would make an effort to secure the tract, but as no one took the initiative in the matter, Mr. and Mrs. Greenough decided to buy the land and give it to the city." Although they had a struggle to get "all the owners to part with their holdings at a reasonable price," they were not deterred.[12]

The Anaconda Standard writer credited the donors with saving this beautiful place from destruction "by vandals and careless campers."[13] Visitors appreciated being able to enjoy the creek and its environs so close to town. The only time it couldn't be used was during May and June, when the "freshet," as the spring runoff was commonly called, flooded the area. During that season, many visitors went to the upper east edge to view the rushing waters from the safety of a high terrace. The reporter told of an immense volume of water during that season that could carry downed trees in a rush to the "Missoula"—now Clark Fork—River. Local citizens remembered small buildings being washed from the banks by the spring runoff.

The park's "chiefest charm," according to a *Missoulian* writer, was its "unaffected naturalness." The writer celebrated the absence of elaborate gardens of flowers, "Keep off the Grass" signs, and restrictions "as to where to go and where not to. . . . There is plenty of room for everybody in Missoula's Park," the journalist continued, noting especially the "room to breathe, room to feel as if one were far away from everything and everybody." And all this was only five minutes from the bustle of town.

The *Missoulian* reporter touted "the nucleus of a good zoo" at the entrance of the park, with cages and enclosures for two black bears, some deer, and other native fauna. The writer failed to note that this feature was not in keeping with the wishes of the Greenough family. In fact, Thomas Greenough was none too happy about the menagerie at the entrance to the park, which he believed was "a nuisance from the time it was started." The location "was not a proper one for anything of the kind," he complained in a letter to the editor, and the annual cost of $150 to keep the bears would be better spent on new bridges and trails. He also had strong objections to the cutting of trees and native vines in the park.

Improving, Maintaining, and Preserving

Once the deeds were signed, the city got right to work on consummating its responsibilities. In March 1903, the Parks Committee chairman asked for a custodian to be appointed to protect the park and to look after improvements. The committee would seek bids for fencing and for two rustic bridges.[14] In May, they reported on their plans for a caretaker to protect improvements "from trespassers and vandalism." Beautiful and valuable trees in the park had already been destroyed or damaged.[15] Trespassers, in this case, were adjacent homebuilders who encroached around the edges of park lands.

The Greenoughs continued to acquire tracts to expand the park. From the start, they had engaged partners to contribute additional lands, including the Missoula Water Company and the Missoula Real Estate Association.[16] They continued their struggle to get landowners on both sides of the creek "to part with their holdings at a reasonable price" but managed to assemble a large number of parcels.[17]

One property owner held out and prevented the Greenoughs from securing contiguous lands on the east side of the creek. This one owner of a triangular piece of property, according to Tennie, "would place no price upon it and would not sell. Suddenly, one day, word came out that the owners . . . had sold it to a man named Walcott, who built a pavilion there." The two-season pavilion was used in the summer as a dance hall and in winter it served as a skating rink.[18] Walcott "allowed no one to pass over a corner of his land," according to Tennie, so to provide access from the pavilion to the park, she and Thomas eventually bought a house and lot on the terrace above, "and deeded enough to the city for the establishment of the road."[19]

The Missoula Chamber of Commerce got involved in park management in 1906 with a two-year beautification plan. A *Missoulian* editorial voiced strong support. "Nature," they espoused, "has endowed it [Greenough Park] with all the attractive environs that are necessary to make it a beauty spot . . . one of the most charming spots in all of the West." Nature, however, in their way of thinking, needed "a few artificial embellishments from the hand of man."[20] One of the most interesting ideas to spring from the chamber's brainstorming was to ask Michel Pablo to donate two bison from his herd on the Flathead Reservation. "Should he not desire to present the animals to the city outright," recounted the chair of the chamber committee, "it has been suggested that he leave a herd of them to pasture in the park." The naïve committee couldn't imagine anything that would add more to the attractiveness of the park "than a few head of buffalo."[21] Clearly, they knew nothing of appropriate habitat for bison or the kind of stout fencing required to keep them contained.

The *Missoulian* reported that the chamber recommended a park commission be appointed by the mayor and proposed an affordable means to make all this happen. By June, the chamber's plans were moving forward. They had an estimate of $300 for a "permanent place of habitation" for the two bears already there "and others which may be donated to the park."[22] They were considering "a number of swings" and "a number of attractive flower beds" to be scattered through the park. Beautification was the goal.

The Greenoughs had other things on their mind at the time. In November 1906, their oldest daughter, Estelle, was married in an elaborate ceremony in their home. In 1907, Thomas Greenough and his brothers had invested large sums in a Wyoming mine that turned out to have been "salted," misrepresenting the quality and abundance of the ore. They lost more than $100,000 in the swindle. Meanwhile, the Chamber of Commerce moved ahead with its "improvement plans" for the park.

In late March 1908, a *Missoulian* reporter went to the park to interview people about proposed improvements. Strollers had strong feelings about the zoo at the main entrance. Most wanted it removed or relocated to "some secluded section of the pleasure ground," where it would "give no offense." Some people thought that the entrance would benefit from the work of an experienced gardener to create a formal garden there, or, perhaps, more of "the wild-garden idea." One man reported that he had never seen a park with "so many natural advantages . . . a priceless treasure."[23] The two perspectives—nature park versus recreation park—reflected a larger conversation happening throughout the country.

In May, George Walcott, proprietor of the pavilion on the east side of the park, ignored state law and held a dance on a Sunday. He was arrested for "conducting dance hall on the sabbath." The *Missoulian* reported how Walcott held the dance on Sunday under rather unusual circumstances. "It is said that ice cream and cake were served to ladies and gentlemen at $1 per order, and that after purchasing they were allowed to dance as many times as they chose without extra charge." Reportedly, Walcott purposefully invited arrest as a test case of the law. According to the reporter, this particular law was "very strict, and sets forth that anyone aiding or abetting such a violation is as guilty as the proprietor of the place and equally open to fine." It was possible that the orchestra members could have been fined as well as everyone who came to the dance.[24]

Progress in the park got waylaid as the wet spring of 1908 continued. Then, on the morning of June 7, Missoulians woke to the worst flood in memory. Although bridges up and down Rattlesnake Creek and the Clark Fork River gave way to the raging waters, Greenough Park generally fared quite well. The welfare of the bears was at risk when their pit became filled with water. One of them found refuge on the post in the center, but it was going hard with the other. His plight was discovered by the police chief, whose arrival coincided with the cessation of flooding.

The *Missoulian* reported that a few trees had been uprooted near the park entrance and "the grassy flat was stripped of its soil and verdure to the bare rocks." The flood also damaged the north end of the wagon road, and three small foot bridges, wooden benches, camping tables, and parts of the park fence "were swept clean." The east-side road was damaged. The creek itself split into three separate channels.[25] Fortunately the many trees protected the soil from washing away.[26] The flood caused serious damage to the Greenoughs' stone wall.

By 1909, the well-loved park was just what the Greenoughs had envisioned. The Montana Horseshoers' Protective Association held their annual picnic there, as did the Buckeye Club. Sunday schools used Greenough for day camps, and local families took visiting relatives there to cool off on summer afternoons.

1908 flood damaged a retaining wall at Greenough mansion. PHOTOGRAPH BY NORMAN A. FORSYTH, COURTESY OF THE UNIVERSITY OF MONTANA ARCHIVES.

In the spring of 1910, the Greenoughs offered the city an additional 8.5 acres along the creek.[27] A March 22, 1910, *Missoulian* editorial explained how the vision behind Greenough Park fit well within a small parks and "recreation ground" movement that began at the end of the nineteenth century.[28] Earlier parks tended to be large-scale preserves located at the edges of urban areas. Progressives back East noticed that many people were unable to enjoy the benefits because they could not afford the transportation costs to get there. Small parks within urban areas would make open spaces—"breathing places"—available to all. As old photos reveal, Missoula's air quality had diminished with the first sawmill and continued with each new wood- and coal-burning building. The Northern Pacific added soot to the mix.

The *Missoulian* advocated for the city to acquire ground for small parks while it was affordable. Funding for these parks in eastern cities often came in the form of cash or land donations from their wealthy citizens. Only one such "instance of splendid philanthropy had come to Missoula," the editor declared, and that was Greenough Park. With the extensive addition to the park, "Greenough park will be as fine a breathing place as is owned by any city in the west."[29]

The pavilion became available for purchase in 1910 when George Walcott, the pavilion operator, died in an insane asylum and Mrs. Walcott "met violent death in one of the towns on the Coeur d'Alene branch." The Greenoughs bought the property for $7,500, a small portion of which was transferred to the city for Greenough Park, squaring up the east side.[30] "The deed which was handed to the mayor yesterday helps the park and ensures Parkside lot owners the delightful contact of the Greenough park." There was an immediate rush for the Parkside lots, offered from $75 to $250.

The Greenoughs offered nearly twenty-four acres at the north end of the park in June 1910, with a contingency that within three years the city would purchase the land between the park and the donation. The city accepted the offer.[31]

A BARGAIN

$2,600

Five-room house, corner Jackson and Cherry streets; size of lot, 130 x60 feet; good cellar, large barn, chicken house and woodshed. Beautiful shade trees and six fruit trees. Fine garden and lawn. Only two blocks from Greenough park. Terms, cash.

Real estate advertisement for lower Rattlesnake, the Missoulian, *1909.*

At the same time, Mr. Greenough asked the city to remove the caged deer from the park, "as they were practically destroying the verdure and the trees where they were confined." At least five of the seven deer were shipped by rail to the National Bison Range in the Mission Valley, established just two years before.

Thomas Greenough left Missoula toward the end of 1910, in poor health and angry at the city over the state of the park.[32] He spent time in Arizona and California that winter and then joined his brothers in Spokane.[33] One of the last things he did "before leaving Missoula the last time was to urge the city council to preserve this pleasure ground for the people in all of its natural beauty."[34] He had considered reclaiming his gift, he said, because he was so frustrated over its management by "people who do not know anything about parks, and who are advocating the trimming of the trees and cutting of all undergrowth, thereby destroying all natural beauty of the park." He reminded the city of the irony that other cities in the country were undertaking the difficult and expensive work "to make their parks looks natural," while Missoula already had been gifted just such a park.[35]

Thomas Greenough died in a Spokane hospital on July 23, 1911, after a long struggle with "the grip" (influenza) and pneumonia. While he lay on his death bed, he would have been pleased had he known that twenty little girls from the Congregational Church were enjoying a happy day at Greenough Park.[36] The *Missoulian* extolled his generosity. They called on Missoulians to take good care of this gift and to honor the ideals of its donor. The short article concluded by saying that "Missoula will miss Tom Greenough greatly; but he will always be remembered; the city's playground is his enduring monument."[37] Two weeks later, the city finally honored his longtime wish to remove the bears, playfully noting that no local flags would be flown at half-mast in honor of their removal.[38]

A year after Thomas's death, bears were back. The city council overrode public protests and Tennie's objections and approved the offer of two bear cubs to be kept in the park "to amuse the children." One of the councilors had strong objections but lost the vote. Not only did he object to the expense of keeping the bears year-round, but he also complained that the city was already facing legal action "on account of a runaway caused by the former inhabitants of the pit."[39] The location by the main entrance made the situation more dangerous than if they were kept in a more out-of-the-way spot. The *Missoulian* sided with Mrs. Greenough, noting "a persistent disregard" of her wishes.[40]

By the summer of 1913, growth and increasing prices in the lower Rattlesnake along the creek threatened potential for future park expansion. With more than 12,000 people living in the city, areas once considered too far from town were in increasing demand. A *Missoulian* editorial accused the city of neglecting opportunities to expand on this "40-acre" gem.[41] The editor warned that "in a very few years Missoula will look back and see her mistake" and will mourn the irretrievable loss. It would soon be too late. With the strong "spirit of civic improvement and beautification" sweeping the country, the editor emphasized that this would be a good time to act. But the city's bare coffers prohibited further acquisitions.

The park continued to see improvements, including a more flowing and attractive entrance. A "splendid lawn with several flower beds," although certainly not natural, could be enjoyed from benches scattered around the area. The main picnic grounds on the east side were cleared of brush and weeds, and a plan was in place to add a bandstand at the north end of the park. The route had already been cleared. One touted improvement that would have a significant and long-lasting impact was the decision to plant non-native maple trees, which were "growing splendidly" that spring. Of the park's half dozen natural springs, one had been developed into a concrete drinking fountain to serve as a watering hole for horses and dogs.[42]

High water in the park during the spring of 1913 created a new channel that flowed into the eastern section of the park. The remedy was to place riprap at several locations along the main channel to control the flow and protect threatened property and streets. Logs had already been hauled in for that purpose.[43] By August, retaining walls had been extended for about 200 yards, along with some solid wing dams to keep the creek in one channel on the west side.[44]

The *Missoulian* always championed the park. In June 1917, when automobiles were becoming commonplace around town, some citizens complained the upkeep of the park was a waste of city funds. The paper ran an editorial celebrating the fact that the pleasure found in Greenough by so many kept it from succumbing to the whims of those who preferred to peer from their automobile windows at "green boulevards and stiff little half-acre gardens."[45]

Disturbing the Sleeping Buffalo

A week later Missoulians were greeted by a compelling headline: "Greenough Park's Sunday Services Open to Everyone."

> For the rare Missoulian who hasn't an automobile of some kind, Greenough park extends an invitation to spend at least a few hours today in its "temple"—one of the kind Bryant referred to when he began, "The groves were God's first temples." The musical program, which will continue throughout the day, will consist of a solo by the Rattlesnake with its rush of water against boulders, accompanied by the rustling of leaves in tree tops. The combination is said to be particularly effective as a lullaby. The musicians are not so temperamental as to stop when persons in the audience read or chat or even sing or play. For those who will but lie on their backs on the lawn a rare exhibition of fantastic designs in fleecy clouds sailing in a sea of restful blue will be furnished. (This part of the program is subject to change without notice, black clouds, thunder, lightning and rain sometimes appearing on the scene.) Fish will furnish diversion to those so inclined, swings to others and enticing paths winding through the shrubbery to others. The park will be prettily decorated with green foliage and the white blossoms of the wild cherry and the briar. Because the English language is regrettably deficient in adjectives describing odors, the park can only promise that it will be perfumed with an indescribably pleasant fragrance. There is room for everybody without crowding and there will be no charge for admittance.[46]

The park might have been particularly important during that summer of 1917, after the United States entered World War I. That difficult time might have been what prompted Jim Caras of the Garden City Fruit Company to sponsor the first annual melon picnic by providing 8,000 pounds of watermelons to be enjoyed by the whole town. The next year's event was even bigger. Caras, who acted "the part of the fond parent for the second watermelon orgy," hosted the whole town in Greenough Park for the picnic and games. Along with the melons were apple races, watermelon-eating contests, and nail-driving contests for women, with assorted prizes for the winners.[47]

Relatively sparse information is available about the park for several decades after 1918, the year when 5,000 Montanans lost their lives to the Spanish flu, while the war dragged on alongside a depressed economy. The only park story to make a splash in the news was the biggest carnival ever held there, in July 1922. The purpose of the carnival, along with a dance, was to cover the costs to bring the Fourth Infantry regimental band to town. "All past carnivals," according to the *Missoulian*, "were mere side shows" compared to this one.

Local organizers played key roles that made this carnival special. A line of tents offered intriguing opportunities for attendees, such as fortune-telling by Madame Kiwadary, the disguised wife of the city clerk. Another booth featured Madame Frankie Trotzski, whose identity was kept secret, but was hinted to be a prominent businessman. Inside the pavilion, carnival-goers could see "Dobbin, the Shetland Pony with his tail where his head ought to be." Men jostled for a spot in the line to view the "For Men Only" exhibit, while women were less obvious about their interest to see what lay behind the curtain of the booth "For Women Only." The paper didn't reveal what viewers found behind those curtains. Games, including a fortune wheel, provided fun for the children, and families had their portraits made for a cost of ten cents. The dance was a wild success.[48]

Many constructed additions were introduced in the park as time passed— a large picnic area with a stove, tables, swings and a merry-go-round, a fish hatchery, and, later, a wading pool and three children's fishing ponds. The bear pit remained active through most of the 1920s.

Missoula marked the end of an era with the closure of the dance pavilion after two decades of operation. The final dance at the pavilion was held at the end of September 1925. The pavilion was to be torn down, explained Mrs. Greenough in an interview. Her decision was regrettable, but she was tired of all the criticism directed at her through the years by those "who presume that the place has been run to make money," and that she was making a profit. When she and Thomas purchased the property in 1910, they made substantial investment in upgrading the facility. Tennie had managed the pavilion along with the family's varied business concerns since Thomas' death. She

Bear cage at the entrance to Greenough Park. PHOTOGRAPH COURTESY OF THE UNIVERSITY OF MONTANA ARCHIVES.

had hired a couple to run the place, following policies she had established, including "strict supervision over the dances" by a policeman and a matron. Mrs. Greenough asserted that "profit never was the aim of the pavilion." She found the accusations especially exasperating because "not a cent has been realized" from the pavilion. "It was run so that the people of the city would have a place to go," Tennie explained. She wanted somewhere for "respectable people" to be able to enjoy themselves. Mrs. Greenough, almost seventy, "decided to be done with it and after the close of the season to tear the place down."[49]

As a widow, Tennie lived the rest of her life in the mansion on Vine Street. She died of a stroke at the age of eighty on July 31, 1937.[50] Through the years, she had to witness some benign neglect in the park. A smoldering rubbish fire in 1929 resulted in a good-sized blaze brought under control only because of rapid action by the fire department.[51] Throughout the course of her adult life, she read and heard all about her husband's legacy, when it was every bit as much hers, and probably more. Early Missoula historian Will Cave attributes the preservation of the park entirely to Tennie Greenough. "That we now and posterity shall continue to enjoy a modicum of the pristine charms of the stream and its environment," he wrote, "a debt of gratitude may endure to Mrs. T. L. Greenough in whose mind was conceived and by whose hand was executed the plan of 'Greenough park.'"[52]

Fast forward to 1948 and it seems that the park had been left largely to its own devices—nature had taken over, and vandals had been at work. Tennie and Thomas would have been horrified. The *Missoulian* ran a long article documenting its condition.[53] The park, "once beauty spot, now overrun," was in need of some TLC. Lloyd Stimson, a local resident, rallied volunteers to clear underbrush and make the upper part of the park accessible again. "At the present time," according to park board member John Toole, "the park is virtually a park in name only. The only recreation it offers is the drive around its border. . . . The drive itself doesn't offer any view to speak of, because of the high wall of overgrown shrubs and various collections of debris along the route of travel."[54] A concrete wading pool had been created for children, but there was a question about the willingness of mothers to allow their children to use it. "It is doubtful," expressed Toole, "that parents will feel perfectly at ease while their children are playing in an area that can conceal and protect perverts and criminals." Older Missoulians remember their mothers warning them not to walk through the park.[55]

That a person could disappear in the heavy undergrowth had been proven in 1930, when the park was still in regular use. The decomposed body of a man was discovered one hot August day in the park's interior.[56] Apparently, he had hanged himself in a clump of bushes only a few feet from the main path leading to the fish hatchery, about five or six weeks before his body was discovered.

According to the 1948 news piece, some Missoulians "want to keep the park in its primitive condition." But the intentions of Stimson's volunteer group were to "clean it out, build bridle paths, develop the picnic ground and make it an improved natural park." A. J. Mosby, park board president and second husband of Thomas and Tennie's daughter Ruth, told the volunteers he was "surprised at the improvement shown in the park's appearance following just one day's work." Plans included a kids' fishpond on the east side of the park where the fish hatchery had been. The committee would build small dams in the stream to create pools for fish. The park improvement plan was estimated to take ten years, with some goals to be accomplished more quickly than others.

In May 1951, those responsible for park management prioritized removal of dead and rotten trees after one large snag fell in an area where children were playing.[57] That same summer the Montana Fish and Game Association stocked the kids' fishpond with 2,100 fish at season's start, with a plan to add 600 more every other week.[58]

In 1954, Stimson and his volunteers were still at it. They had expanded the kids' fishing access to three ponds with 1,000 feet of shoreline. May 16 was scheduled for opening day for grade-school children. To be ready in time for the fish delivery from the Arlee hatchery, the volunteers used a bulldozer and other equipment to clean out the ponds.[59]

After one too many abuses of the original agreement, the Greenough heirs filed suit in 1954. They claimed the city had violated the terms of the deed by not preserving the forest and natural growth of the park. "The city has cleared underbrush in some areas to plant grass and establish a picnic area and playground." Other areas had already been cleared. Bulldozing trees to make way for a baseball diamond was the action that propelled the Greenoughs to initiate their claim.[60] The heirs complained that the cumulative actions had left "ugly barren scars fit only for the growth of weeds," not in keeping with "a comfortable, romantic and poetic retreat" their parents had imagined. The family had repeatedly protested these violations and "following a policy of 'progressively and deliberately' converting the park into a public playground rather than keeping it as a natural park."

By September 1955, the litigants had informally agreed to drop the suit if the city followed the recommendations of the former park board that "no more of the park [would] be torn up and that it [would] be brought back to its original state."[61] Arbitration led the sides to agree to "13 Points" for managing the park in perpetuity. They would close roads, provide parking, stop constructing recreational facilities, remove concrete culverts, create natural-seeming paths, control creek erosion, and form a committee of citizens with botanical and hydrological knowledge for better long-term planning and management of the park's natural assets. Subsequently, many citizens have volunteered their time and talents through the years to help care for this beloved park.

The 120-year history of Greenough Park encapsulates the story of parkland preservation in America, with all its conflicts over the value of nature, in and of itself, versus "improved" lands. The Greenoughs' visionary foresight is surely something for Missoulians to celebrate. Its management, however, has never been easy. Throughout all the many decades since the park's creation, the city has continued to grapple with its understanding of the donors' intentions. Fortunately, enough good citizens continue to step forward to protect their dream.

Here's to you, Tennie and Thomas Greenough, for the gift of a nature park—a "breathing space"—in the heart of Missoula. It surely is that, and so much more. Now the bears are uncaged, and birdwatchers come from far and wide to enjoy dippers, kingfishers, pileated woodpeckers, great horned owls, and some 120 other bird species, including multitudes of migrating songbirds.[62] Park managers continue to wage a battle against the Norway maples planted in 1913. In 1997, the most recent time the creek forged a new (old) channel on the east side of the park, it was allowed to have its way, and pedestrians gained a new bridge to accommodate the altered landscape. A beaver moved in during the winter of 2022–2023 to do some landscape alteration of its own. All winter long, visitors stopped to share their stories of sightings of the flat-tailed marvel, then smiled and greeted others as they continued their loop around this gift of a park. The Greenoughs would be proud.[63] ✢

TRAVELS WITH JUMBO

When the Confederated Salish and Kootenai Tribes joined in Montana's case against ARCO for losses on the Clark Fork River in the 1990s, I served as an expert witness to help document their losses due to the pollution caused by mining and smelting at the headwaters. The tribes still hold off-reservation treaty rights to practice traditional activities in their aboriginal territory, including the Clark Fork basin. In addition to learning from elders about traditional uses of the Upper Clark Fork, I interviewed homesteader families between Butte and Bonner. Their collective recollections echoed those of the Salish, helping to document many particulars about aboriginal uses that otherwise would have been difficult to verify. In addition to information relevant to the case, I heard many little gems of Montana history that have never found their way to paper. The following is one of my favorites.

Travels with Jumbo

Bud Weaver's family moved to the Bearmouth area from Philipsburg in the late 1920s, when Bud was a young child. He remembered annual visits by people from the Flathead Reservation in those early years, and he also remembered a fellow, "tall and thin," coming by their ranch when he was a kid. The man drove a cart pulled by his buffalo-cow cross, "Jumbo." Buffalo were animals of history. Bud had never seen one, so this occasion was never forgotten. Surprisingly, the man encouraged Bud to get on the beast and ride him.

He complied and rode a little way before the man told the animal to "buck him off"—which Jumbo obligingly did.

Ernie Hunt's family settled along the Clark Fork in 1922, between Piltzville and Turah on the north side of the valley at the location of an old Salish village site. Ernie remembered the beefalo-drawn cart coming to their place in the 1930s. According to Ernie, the cart-man put heavy leather shoes on his critter—probably of buffalo skin—and would change them out, as needed.

Dale Karkanen, born in 1929, descended from a Finnish family that homesteaded around Bonner in the late 1800s. Dale remembered the man with his beefalo and found an old photograph of this unusual scene from their family collection.

A catalo or beefalo hitched to a cart in Bonner, Montana. PHOTOGRAPH COURTESY OF DALE KARKENAN.

By zooming in on the wagon cover, I was able to determine the name of the ranch from which they traveled and, through the name, was able to learn some interesting background information on these beefalo cart trips up the Clark Fork.

The tall, thin man was Leland C. Wilson, born in Kansas in 1902. As a young adult, he made his way to the Grandview Ranch in Colville, Washington. By the late 1920s, he was raising Jumbo, a cross between American bison and beef cattle. Wilson wasn't the only person trying to breed a stronger species than cattle.

On March 7, 1929, Frank Thone published an article in the *Miami Daily News Record* entitled "AMERICA MAKES SOME NEW ANIMALS." Apparently, cattle hybridization was all the rage in the late 1920s because cattle didn't appear well-suited to the West, at least not in the modern economic sense, according to the author. The problems were due to climate and geography.

> The breeds of beef cattle that have become standard in this country originated in western Europe, on rich pastures where blizzards never howled, and where there was shelter from even the relatively mild storms that did come. Their names tell that: Angus, Durham, Hereford, and so on. They have furthermore been bred in this country to meet the needs of the moderately humid east and not to face the sterner life of the thin-grassed western range where they must shift for themselves as best they can even when a "norther" catches them in the open.

The author went on to explain that although the Texas longhorns were better adapted to the drought and cold of the West than Herefords and other northern European breeds common in America at the time, the longhorns "were not shaped right for modern beef fashions. Ranchers expected breeds that "carried more meat aft."

At that time, cattle across America suffered terribly from tick-borne fever, causing stockmen to cast about for "possible hardy mixtures to add to their blood." Of course, their first thought was of American bison. Like people of the Flathead Reservation, Thone reported that a few cattlemen, "either more sentimental or more farsighted than their contemporaries, had kept small private [bison] herds going on their ranches." They recognized that bison, unlike cattle, were "able to travel and feed at the same time," could face blizzards head-on with the protection of their long shaggy manes, and were much more resistant to disease than cattle. They were made for the plains of the American West; they had evolved alongside the short-grass prairies.

The first attempts to cross bison with cattle were less than successful, but eventually viable hybrids emerged. They carried the greater immunity of the bison, generally had the thick manes, and although they weighed more, they ate less. They were "easy keepers," as stock growers refer to those that hold their weight despite adverse conditions. Their meat was better. Charles Goodnight, a pioneer breeder of Texas, noted that because "they rise on their fore feet instead of their hind feet," they are able "to rise when in a weakened condition," an important trait of resilience. He further noted that "they never lie down with their backs downhill, so they are able to rise quickly and easily." This habit, he noted, was the opposite in cattle. These early cross-breeders decided to name their creations "cattalo," a term accepted by the American Genetic Association, of Washington, D.C.

In July 1935, Wilson took one of his crossbreeds to market in Spokane for sale, according to an article in the *Tacoma Daily Ledger*. Meat from the two-year-old, 1,370-pound steer would be "wrapped in wax paper and sold at from 25 cents to 75 cents a pound, depending on the cut." Eager to become a success with this promising new crossbreed, in 1935 Wilson hooked up 1,200-pound Jumbo to a covered wagon and together they visited twenty-three states and traveled more than 10,000 miles around the country, moseying along at the rate of two miles per hour and an average of ten or fifteen miles a day. This tour appears to have lasted four years, based on souvenir postcards. One postcard shows Wilson and a woman alongside Jumbo and the wagon. Another, dated to 1939, showing Jumbo yoked to the wagon, is signed on the back by Wilson, noting himself and his wife, Dotah Cha Rayinbir.

Perhaps the years of traveling put too much strain on their relationship; the 1940 census records show that Leland was, by then, a single farmer, renting a home in Arden, Washington.

Leland Wilson and Dotah Cha Rayinbir stand with Jumbo, 1939. PHOTOGRAPH COURTESY OF HARRIET BAKAS.

Apparently, these early hybrids, along with Wilson's marriage, seem to have failed, although Leland continued in the same general line of work. The 1950 census shows him married again and working as a "Wild Life Farmer." Cattle remained the dominant herd animal on the plains. In the 1970s and 1980s, ranchers once again experimented with the hybrids, which they called "beefalo." They never secured a good niche in the American meat market, but their ancient ancestors, the American bison, sure did. Buffalo burger, anyone? ✛

PART V

ROCKY MOUNTAIN FRONT

ANCIENT CLIMATE REFUGEES
ON THE SUN RIVER

My doctoral dissertation (University of Colorado, 1980) explored how indigenous people on the Great Plains adapted to major changes in climate since the end of the Pleistocene. At that time, I never imagined how big a topic climate change would become in our lives.[1] What I learned about the past, in short, is that people relocate to the mountain fringes during long dry periods. By sheer happenstance, after moving to Montana, I got the opportunity to delve more deeply into the subject through an archaeological site on the Sun River.

The Sun River location has a good pre-industrial baseline of characteristic fauna that can be identified through the records of the Corps of Discovery. When Meriwether Lewis explored what was then called the Medicine River in June 1805, he witnessed deer, pronghorn, and great numbers of buffalo. The following summer, on July 9, 1806, during a day when he and his men took shelter from a thundershower in some old Indian lodges, Joseph Field killed a bison and two deer, and also saw pronghorn and wolves as they traveled along. The next day, after camping near the mouth of Simms Creek, they noticed "several gangs of Elk," and managed to kill three that evening. One of the hunters shot a grizzly bear who had his eye on an elk carcass. They butchered their elk and the bear (valued for its fat) and proceeded downriver to their next camp, in a cottonwood stand.

On July 11, Lewis sent the hunters down the Medicine River, again, to hunt for elk. He aimed his own course a little east of south across the broad valley toward the White Bear Islands, about eight miles away. They passed immense herds of buffalo. Lewis made note in his journal that they heard the "tremendous roaring" of the bulls before they saw them, for it was the beginning of the rut. Wolves were plentiful. When they reached the river bottom, he was astonished by the number of buffalo there. He estimated "not less than 10 thousand buffaloe within a circle of 2 miles arround that place."

On that July day, Lewis and his party passed near the area of what today is known as the Sun River archaeological site.[2] The explorers had no way of knowing that detritus of ancient camps lay deeply buried under their feet. Nobody knew of this archaeological treasure until the spring of 1982, when Historical Research Associates (HRA), with Weber Greiser (my husband at that time) and myself serving as co-principal investigators, explored the floodplain of an oxbow about three miles up the Sun River from the confluence with the Missouri River at Great Falls. This Missoula-based business had been contracted by the Omaha District of the U.S. Army Corps of Engineers to determine whether any significant archaeological remains were present in an area being considered for excavation of gravel to build a levee. Previous survey and testing of the area found evidence of shallow Indian encampments and established that soils were very deep. More information was needed prior to impacting the site.

Testing the Site for Archaeological Evidence

Our field effort required deep testing using heavy equipment. We established our datum point for future reference and got started. The plan was to transect enough of the area to either find indications of past human use or to clear the area for gravel removal. The backhoe operator dug twelve trenches, one after another and each about ten feet deep, peeling back layers like a highly skilled wood-carver. Most of them revealed small lenses of charcoal scattered through the layers of overburden deposits from the river, but none of them revealed anything clearly cultural.

"Let's do one more," I told him, hoping thirteen would be our lucky number. We watched the profiles of the sidewalls as the dirt was removed. This trench

Backhoe at Sun River site, looking north (river is to the south). PHOTOGRAPH COURTESY OF SALLY THOMPSON.

looked like all the others. I started thinking about wrapping things up. We would need to fill in the trenches and let the Corps proceed with their levee project. I started thinking about dinner and my schedule for the rest of the week, when the bucket came to an abrupt halt.

"Is that what you're looking for?" the equipment operator asked. Wide-eyed, we enthusiastically grabbed a few trowels to sort through the back dirt just delivered to the growing mound. Bone, charcoal, and some stone flakes grabbed our attention. Bingo! About two meters (6.5 feet) below the surface, we had an archaeological site. We would write a report to the Corps of Engineers to inform them of our finds. By law, under Section 106 of the National Historic Preservation Act of 1966 (NHPA), the Corps would need to decide whether to mitigate impacts to the site or to move their borrow pit elsewhere.

The Corps chose to mitigate impacts to the part of the site to be affected by their project. In other words, rather than abandon the project, they would contract for archaeological work to retrieve and analyze the evidence of past use before disassembling the deposits. HRA got the contract to excavate what became known as 24CA74, the Sun River site. Before the skilled work of hand excavation could begin, tons of sediment needed to be removed from the roughly 8 by 8 meter area (about 100 square yards) to be impacted by the Corps. A test trench revealed three clearly distinguished occupation levels, each one marked by a dark clay matrix separated by lighter and siltier clay layers. Sun River turned out to be one of the most important archaeological sites in Montana.

Hand excavating the "Grotto" at Sun River. PHOTOGRAPH COURTESY OF SALLY THOMPSON.

Oxbow points from the Sun River site. PHOTOGRAPH COURTESY OF SALLY THOMPSON.

Early People of the Sun River Country

Dates for the three deeply buried components of the site (which the crew affectionately named the "Grotto") come from radiocarbon analysis, corroborated by the type of projectile points found in all three, known as Oxbow dart points. The dates range from 5,200 to 3,500 years before present (BP). In all three layers, we found archaeological evidence—stones and bones and cooking features—that represents the butchering and processing of meat.

Although the Sun River site turned out to be quite significant in terms of what it contributes to the archaeological record, it is important to keep in mind that the evidence recovered is fragmentary. The crew excavated just "the Grotto," revealing partial activity areas within much larger areas of use. The minimum number of animals known to be processed is determined by the most prevalent bone, such as four left mandibles (lower jaw bones). This number does not account for any mandibles that might have been in adjacent, unexcavated areas. The kill sites, at least in some cases, were elsewhere, as were the shelters of the people. We don't know what type of shelter they used because we found no such evidence. Tipis emerged during this period, and people are also known to have occupied rock shelters.[3]

Using evidence from the Sun River site and other archaeological evidence from the region, let's try to imagine what their lives were like.

First Oxbow Occupants (5,200 Years BP)

Imagine a small band of people whose ancestors have had to leave their home-land to seek food and water. They have to keep moving as the heat gets worse and water sources dry up. Before they were born, during the time of their great-grandparents and earlier, conditions were so hot and so dry that some of their people didn't survive. Their ancestors had to leave their homeland across the prairie because their regular camp locations no longer had reliable water or enough food to support them all. These migrants settled closer to the mountains.

In this country near the Big River (now known as the Missouri), things are a little better but still very difficult. Ungulates, like people, have been forced into fewer water-secure locations than were available before this period of mega-drought. These people have better access to pronghorn than bison because grass remains scarce, while sagebrush (which pronghorn will feed on) is ample. The people must spend almost every day looking for food. Long ago, their ancestors put up food for winter, but now there is never enough.

In this particular year, the hottest months have passed. The women have gathered whatever berries and greens they can find. They have learned to gather chenopod (goosefoot) seeds to grind into flour for cooking.[4]

Fall is the time to focus on bringing in whatever meat they can. They move to the sagebrush flats a few miles up a tributary from the Big River, not far from the high mountains, where pronghorn can usually be found. Their dogs haul their belongings lashed between two long poles. When they find the right spot, the women set up the lodges in a grove of struggling cotton-wood trees clustered around a small spring. The men split into small groups and go in search of food. Some days are better than others. During their time in this camp near a big bend in the river, the men kill four pronghorn, one buffalo, and a deer. Boys manage to snare a bird and kill a jackrabbit.

The women get right to work on processing the food. The bison is a scrawny old bull, with little meat to give. The four pronghorn are thin but still provide them with almost 100 pounds of fresh meat, along with fat and marrow from the long bones. This food, along with the mule deer meat, will feed the camp but won't provide extra for their traveling days, and certainly not what they need for winter. They waste nothing.

Dogs whine as they smell meat cooking, but they stay outside the circle of women busy with their tasks. Not only do the women process marrow from the pronghorn long bones, but people break open the jaws and foot bones to suck out whatever they can get, even though none of these bones has much to offer. The Nunamiut people of northern Alaska have an old saying about times like these: "The wolf moves when he hears the Eskimo breaking (caribou) mandibles for marrow." In other words, the wolves sense the extreme hunger of the people when they hear them breaking jaw bones for food. The broken mandibles at Sun River attest to the hunger of its occupants.[5]

Men in camp spend time refurbishing their tools. The stone tips for some of their darts are so worn out from previous resharpening that they have nothing left to secure the point to the haft, so they simply leave them behind. Through the months, they have found basalt, chert, quartzite, and agate from river terraces, glacial gravels, and outcrops. They haven't had enough energy to risk a long trip for better-quality material.

Few places can sustain them for long because animals in this long era of drought are too scarce and too easily spooked. The dogs gnaw on what little remains around the fires as the people pack up their belongings. At least, for now, their children are fed. They never know about tomorrow.

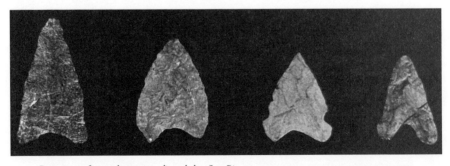

Points worn from resharpening, discarded at Sun River. PHOTOGRAPH COURTESY OF SALLY THOMPSON.

Middle Oxbow Occupation (4,500 Years BP)

Fast forward some 700 years, when a small group of hunters arrives at the same location. It looks different though. In the years between occupations, the Sun River has shifted, and occasional floods during this megadrought have moved vast amounts of sediment. Conditions are more stable now, but food is still hard to find. Like their predecessors, these hunters arrive in late fall or early winter. They are attracted to the area because nearby springs support enough grass to attract bison, and bison are valued more than any other animal. They are their "staff of life." One bison provides more meat than three mule deer or seven pronghorn, and their hides are far warmer than any other. Bison provide not only blankets but also coats and ropes and suitcases, and a litany of other important things.

The hunters are fortunate and manage to kill six buffalo cows and calves. On other days, they bring in one two-year-old pronghorn, an elk, and a deer. The first round of butchering occurs at the kill site, where they leave the heaviest bones behind. They haul the rest of the carcasses in manageable segments to a place close to camp to process. The women work on the bison in one area. Any meat they won't eat that day they slice thinly to be dried on racks. The hot sun cures the food quickly. They process marrow and grease for winter stores. Another day they set to work on the hindquarters of an elk and deer the men have brought in.

These are better times than have been seen for many generations. From the bison alone, this group may process over 2,000 pounds of meat and 176 pounds of grease.[6] Dried, the meat weighs less than a third of the original weight. The parents relish the feeling of satisfaction to know that their children's bellies are full and they will have food going into winter. In this camp, the people don't have to suck on cracked mandibles. They have long bones to suck on for marrow. Their dogs devour what is left. The people pack up the food they have dried and set out for their next stop. They will need more.

Most Recent Oxbow Occupation (3,500 Years BP)

Fast forward again, this time about 1,000 years, when people come again to this beautiful spot on an oxbow bend of the river for hunting in the fall. The world they occupy is much more welcoming than the one that earlier occupants had known. Summers are beautiful. Trees flourish again. Healthy conifers are returning to the nearby mountain slopes. Springs have been replenished and mountain streams flow again. Bison are returning to the area in larger numbers as the grasslands expand back into the pre-drought range. The main difference for these people and those who preceded them is that these folks have more leisure time and less hunger.

Camp occupants butcher and process three bison (one mature adult, one young adult, and one calf of six to seven months in age), along with one prong-horn. The children successfully snare a rabbit or hare. The women roast some of the meat and boil some as well, as evidenced by two types of fire-broken rock. The rocks used for boiling shatter when they meet cold water. Remains of fish or frogs and freshwater mollusks round out the menu.

Where their predecessors appear to have stayed just long enough to process meat, the occupants of this camp are spending time on both the daily and seasonal work of life. Women scrape and finish hides, using an awl to punch holes where laces will go. They likely are also making moccasins for winter and repairing or replacing clothing.

The men take time to refurbish their toolkits by re-sharpening worn tools and replacing those that are beyond repair, using the eclectic mix of stone available nearby. They leave behind four Oxbow points, and a bunch of unfin-ished biface blanks in various stages of manufacture. It seems odd that they would do the work only to leave the points behind. Perhaps they decide to move on to a place with better stone, or maybe they think they will return here, but something happens to divert their course.

Summary

As conditions changed during these three periods of Oxbow occupancy at the Sun River site, so did the types and diversity of animals killed for food. The three deeply buried living floors document the transition from a hotter and drier climate to one quite similar to what we know today. The first two occupations took place during what used to be known as the Altithermal, which paleoclimatologists now refer to as the mid-Holocene Warm Period or the Holocene Climatic Maximum, which was 1° to 2° C (1.8° to 3.6° F) warmer than the average summer temperature in 1950. During this mid-Holocene drought, the lakes of the American Great Basin dried up.[7] The third occupation saw improved conditions for making a living.

The Sun River was probably one of a limited number of oases where food animals remained available.[8] Just over 80 percent of the identifiable bones found in the 5,200 BP occupation were pronghorn, probably because that species' sagebrush-grass habitat had expanded during that time. In contrast, bison had to follow the grass wherever they could find it. Life was hard on the animals as well as for the hunters.

Around 4,500 years ago, site occupants had more foods to choose from. Evidence of their varied diet, including bison, indicates that grasslands were beginning to become more productive and water was more plentiful, causing people to have more confidence that they would get through the winter. Even so, they got every edible morsel out of the animals they killed.

By the time the most recent level was occupied, sometime between 3,800 and 3,500 years ago, conditions likely had become similar to those of modern times. Bison were once again grazing in the Sun River country, as were elk and deer, followed by wolves, just as they were when Meriwether Lewis passed through these same lands in July 1806.

Adaptation to Climate Change on Montana's High Plains

In the big scheme of things, climate is never constant. Humans have always known changes, some within individual lifetimes, some spanning the lives of several generations, and some over long cycles that go unnoticed on the human scale. One obvious response to the long-term aridity evidenced by the pollen sequence documented at the Oxbow site is that people need to locate near reliable sources of drinking water. These adaptations were not limited to the Great Plains. Worldwide, around 5,500 years ago, humans began to cluster in areas of dependable water. The most impressive examples are those "early civilization" sites along the Tigris-Euphrates, the Nile, the Indus, and the Ganges Rivers. People developed irrigation during these centuries to serve growing agricultural communities.

Over time, people in the Great Plains shifted their locations to more reliable water as evidenced by the concentration of archaeological sites along the eastern edge of the Rocky Mountains. Oxbow points, made and used between

5,200 and 3,500 years ago, are commonly found in the Northern Plains to the northeast, even into Manitoba. Their presence on Sun River likely reflects a response to unfavorable climate conditions. People, like animals, had to move. Water was the director of this forced migration. The eastern edge of the Rocky Mountains, with its multitude of creeks and springs and its greater diversity of plants and animals, provided a refuge. It still does. ✢

21

PRAYER ROCKS AND SACRED PAINT ALONG THE OLD NORTH TRAIL

I have been intrigued by the Old North Trail since I first read the account of Chief Brings-Down-the-Sun, as he told it to Walter McClintock in 1905.[1] In the mystery-evoking words of this Pikunni (Piegan Blackfeet) chief:

> There is a well known trail we call the Old North Trail. It runs north and south along the Rocky Mountains. No one knows how long it has been used by the Indians. My father told me it originated in the migration of a great tribe of Indians from the distant north to the south, and all the tribes have, ever since, continued to follow in their tracks. The Old North Trail is now becoming overgrown with moss and grass, but it was worn so deeply, by many generations of travelers, that the travois tracks and horse trail are still plainly visible.

Some people believe this trail dates back to the last days of the continental glaciers, more than ten millennia ago. Many migrations may have occurred in the pre-colonization past. One of the best documented is that of the Athabaskan groups who fled interior Alaska and the Yukon after a major earthquake shook their world around 1,200 years ago. At least some of these groups traveled down the east side of the Rockies to the Yellowstone area, where they split up.

Some groups, including the Navajo and several bands of Apache people, ultimately settled to the west of the Rockies in the American Southwest, while others, including the Mescalero Apache, found a new homeland on the east side. They followed a well-traveled route.

Montana has the best documented segments of the Old North Trail, both in terms of physical evidence and travelers' tales. Upriver from White Bear Island on the Missouri (just south of present-day Great Falls), William Clark followed this old trail, which he referred to as a road. His journal entry for July 18, 1805, included an intriguing mention that the road "is wide and appears to have been dug in maney places."[2] The following year, Meriwether Lewis followed a stretch of the Old North Trail at the base of Lewis and Clark Pass until his party veered off toward their destination on the Missouri, leaving the main trail that continued northward (see Chapter 22, "Lewis & Clark Pass and the Search for Shishequaw: A Roundabout Story").

Brings-Down-the-Sun was personally familiar with the trail. He told McClintock that it transected the continent, north to south. Eventually, its integrity had been obliterated by roads and towns of White men. He had traveled it so often that he knew "every mountain, stream and river far to the south, as well as towards the distant north." He remembered:

Brings-Down-the-Sun and his wife, 1905. PHOTOGRAPH BY WALTER MCCLINTOCK, COURTESY OF THE YALE COLLECTION OF WESTERN AMERICANA, BEINECKE RARE BOOK AND MANUSCRIPT LIBRARY.

It forked where the city of Calgary now stands. The right fork ran north into the Barren Lands as far as people live. The main trail ran south along the eastern side of the Rockies, at a uniform distance from the mountains, keeping clear of the forest, and outside of the foothills. It ran close to where the city of Helena now stands, and extended south into the country inhabited by a people with dark skins, and long hair falling over their faces.

He knew some of these details from a story told to him by his father about a Blackfeet expedition that went south to visit the dark-skinned people with hair falling over their faces. Where Blackfeet and other tribes of the northwestern Plains and their neighbors to the west wore their hair pulled off their faces in braids, some of the Puebloan peoples of the American Southwest, including Santa Domingo on the Rio Grande, wore long bangs across their foreheads. This distinction would have been of interest to the Blackfeet travelers.

The father of Brings-Down-the-Sun told him of the group who went on this journey, including men, women, and children. Traveling with one's family was the Indian way, in contrast to White men who generally left their families back home. Since home was not a fixed location and life was a journey, traveling together was natural to their lifestyle. Brings-Down-the-Sun knew a man named Pemmican who had been on this expedition when he was twelve. He died around 1902 at the age of ninety-five, dating the journey to around 1820. The travelers were away from their people for four years. They took a longer route home by way of the "High Trees"—their name for the "Bitter Root" country. That journey took eighteen moons.

Archaeologist Dr. Brian "Barney" Reeves investigated this north-south trail between the Canadian border and the Sun River using aerial photography and ground truthing. His results included finding dozens of sections of trail tread in addition to cairns and other rock features across this rolling landscape at the base of the Rocky Mountain Front. Remnants of trails indicate two parallel pathways, one close to the mountain fringe and the other farther out. Snow depth and spring runoff were the influencing factors dictating which trail to follow.[3]

The Old North Trail from Black Butte near present-day Augusta. PHOTOGRAPH BY SALLY THOMPSON.

In places where the landscape allowed, family groups and friends rode side by side, rather than single file. These wide flats lack clear evidence of the trail. Other segments contain geographical features that funneled travelers into confined spaces. These are the places where deep ruts formed and cairns kept travelers from straying off course. The Rocky Mountain Front landscape, dominated by north-south trending ranges, creates rivers of a particular east-west inclination, and their numerous headwater streams crosscut the trail. For example, streams that flow into the Marias River from what the Blackfeet call the "Backbone of the World" include the various forks of the Two Medicine River and Cut Bank, Badger, Whitetail, and Birch Creeks. South of those, the trail crossed the various creeks that feed the Teton and Sun Rivers.

In the 1990s, I had the good fortune to be introduced to a Métis man named Lloyd Paul who had grown up around Augusta and knew a great deal about the Old North Trail. The route was still used by the local Métis community in the 1930s, when he was young. Lloyd took me to see a number of trail remnants and told stories remembered from his childhood. He told me about one boulder along the trail to the north of Sun River that he wished I could see. This boulder was huge and flat, he said, "like the hood of a car." What made it so intriguing was that it was covered with fist-sized cobbles. He knew it was a cultural feature, the cobbles left there by people, rather than something that occurred naturally. Although he tried, he was never able to reach the landowner for permission for us to access that remote spot. I carry the imagined scene in my mind.

Prayer Rocks and Sacred Paint along the Old North Trail

A decade later, I was on the trail again and had an opportunity to go onto private land to investigate a stretch of the trail marked by a substantial line of stones crossing a flat on the south side of a steep drop-off to the confluence of the forks of Deep Creek, a tributary of the Teton River. The cold wind coming down the valley and across the flat that day made me speculate that the long row of stones had been placed there as a windbreak so that people could see the trail despite accumulations of blowing snow. We followed the alignment to the edge of the terrace, aiming toward a few well-placed cairns to guide us down to the only accessible place to cross the creek within miles. The canyon is too rugged to the west, and the bluffs below this spot are too steep and unstable for access. No wonder cairns had been placed to guide travelers to this important crossing. We followed a gently sloped, shrub-lined side-cut down into a meadow below where the waters emerge from the canyon, all the while clapping and alerting any bears of our presence. We had been told that an enormous grizzly boar had recently been seen around that area. Thankfully, we didn't run into any bears, but the strong, musky smell on the north side of the creek was enough to tell us that we had explored all we were

going to see of the Old North Trail that day. We turned back the way we came, grateful not to have used our pepper spray.

Knowing of my interest in both the Old North Trail and the Lewis and Clark story, in 2002, my friend Troy Helmick of Townsend offered to show me and a colleague some cairns he had recently found along a trail in the nearby Limestone Hills that seemed to correspond with William Clark's description of lands south of Helena. We met up a few weeks later, and Troy drove us

Troy Helmick and a cairn on the Old North Trail near Townsend, Montana. PHOTOGRAPH BY KIM LUGTHART, UM REGIONAL LEARNING PROJECT, COURTESY OF SALLY THOMPSON.

on backroads to the ancient Indian road that Clark followed between July 18 and 23, 1805, along a slope on the west side of the Missouri. The river in this area is now flooded by Canyon Ferry Reservoir, but trail remnants on the slope above remain clear.

Many things came together for me the day I stood with Troy next to a cairn along that ancient trail. He and I were two people who happened to know a lot about the archaeological record of that particular area. In collaboration with Dr. Les Davis, an archaeologist from Montana State University, Troy had spent years documenting artifacts exposed whenever reservoir levels dropped. Eventually he was able to recognize ten site areas and hundreds of flaked-stone artifacts—spear, dart, and arrow points; scrapers used for hide working and others used on wood, antler, and bone; drills for creating holes in hard material and awls for punching holes in leather—all of which I analyzed. Although site integrity had been destroyed by years of wave action, the artifacts themselves, in the context of that landscape, had much to convey. We determined that these sites clustered around an important crossing of the Missouri, and just upriver from the most important source of red paint in the region. Ten thousand years of intensive use by both east-side and west-side tribes documents the importance of this location.

Meriwether Lewis and William Clark tapped into each of these cultural features—the crossroad and the red clay—but had no context for their significance to the Native peoples of the region. On July 24, Lewis recorded in his journal that "Capt. Clark set out early and pursued the Indian road which took him up a creek some miles." Ironically, the road west, which Clark investigated, connected to one of the most direct routes to the Columbia, the explorers' destination. Had he followed it up and over the mountains there, he would have ended up on the Little Blackfoot River and there met up with the trail John Mullan would eventually select as the best wagon route between Fort Benton and Fort Walla Walla. Some seventy-five miles to the west of the Missouri crossing was the place the Salish knew as Snx̣ʷq̓ʷpuʔsáqs, meaning "the place where the trails separate." Today that place is known as Garrison Junction, where the Little Blackfoot meets the Clark Fork.

Clark didn't go to the top of the divide because the exploring party didn't have the option to travel that way without horses to haul their heavy equipment and supplies. Instead, they focused on finding Sacagawea's Shoshone relatives somewhere south of the Three Forks of the Missouri.

The same day that Clark explored the crossroad, Lewis, traveling by boat, noted seeing "a remarkable bluff of a crimson coloured earth"[4] Patrick Gass recorded in his journal that Sacagawea told them that "the bank of very red earth" was used by Natives "for paint."[5] This particular source of red clay was so vibrant that tribes throughout the region competed for access to it. In April of 1851, when John Owen and Salish companions were traveling up the Clark Fork between Flint Creek and the Deer Lodge Valley, after passing *Senkoposa'* (Snx̌ʷq̓ʷpuʔsáqs) Owen noted that they "passed one of the Indians roads to Buff. Called Vermillion road," referring to the red paint.[6] The Salish name, as recorded by Special Indian Agent Thomas Adams, was "Yeut-so-men."[7] What we now know as U.S. Highway 12 roughly follows the same route that eventually led to the coveted paint. Duncan McDonald, descendant of a Scottish fur trader and a Salish/Nez Perce mother, told *Missoulian* editor Dean Stone about this "deposit of vermilion which furnished the Indians with their red paint in those days. This was, likewise, disputed ground and there was everlasting combat waged over the right to use this iron clay."[8]

Crimson Bluffs on the Missouri River across from Townsend. PHOTOGRAPH COURTESY OF THE NATIONAL PARK SERVICE.

In the 1930s, a Kootenai elder named Ambrose Gravelle from the Canadian side of the Tobacco Plains told anthropologist Claude Schaeffer about earth paint gathered from the plains. They would travel from the Creston area and cross the Swan Range into the South Fork of the Flathead. They would go up that river and cross over the hydrographic divide into the Middle Fork. When they reached that river, they would travel upstream to a trail that would take them to the head of the Teton River or Deep Creek—the Old North Trail—which took them to the prairie. They called their route *namita meksmi* for the reddish-yellow paint they gathered there. They acquired *kamaksmi*, "yellow paint," north of Helena, and red paint, called *namita*, near Helena (probably at Crimson Bluffs).[9]

With all I had learned from the artifacts found at Canyon Ferry back in the 1980s, I had never known of the Crimson Bluffs and their importance as a paint source to the tribes of this region. The crossing was more than a good ford on a trail to buffalo. The people were there for the paint. This was the paint a Nez Perce and Salish contingent stopped to gather on their way to the peace council with the buffalo hunting tribes in August 1855 (see Chapter 7, "A Summer Like No Other").

The Crimson Bluffs were a sacred place where Mother Earth's paint was made available. Whenever I attend ceremonies with the Blackfeet, I wonder if the paint might have come from there. I never ask. That information is not mine to know unless someone chooses to tell me. They have explained that only women gather paint and only when it shimmers for them, giving them permission. There is a place on the Judith River where long ago several women lost their lives while gathering yellow paint. Perhaps they failed to ask permission. The riverbank collapsed and buried them.

⊕ ⊕ ⊕

Although I never set out to learn about paint, red ocher kept finding me. At a gathering of Kootenai elders in 2009 at Yellow Bay on Flathead Lake, John Mahseelah told a story that mentioned collecting red paint on the other side of the mountains from their Tobacco Plains homeland. My jaw dropped when I heard what came next. He mentioned that when his ancestors safely crossed the divide and reached the foothills of the Sun River country on their

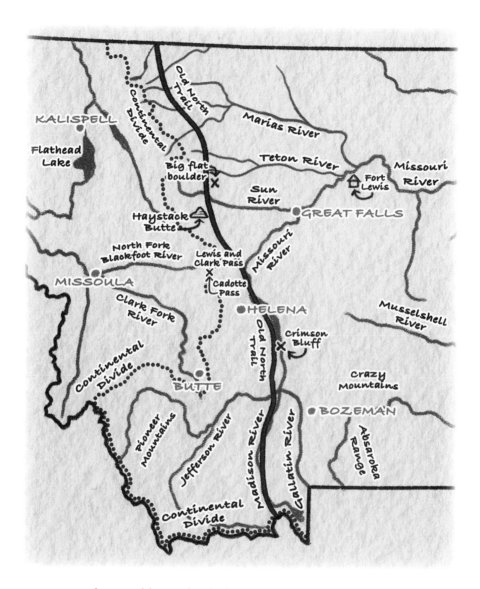

excursions, they would give thanks by placing a cobble on a huge rock long used for that purpose by their people. I had finally learned an explanation for the archaeological feature north of Sun River that Lloyd Paul told me about a decade before—the flat boulder, the size of a car hood, covered with cobbles. I've never visited that place made holy by so many prayer-filled cobbles, and have never seen a photograph, yet the picture formed through Lloyd's words remains vivid in my mind. Now I see Kootenai travelers stopping there, as well, stopping to give thanks for their safe journeys, and I try to remember to express gratitude when I complete a journey.

Volunteers for The Old Trail Museum in Choteau, led by local Métis elder Al Wiseman, have marked the trail in a number of places with inscribed boulders as a way to acknowledge this ancient road and to honor the past. The museum has an exhibit about the Old North Trail, and tour guides occasionally take visitors to interesting locations along the trail. Call before you go. ✛

Lewis & Clark Pass and the Search for *Shishequaw:* a Roundabout Story

During the Lewis and Clark Bicentennial I had the good fortune to direct the Regional Learning Project at the University of Montana. We focused on Native people along the trails followed by Lewis and Clark, rather than the explorers themselves. Their journals and maps oriented us along these old trails, like the one across Lewis and Clark Pass. When the explorers reached Travelers' Rest on their return trip to the States in early July 1806, Nez Perce guides helped Clark create a map for Lewis to follow from the Bitterroot-Clark Fork confluence, up the Blackfoot to the Sun River country, and on to the Missouri. The map shows rivers, creeks, and landmarks, including a mountain called Shishequaw, known today as Haystack Butte, a prominent cone-shaped knob southwest of Augusta, visible to the north from Montana Highway 200. This is the story of Lewis' journey on the trail to Shishequaw Mountain and the unusual sequence of events that led to an explanation of its name.

Following an 1806 Map Across Lewis & Clark Pass

Before I became acquainted with this 1806 map, I was already aware of the Blackfoot River trail to buffalo used by the local Salish and Pend d'Oreille tribes and by the Nez Perce. A few years earlier, I had been hired to examine cairns along an old trail at Lander's Fork. While I was trying to get oriented,

Eneas Vanderburg, one of the Salish elders, whistled me over to him and then proceeded to demonstrate how much more he knew about old trail markers than I, the paid professional. From one feature to the next he followed the trail, pointing out a variety of clues that often go unrecognized by archaeologists, such as trees with a strange bend a few feet off the ground. These had been bent when they were young to mark the way. They call the top of that trail *Smítu Sxʷ cu sí,* "Indian Fort Pass."[1] The Nez Perce call it *Qoq'aalx 'Iskit,* meaning "Buffalo road." I wanted to know more, and the Lewis and Clark journals and maps provided me the opportunity.

Initially I focused on the source of the name Shishequaw. The Nez Perce guides were the ones most likely responsible for the name since they had provided the geographical information for the map. But when I asked elder Horace Axtell about it, he shook his head. This fluent speaker of Nez Perce explained that even considering poor translation, the name wasn't a Nez Perce word. The sounds weren't right. Salish-speakers didn't recognize it either, and Lewis and Clark had no contact with Blackfeet up to that time, so the word was not likely to be theirs. Maybe I would have more luck exploring the trail itself.

⊕ ⊕ ⊕

A friend and I headed out for this adventure on Lewis and Clark Pass in early July 2001, the same time of year Lewis was traveling. In my pack I carried a copy of the map Lewis carried 195 years before, along with the USGS quad map for the area. We drove up Montana Highway 200 to Alice Creek, where a long, bumpy drive on a gravel road brought us to a poorly marked trailhead.[2] The plan was to compare our journey to the top of the pass with that of Lewis and his crew of nine men and seventeen horses, and, from a good vantage point, to see what we could see of the trail down the east side.

On July 5 and 6, 1806, Lewis and crew traveled up the Blackfoot River without any guide, noting the good trail, wildlife, and interesting landforms. Lewis' journal entry for July 7 is brief. The Nez Perce that accompanied him over Lolo Pass and to the Clark Fork had told him to follow the left fork as they approached the pass. That option is now known as Lander's Fork, named for one of the surveyors with the Pacific Railroad Survey crew in the 1850s.

From Lander's Fork, the trail veered eastward toward Alice Creek and on to the pass now known as Lewis and Clark (even though Clark was never there). The other trail led over an optional route across the divide, later named for Pierre Cadotte, an early settler at Fort Benton. These trails, used since time immemorial by indigenous people, now carry other names.

Lewis briefly noted that they followed up the creek "through a handsome narrow plain," and soon found themselves "passing the dividing ridge between the waters of the Columbia and Missouri rivers." He described the gap as low and an "easy ascent on the west side." From the top, "the fort mountain" was visible to the northeast, referring to Square Butte.[3]

Sergeant Gass provided more details. After a three-hour lunch break somewhere on Alice Creek, they traveled four more miles up that drainage to reach the top of the divide. On the Missouri side of the ridge, along what is now Green Creek, they found "a fine spring" where they camped for the night.

On July 7, 2001, after passing through a herd of Herefords, an easy hike of less than two wildflower-studded miles along an old two-track brought us to the top. I remember the red of Indian paintbrush alongside the fuchsia of sticky geraniums. Much of the way we followed Alice Creek, one of the many headwater streams that ultimately form the mighty Columbia River. Traces of travois trail treads were visible in places along the way. Almost to the

top, I noticed a partially buried, lichen-encrusted, stone alignment shaped like an arrow, an anchor, or a cross. It reminded me a bit of early Spanish crosses or the Camargue crosses from southern France with the crescent shape at the bottom. Clearly old, I wondered if it had been here when the Lewis party passed

The stone feature near the top of Lewis and Clark Pass. PHOTOGRAPH COURTESY OF *SARA SCOTT.*

through.[4] The top of the pass was covered with kinnikinnick, limber pine, and lupine. Visibility was limited by the gnarled pines—krummholz—at this windy spot at nearly 6,500 feet above sea level. Some of the limber pines that were struggling to survive may have been there when the explorers passed through.

We followed up a ridgeline to find a viewpoint and soon found ourselves looking over a magnificent expanse eastward across fifty miles of a dramatic glacial and volcanic landscape. White phlox and other low-growing cushion plants covered the rocky windswept slopes. The old map made perfect sense from that high vantage point. To the east, we too could see a butte, which we thought was Crown, rather than Square. To the north, we could see the very top of Haystack Butte beyond a ridge. Down below us, where the creeks are flowing toward the Missouri, the Mississippi, and the Gulf of Mexico, we saw a winding ranch road carved through the steep, tree-covered hillside. One area stood out because of the bright green of deciduous trees, which might indicate the spring where the Lewis party spent the night.

I would have loved to hike down from the top but knew better than to traipse through private property. Besides, a storm was brewing. As we loped back down the trail, scattered drops turn into a deluge. I prayed to Lightning-Maker to hold off until we were further downslope and out of this open, vulnerable terrain. The bombardment of pea-sized hail gave us a slight inkling of how Lewis' crew felt when they were pummeled by apple-sized balls near Great Falls that knocked some of them out cold! The rain stopped before we reached the rig. We dried off, replenished our water, drove back out the long bumpy road to pavement, and headed home. It was late. The other side of the divide would have to wait.

A few weeks later, I headed back to the pass, this time with two colleagues, Kim Lugthart and Ken Furrow. We left early to allow plenty of time to explore the trail on the east side of the mountains. A beautiful day greeted us, with a completely different array of wildflowers. This time the ridge was covered with pink mountain heather and blue alpine forget-me-nots, set off by the bright yellow of low-growing sulphur buckwheat. Once we reached the top, we spread out to look around. I almost stumbled over a couple of stone features that turned out to be collapsed ramparts—low stone walls, each approximately ten feet across. These must be the source of the Salish name "Indian Fort Pass."[5]

We enjoyed lunch overlooking the sea of near and distant knobs and then hurried back down to the rig, with miles to go before we slept.

A visit to the landowner was our next stop. I love the expansiveness of the east side of the Continental Divide and relished my first glimpse of the magnificent landscape we were about to enter as we crossed Rogers Pass. We followed along the Middle Fork of the Dearborn River, named on their west-bound trip by Lewis and Clark for the Secretary of War, Henry Dearborn. The first left off Montana Highway 200 is the Bean Lake Road. We took it and looked for the driveway to the house we could see at the base of Lewis and Clark Pass.

Steinbach was the name on the mailbox. We were greeted first by dogs, as is the way in this country, followed by the ranchers, Buz and Verna Steinbach. I told them about our interest in the old trail and how we tried to figure it out from the top but couldn't quite see what we needed.

"Well, let's go," Buz offered. "I'll show you this side of the pass." We jumped into his pickup and headed up the ranch road we had seen from the top. He told us where the road diverged from the old trail and shared stories about the area. His family roots are in this wild country at the edge of the Scapegoat Wilderness, a landscape made famous by A. B. Guthrie and Ivan Doig.

Back at the house, I showed the old map to the Steinbachs and talked them through the description in Lewis' journal. On July 8, 1806, at 6 A.M., Lewis and his men set out from their camp on a "small run under the foot of the mountain." He reported that the road descended the hill for one and a half miles and continued "down a branch over several hills and follows along the foot of the mountain hights passing five small rivulets running to the wright."[6] Sergeant Gass reported that they continued eastward another mile or so from their camp before turning north, then proceeded for "eight miles, passing a number of small streams or branches." Three miles along their northward course, from the top of a hill just before the trail drops into the canyon of the Dearborn, Lewis reported that they were able to see "the Shishequaw mountain," an estimated eight miles ahead of them.

We all agreed that Shishequaw could only be Haystack Butte. I asked if they have ever noticed any cairns marking a north-south trail, or ruts running that same general direction. Travelers frequently placed cairns at the edge of a terrace, where otherwise the trail trace might not be seen. Especially with so many willow-lined creek crossings, travelers wanted to be able to look ahead to see where they were going. A simple cairn saved time otherwise spent doing course corrections.

"Nope," Verna responded. "Nothing like that around here." She told us that she grew up across the highway and had ridden horses through this country all her life. She had never seen anything like what I described. Disappointed, I handed her my card and asked if she would call me if she ever happened to find any trail evidence. We headed on our way.

We drove slowly northward along the Bean Lake Road hoping to see evidence of the old trail, counting creek crossings as we went. I was convinced the trail Lewis followed northward from the base of the pass was part of the Old North Trail, and evidence should still exist (see Chapter 21, "Prayer Rocks and Sacred Paint along the Old North Trail"). I had seen cairns and trail treads on both sides of the Sun River to the north, and there was no reason for this major thoroughfare to have stopped near the base of Lewis and Clark Pass. Besides, the Lewis party followed a well-worn trail to the south. Private land on both sides kept our exploring to a minimum.

Haystack Butte from the southwest. PHOTOGRAPH COURTESY OF THE U.S. GEOLOGICAL SURVEY.

Like Lewis, after five creek crossings we saw Haystack looming straight ahead. From this angle, its shape is a perfect cone. We were either on or very near the old trail. New trails follow old. Native people in the region explain that their ancestors followed the animal trails, then the surveyors came and learned the routes of travel from the Indians. As we approached the deeply incised Dearborn, we looked for clues about the most likely place for a river crossing in the years before 1897, when engineers with steel beams constructed the high bridge over the river.[7] We parked and got out of the car to sleuth out this puzzle. I spotted a cairn at the lip of a shallow drop-off above the road. Its position helped us estimate where the trail crossed the river downstream from the bridge.

Dearborn River High Bridge. PHOTOGRAPH BY JET LOWE, COURTESY OF THE LIBRARY OF CONGRESS, HAER MONT, 25-AUG.V,1--12 (CT)Y.

⊕ ⊕ ⊕

In his journal, Lewis described Shishequaw as "a high insulated conic mountain standing several miles in advance of the Eastern range of the rocky mountains." His party left the broken and mountainous country through an open plain to "Shishequaw Creek," known today as Elk Creek. The route they were following continued "to the West of north" along the foot of the mountains. Since this was not the direction they were heading, they left the road and "steered through the plains." They ended their day when they reached the confluence of Shishequaw (Elk) Creek and the Medicine (Sun) River and camped on a large island. Today, this location is a short distance northeast of the town of Augusta.

⊕ ⊕ ⊕

Fast forward a year to when I stopped by the Steinbachs to return a book. I noticed an odd look on Verna's face when she opened the door.

"I've had your card by my phone for weeks," she told me, then paused before making her confession. "But I hate to be wrong," she said, with a twinkle in her eye. Her whole face lit up as she revealed that she did, in fact, find both cairns and treads as she explored northward from their place and onto the neighbor's.

"Yes!" I thought, a little smugly. Following old trails is a bit of an obsession with me, and when I find actual physical evidence, I feel like I've hit the jackpot. This was very exciting news, indeed.

Her discovery started when she noticed a small pile of rocks on a ridge to the north of Little Skunk Creek, the one that runs through the ranch. Instead of just thinking about it as a pile of rocks, she took the time to investigate whether this might be a trail marker. That clue led her along an obvious, yet faint, old trail.

"Come back when the snow melts and I'll take you out to see them," she invited, much to my delight. "We'll just have to be careful of the big old grizzly I almost ran into." She told me how she encountered its bedding area, strewn with some elk bones, right in the willows near the crossing. "Which would you prefer?" she asked. "Horseback or four-wheeler?"

"Definitely horseback," I replied. Now, a decade later, I hope to still have the chance.

History of Lewis and Clark Pass Trail
and the Mountain Known as Shishequaw

For forty years following Lewis' crossing of the pass, the written record about this trail is blank. Although the tribes continued to use this important route to buffalo, it appears that White travelers, at least those who kept journals, were following other trails. The absence may reflect choices Lewis made in Blackfeet country in late July, just two weeks after he crossed the divide. He, the Field brothers, and George Drouillard camped with a party of eight young Blackfeet on the night of July 25, 1806. Lewis awoke from a deep sleep around 3 A.M. to find some of their new companions attempting to steal their rifles, while others were driving off their horses. In the ensuing chase, Reubin Field stabbed one of these Pikunni to death and Lewis shot another. Lewis made his mark by hanging a U.S. peace medal around the victim's neck.[8]

The Blackfeet have their own versions of the story. Wolf Calf was a boy of thirteen when he joined the raiding party that would meet these White men trespassing through their country. He remembered they were friendly, and they camped together. The leader of the Blackfeet group directed the young men to steal some of the Americans' things, which they did. Wolf Calf saw the White men kill Calf Standing on a Side Hill with their "big knives." Afterward the Blackfeet ran off some of the White men's horses. Wolf Calf was 102 years old in 1895 when he shared his memories of these events with naturalist George Bird Grinnell. "When Grinnell asked why the Indians didn't pursue Lewis to retaliate for these deaths, Wolf Calf said they were frightened and 'ran away'—just like the white men, only in the opposite direction."[9]

Wolf Calf in 1895, 102 years old, one of the Blackfeet group whom Captain Lewis and party fought with on headwaters of Marias River in 1806. George Bird Grinnell gave this image to Olin D. Wheeler, who then published in his book, The Trail of Lewis and Clark, 1804–1904.

Wolf Calf's story tells of only one death, yet there were two. The man shot by Lewis was named He that Looks at the Calf. The story of his death was told to Alexander Culbertson of the American Fur Company in 1833, and the account, which generally conforms to Lewis' report, was recorded by James H. Bradley in the 1870s:

> Capt. Lewis had gone into camp on the Marias unfurling his flag according to custom. In the evening a number of Piegans came into the camp and were kindly received, but during the night a part of the Indians ran off with some of Capt. Lewis' horses, when the rest were detained by him as hostages. The next morning one of the hostages, watching an opportunity, seized a horse, mounted him and dashed away, when he was fired upon by a soldier and killed.[10]

After these killings, the Blackfeet were very aggressive toward Americans. The Blackfeet called them "Long Knives" to distinguish them from Canadians, based on the six-foot-long espontoons carried by American soldiers. A few years later, Canadian fur trader David Thompson learned the Blackfeet were keeping the Long Knives out of the area because of these killings.[11]

American fur traders eventually made their way into Blackfeet Country. Each fort was built a little farther up the Missouri than its predecessor. In 1846, the American Fur Company established Fort Lewis across the river from what would soon become Fort Benton. From there, the head of navigation, they began to look for ways to expand their business. One of their traders, Charles Larpenteur, tried to locate Lewis and Clark Pass in October of 1848. He left Fort Benton bound for the Bitterroot Valley to establish direct trade with the Salish. The party of eleven men, plus a young Blackfeet guide, traveled with carts and wagons and the horses to pull them. From Fort Benton, the traders traveled to Sun River. The steep crossing required them to modify the bank to get the wagons down and into the water. They ate their dinner, then made an easy crossing of the river and set up camp below the ford. Their young guide was nowhere in sight. By morning it was clear he had abandoned them.

Larpenteur decided to leave the outfit where they were and, with his hunter, set out to find the trail to the pass. They traveled with only a little sugar and coffee, expecting to find meat along the way. However, like Lewis and Clark learned when crossing the Bitterroots in October 1805, Larpenteur found that "when one gets in the mountains he is out of the range of game." On the fourth day out, having reached the summit of a mountain—presumably Lewis and Clark Pass—they encountered heavy snow. With no food and no practicable wagon road in sight, they had to turn back.[12]

A fortuitous meeting at Fort Benton on his return in late October provided the trader a second chance.[13] Some of the Small Robe band of Blackfeet had arrived and "among them was a small Indian named Sata, a half-breed Flathead and Blackfoot," who had grown up with the Salish, his mother's people. He and his father had often crossed the Continental Divide for bison with the Salish and, in 1846, they guided Fathers De Smet and Point from St. Mary's Mission to Fort Lewis, where they briefly overlapped with Larpenteur. Sata told him he could find a wagon road and would show him the way. Larpenteur's eagerness to meet with the Flatheads—"wagon road or no wagon road"—got the better of him, despite his recent experience of snow atop the pass. He "determined to try that famous guide." Three days later, they were on their way again. Two days travel got them to the base of the mountains, when their plans, once again, were about to change.

> Sata remarked that we had best try to get some meat, as game was scarce in the mountains, and now was the time to provide for ourselves. Thinking myself somewhat of a hunter I went a little ahead of the party next morning, and soon saw some objects crossing a small brook, at so great a distance that I was unable to distinguish whether they were men or game. Hoping they were deer, I slipped the cover off my double-barrel, and went after them. When in the act of shooting, I discovered on my left, behind a small hill, an object which I could not make out, but thought was probably a wolf. Sata and my man, who had come up by this time, asked me, "What have you seen?" I replied in Blackfoot, "Matahpey," meaning "people."[14] On our advancing

a few steps, fifteen naked Indians, with guns, bows, and arrows rose up before us, ready to shoot; but Sata cried out, "My brothers! my brothers! don't shoot! It is I." Hearing this they put down their arms, came up, and shook hands. They said, then, that they had discovered us, taken us for beaver trappers, and had made arrangements to kill us. As to myself, whom they took to be the chief, they had me killed already in imagination; one was to have my stuball horse, one my sky-blue coat, another my gun, and so on in the partition of my effects. The object I had taken to be a wolf was one of the Indians, who remarked himself that he had got a little nearer me than the balance of his party, and that I might be glad his gun was hard on the trigger; for he had aimed well at my breast, and I surely would have been a dead man, had he got his gun to go off. On learning where we were going, they told my guide that it was impossible for us to cross the mountains; that they had had great trouble to return, and that our animals could not get over. Thereupon, my Sata gave up the idea of going any farther, and concluded to turn back with them.

Larpenteur never did make it over Lewis and Clark Pass. That winter, when the Blackfeet learned of the American Fur Company's intentions to establish trade with the Salish, they made it clear that they did not approve. The next summer they would "remain south of the Missouri, with the intention of carrying on war with the Flatheads." With that warning, the fur company traders abandoned their plan.

Members of the Pacific Railroad Survey team surveyed the various passes across the Rockies in the mid-1850s. When it came time to select the route for a military road to connect Fort Benton to Fort Walla Walla, John Mullan argued for the Little Blackfoot route over the Blackfoot River options and won, shifting commercial traffic southward after 1861. For those still aiming for the Sun River country from the Blackfoot River valley, Euro-Americans seemed to prefer Cadotte Pass, but the Indians never stopped using the old trail followed by the Lewis party. It became known as the Pend d'Oreille Trail.[15]

General John Gibbon was head of the U.S. Army in Montana during an interlude between the Sioux Wars of the 1860s and the Nez Perce flight of 1877. Based at Fort Shaw in the fall of 1871, his troops rediscovered, surveyed, and mapped the two passes in the vicinity of the mountain that had become known as "The Haystack."[16] He compared his observations with compass readings and the description provided by Lewis and concluded that the more northerly one was the one that Lewis had crossed.[17] Soon after, however, the association of Lewis with the trail once again faded and wasn't resurrected for another two decades.

Elliot Coues, the ornithologist, surveyor, and historian who published the first edited volumes of the Lewis and Clark Expedition, made news on October 17, 1893, when he rediscovered Lewis and Clark Pass. By that time, it would seem, the name for the pass was unknown, at least by locals. Coues' story, as reported in the *Helena Independent*, holds important glimpses into a history otherwise lost. "When I started from Cascade to climb the main chain of the Rockies," he reported, "I had nothing to go upon but a mental image of Lewis & Clark Pass, on top of which I proposed to stand." He had asked "the natives of what had long been Lewis & Clark County" (since only four decades had passed since the earliest non-Indian settlers arrived in Blackfeet Territory, it is unclear what "natives" he asked), but none of them recognized a pass of that name. They told him that Cadotte's Pass was the only route over the main divide. Then one person mentioned another pass, somewhere north of Cadotte's, that was known as Pend d'Oreille Pass. Coues knew he finally had a lead. When he was told that an old Indian trail from Sun River led to this Pend d'Oreille gap, he felt confident that this was the Indian trail Lewis had followed. A young man named Michael Casey told him "he knew nothing of any pass," but nonetheless, could get him to the old trail. That was enough for Coues to agree, and they began their adventure, approaching from the southeast. The first thing he recognized "was Shishequaw mountain of Lewis and Clark, which stands out so strongly as Heart mountain on John Mix Stanley's bird's-eye Pacific Railroad Survey lithograph, but which Casey called Haystack butte."[18]

Despite the challenge for historians to relocate the pass, Native people continued to visit familiar places along that route. A full century after Lewis passed through, and a couple of decades after the buffalo were gone, a homestead family on Alice Creek would see Indian people traveling along the old trail. Old habits die hard, and ancient ones even harder.[19]

Serendipitous Discoveries

A year or so after this field trip with Lewis' journal, when I had moved on to other subjects, I ran across a word in a trader's journal that took my breath away. I did one of those head-jerking double-takes and re-read a passage in François-Antoine Larocque's 1805 *Yellowstone Journal*. The word was "*Shiskequais.*" On August 26, 1805, one day after the Crows had skirmished with another tribe, Larocque reported, "The young men paraded all day with the scalps tied to their horses bridles, sing[ing] and keeping time with the Drum and Shiskequais or Rattle." *Shiskequais* was old French for rattle.[20] Of course! I had long heard some of the landforms in the vicinity below Lewis and Clark Pass called the Rattle Hills. I had come to believe the name referred to Crown Butte and some of the other volcanic remnants around that magnificent form. But here was evidence that Haystack was known as "The Rattle."

Fast forward again to 2021, when I was attending a medicine lodge ceremony in the lower Two Medicine valley on the Blackfeet Reservation. During a break, I visited with a friend who is a member of the Crazy Dog Society. I mentioned a painting done in 1846 by Jesuit missionary Nicolas Point of the leader of the Crazy Dogs along with a description of the rattle he carried. My friend listened quietly, nodding when I was finished, and then told me that special rocks for use in those rattles are found down around Augusta on Haystack Butte. *Awanáán* is their word for rattle. They call Haystack Butte "Rattle Mountain."

The explanation took twenty years for me to discover, but it was well worth the wait to understand the rich history embedded in the name Shishequaw. I realized that looking for answers in the written record alone could never tell the complete story. Even a decade of on-the-ground exploration didn't solve the riddle. In the end, the cultural continuity among the Blackfeet and the Crazy Dog Society provided the key link to understanding how this name, whether in French, English, or Blackfoot, became associated with what western Montanans know as Haystack Butte. ✤

Crazy Dog with rattle, circa 1930s. PHOTOGRAPH FROM THE BLACKFOOT PAPERS, VOLUME ONE: PIKUNNI HISTORY AND CULTURE, *BY ADOLPH HUNGRY-WOLF. PHOTOGRAPH PROVIDED BY SALLY THOMPSON WITH PERMISSION OF ADOLPH HUNGRY-WOLF.*

23

BADGER-TWO MEDICINE
CONFESSIONS OF A NAÏVE ANTHROPOLOGIST
IN A BLACKFEET HOLY LAND

West of the Blackfeet Reservation and south of Glacier National Park lies an area of some 130,000 acres called "the Badger-Two Medicine," after the two rivers within its boundaries. These lands are now within the domain of the Lewis and Clark National Forest, but prior to 1896 the mountains were part of the Blackfeet Reservation and the aboriginal homeland of the southernmost band of the Blackfoot Confederacy, Amskapi Pikunni, the Blackfeet of Montana.[1] At that time, and again a hundred years later, non-Indians were drawn to the area's potential mineral wealth and sought ways to exploit that possibility. Both attempts at exploitation have been heart-wrenching to the Blackfeet. The complicated history presented here highlights the contrasting cultural values of the Blackfeet and values brought to this continent by Europeans. My own history with the Badger-Two Medicine seriously rocked my understanding of the world. Like a seismic tremor, glimpses into the contrasting realities of my world and theirs destabilized the foundations of my education and even my experience.

Risky Business

In the early 1990s, I found myself bearing a weighty responsibility for influencing the decision as to whether these lands should be protected from gas

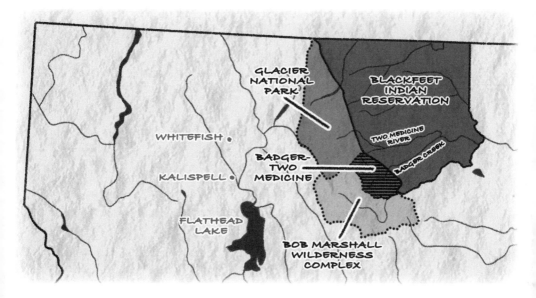

and oil exploration. The magnitude of this responsibility didn't hit me at first. My co-investigator (and husband at that time), Weber Greiser, and I were eager to have the opportunity to conduct research under a new process—the investigation of Traditional Cultural Properties (TCPs)—enacted in 1990 under the National Historic Preservation Act. The Badger-Two Medicine area was threatened by a plan to develop numerous gas wells and a processing plant, all linked together with interconnecting roads. Federal law requires such projects to consider cultural impacts to places deemed significant according to the National Register of Historic Places standards. At issue in this case was (and continues to be) the relative value of unimpeded Blackfeet cultural practices compared to gas development.

Looking back, I cringe at the memory of how naïvely we began our work. We posted a notice in the local paper, announcing a public meeting to be held in the Browning High School gym. On the appointed evening, I found myself standing in front of a small crowd—twenty or thirty people—looking into their unwelcoming faces, and began to tell them the requirements of our contract with the Lewis and Clark National Forest. We let them know that we would be conducting interviews in the community about important cultural places within the Badger-Two Medicine and wanted their input. When I'm nervous,

I tend to talk more than necessary. Maybe if I re-stated what I just said, it would come across better. It didn't. Finally, someone in the crowd spoke.

I don't remember too many details of that evening, more the feelings. Someone expressed that the Blackfeet people were tired of outsiders coming in and taking their stories away. The individuals who were the most knowledgeable preferred to speak in their own language and wanted their stories protected. On reflection, I wondered why we didn't have a translator working with us, and why we had not considered how to ensure that their traditional cultural knowledge would not be made public. We were beginning to realize how inadequately prepared we were to do this job and how presumptuous it was to expect traditional elders, whose first and best language is Blackfoot, to speak to us in English.

We accomplished little on that first trip, except to learn that we needed to start over. In the meantime, Floyd "Tiny Man" Heavy Runner, head of the Crazy Dog Society, approached the Blackfeet Tribal Business Council to request that authority for the project be handed over to him. According to traditional leadership protocols, he had the responsibility for protecting those mountain lands—Mistakis, "the Backbone of the World." The council agreed. From that point on, Tiny Man directed our effort and approach, to the extent the contract allowed.

To get us going on better footing, Tiny Man suggested that we host a "feed." That occasion would bring people together and give us time to get to know each other. Again, I have forgotten most of the particulars about the gathering except the shift in receptivity. The community center was full. Berry soup was on the menu along with bison stew and fry bread. Weber and I had instructed our children about not refusing food. I watched the surprise come to the face of our youngest, Ingrid, after biting into a spoonful of the berry soup and finding it laced with bison fat. Tim and Sarah, too, put down their spoons and wondered what to do, remembering not to be rude. Eye contact was being made from across the table and soon the bowls found their way to some elders, eager to enjoy a second helping. After the meal we had fun learning to play a stick game, while we all got to know each other. Faces opened, relationships formed, and people stepped forward to schedule interviews.

Tiny Man Heavy Runner and Mary Ellen Little Mustache. PHOTOGRAPH COURTESY OF MARY ELLEN LITTLE MUSTACHE.

With Tiny Man, we discussed our Forest Service contract, in which we were required to identify Traditional Cultural "Properties," with all that the term conveyed. The language of the regulations directed us to draw lines around important properties so that proposed impacts could avoid identified places of significance. We soon learned how much this work would require us to stretch beyond the bounds of our archaeological training with its focus on tangible evidence of past and continuing site use. Tiny Man helped us understand the conflict resulting from the contract's emphasis on physical places. In their world, he explained, some places matter because they have *not* been changed by human agency. For most non-Indians, a church, mosque, or temple is where sacred rites take place. These are much easier to observe and evaluate than places where ritual rocks were gathered for a sweat in preparation for a fast, for example, or places where spirit beings have been or might be accessed. Such places are not so much archaeological sites as they are places that are powerful in a spiritual sense, what White culture might call intangible.

Tiny Man patiently and kindly helped us negotiate this foreign landscape. To be patient, kind, and generous is part of Blackfeet ways, and, in this case, it was also the best way for this Crazy Dog member to get the results that were so needed to protect these lands. The more we understood, the better we would represent their perspective. He helped us to begin to understand the awesome responsibility we carried, for we would be asking people to disclose the foundations of their religious and cultural beliefs in order to prove that the area in question was (and is) important enough to be protected from desecration. They would have to translate into a foreign tongue and worldview that which is most sacred to them. This is risky business. Participants would risk loss of personal powers acquired through religious practices, and perhaps contribute to wider cultural damage.

For people who have never left their homelands, 100 years is not so long ago. In Blackfeet oral history, a strong cultural cord binds one generation to the next. Also, for many tribal members the memory is fresh of what was lost through the "Ceded Strip" negotiations of 1895. The strip contained what became Glacier National Park as well as the Badger-Two Medicine. From experiences related to both areas, and many others, this tribe has learned not to trust representatives of the U.S. government. For example, their elders passed down a story of how the White men tricked their leaders by distributing liquor when they went "off record" one night during the negotiations. Deals were made that night that negatively changed the course of their history and their lives today.

The questions we asked put our respondents in a bind: If they didn't tell, then there would be no documentation of traditional cultural practices, and thus, nothing to protect. If they did tell, the mystery that sustains them might be compromised. For way too long—until the passage of the Native American Freedom of Religion Act in 1978—they had held their ceremonies in secret because the rites had been outlawed by missionaries and then the government for more than 100 years. For them to reveal more about their practices was of concern to them because they had already lost so much, starting with testimony given by their leaders during the 1895 negotiations, which resulted in their loss of authority over those mountain lands. The people we interviewed were understandably worried that history might repeat itself, and fearful that the more they told, the more they would lose. The more we understood of their dilemma, the more sensitive and respectful we became.

Interviews we recorded as part of the TCP process echoed back to the testimony given in 1895. Participants generally agreed that they went into those mountains for many traditional activities such as ritual gathering of plants and paints. This land, they said, is their church. The high mountain peaks have always been places to seek connection with spirit helpers. Napi, the incarnate Creator, told the first dreamer to seek a place several days away from other people; that is, a remote area. He gave instructions for a sweat lodge ritual as part of the quest. This activity requires the presence of particular rocks and pure water. The best location of a dream bed is one that requires great bravery, either due to its proximity to fierce predators, such as grizzlies, or because of situating the dream bed on a high, narrow ledge. Many such places exist in the remote mountains of the Badger-Two Medicine area, but Tiny Man encouraged us not to focus too much on the particulars. In and of themselves, they were not what mattered. We should focus, instead, on the integrity of the whole area, the landscape fed by these waters.

The mountains, he explained, hold gifts from the Creator, gifts that provide for the people's long-term health and well-being. Many plants, animals, and minerals found there are used in Blackfeet customary practices—religious rites—and the high peaks allow seekers to bridge Earth and Sky. The spirits of these mountains remain unsullied by the modern world. Pure water still flows from springs and meltwater, and medicine plants remain uncontaminated. Mistakis provides a refuge for spirit and body.

People gather at a medicine lodge, 1903. PHOTOGRAPH BY WALTER MCCLINTOCK, COURTESY OF THE BEINECKE LIBRARY, YALE UNIVERSITY.

The two stream valleys are often selected as sites for the Okan—the Medicine Lodge ceremony—and always have been. The name Two Medicine comes from a time, long ago, when two medicine lodges were erected on that creek at the same time.[2] The traditional name for the month of July is Coming Together Moon because of this important ceremonial time for the people to gather together.

I realized that theirs is a spiritual reality while the government's is material, measurable, separable. We needed to understand that, in the world of the Blackfeet, discrete lines could not be drawn around individual parts. An analogy might be helpful here. If we were considering the human body instead of a landscape, the government's approach would have us protect only the organs. The flaw in that model is that by focusing on the parts, we ignore the interdependent whole. To isolate significant areas (i.e., "the organs") for protection would be to open every other place to development.

A Blackfeet seeker would be unable to purify himself with water contaminated from drilling activities, and it would be impossible to fast and pray for four days while listening to a drilling rig buzzing down below. The integrity of the entire animate landscape would be destroyed.

The Badger-Two Medicine is not only the tribe's last refuge for matters of spiritual well-being, but it also serves as the best remaining place to hunt; in a sense, it is their "bread basket." Activities associated with gas and oil development would interrupt traditional hunting and other gathering activities. Again, under the guidelines of the TCP process, the Pikunni world and the one imagined by the authors of the regulations were incompatible. We couldn't draw lines around important hunting and gathering areas without compromising the integrity of the whole living system.

I did my best to understand. Even listening, though, I couldn't really hear. The world in which I grew up held such dramatically different views of reality that I literally couldn't understand much of what was told to me—I knew the words but could not fathom the meaning in terms of *their* understanding. Thankfully, through the contributions of some extraordinarily patient individuals as we worked through the process, enough sank in for us to realize that we could not segregate one cultural use area from another. Curly Bear Wagner, the Cultural Preservation Director, was particularly helpful, as were the many elders and practitioners who had spent so much time in those mountains. Based on the results of our study, along with previous studies, we prepared a Cultural District nomination to the National Register of Historic Places, to protect the whole sacred landscape.

Being Changed

More than thirty-plus years have passed since I undertook the life-altering Badger-Two Medicine cultural preservation work. I have continued to spend time in the Blackfeet community, including attending three five-day Okans on those two streams over the last decade.

To sponsor a medicine lodge means that a woman and a man will "sit holy" for four days, expressing gratitude for the sun's daily blessings and praying for the people, while fasting. Word goes out in advance, and by the time the couple enters the lodge, the community has set up their painted tipis in a

Okan camp on Badger Creek, 2014. PHOTOGRAPH BY SALLY THOMPSON.

large, embracing circle. In 2013, more than two decades after the TCP work, during the first Okan I attended, I began to fathom the differences in the ways Blackfeet and White people know the world.

Close friends of mine were the sponsors of the gathering in the valley of Badger Creek. I set up my camp with the family—my adopted family—and helped prepare food for the many people who would visit each day while the couple fasted in the holy lodge. Each morning, as the sun rose higher, heat waves danced like mirages. We moved slowly as the thermometer passed 100 degrees, and we prayed for our loved ones, sitting by the fire as they prayed for all of us and all creation. Around the camp, adults visited quietly, while laughter rang out from the children playing in the cold creek waters.

On the fourth and final day of prayer, I was visiting with a friend who is a leader in the Crazy Dogs Society[3] (see Chapter 22, "Lewis & Clark Pass and the Search for *Shishequaw*"). He was taking a break from his responsibilities as camp manager. Our chairs were facing north. "Look at that," he said, nodding ahead of us. I looked up and saw a thick band of clouds, a weather front, steamrolling straight toward us. "The white band in the middle is hail." He's a science teacher, so I took his word for it. He's also a keen observer of the natural world, like most Native people I know.

Others began to take notice as a breeze started to flap the awning behind us, over the cookstove. One of the men seated nearby had been introduced to me on the first day as a famous weather dancer from one of the northern tribes of the Blackfoot Confederacy. These men play an important role in camps such as these because of their power to influence the weather. As the storm was beginning to bear down on us, I didn't understand why he remained seated. Suddenly one of the women jumped up, ran into her tipi, then appeared before the weather dancer with an offering of tobacco, which he accepted, then got right to work. He went to the north edge of camp and began his prayers. He offered tobacco to Mother Earth and held an eagle feather skyward. As he danced, with a fierce wind blowing the fringe of his shirt, I marveled to see the storm take an abrupt ninety-degree turn. It jogged to the east and then back to the south, barely skirting the outer edge of the camp. It took down an unoccupied outhouse but left the supplicants to continue their prayers undisturbed in their tipi. I learned later that they were completely unaware of the storm. If I hadn't witnessed this unnatural shift in the course of a storm, I might not have believed it. Afterward, a double rainbow appeared and lingered, like a blessing over the camp.

For the Blackfeet and other American Indian nations, the weather dancer's influence over the storm was not unusual. In their reality, many people have active relationships with some aspect of nature. One only needs to sincerely seek it for the spirit world to respond. In fact, the very reason for this Okan stemmed from such an event. Two years before, a grass fire had rushed toward my friends' home on the prairie below the towering peaks of the Two Medicine country. They watched from their relatives' house on the ridge above and prayed that somehow their home would be spared. When the fire split and went around their beloved abode, my adopted sister, out of her deep gratitude, vowed to sponsor a medicine lodge, as her way to give back to the world that cares for her and her family.

Watching a human being redirect a storm is antithetical to the part of me raised in a world explained by Aristotle, Euclid, and Newton. Another part of me, though, the one influenced by some mystical events in childhood and an increasing number of unexplainable experiences through my adult life, was able to accept what I saw, even though I didn't understand it.

Last summer, I attended another Okan on Badger Creek, in a protected prairie overseen by Heart Butte and Feather Woman Mountain. I could feel the presence of those mountains like I had never experienced before. If I had to describe the feeling, I would call it a heart-connecting force that radiated from those mountains. During this third experience of the Okan, I found myself more immersed—no longer self-consciously looking for ways to fit in and to not be in the way. I have come to know that Native people, raised in keeping with their traditional beliefs, have a different understanding of the living world and the spiritual forces that hold it all together. I don't understand it, but I have come to accept the unexplainable. I saw a weather dancer move the storm and felt love from a mountain.

Heart Butte and Feather Woman Mountain. PHOTOGRAPH BY TRACEY VIVAR, USED WITH PERMISSION.

Looking back to 1991, I realize how much I have absorbed of what Tiny Man and Curly Bear, so long ago, tried to teach me. They are long gone from this world, but, somehow, I think they know.

Afterward

In 1994, Tiny Man decided to go straight to the largest lease-holding corporation on Badger-Two Medicine lands to try to influence the outcome. If they understood the consequences, perhaps they would withdraw their leases. This humble man traveled to the Netherlands to meet directly with managers at Royal Dutch Petroleum. Against what seemed like hopeless odds, he successfully influenced them to retract their leases. In 1997, based on both environmental and cultural concerns, then-Lewis and Clark National Forest Supervisor Gloria Flora declared a fifteen-year moratorium on all future oil and gas leasing. Since then, the Blackfeet Nation's Historic Preservation Office, under the leadership of John Murray, has continued to work for the protection of these precious lands.

In 2002, after thorough review, the federal Advisory Council on Historic Places approved the Badger-Two Medicine Cultural District nomination in its entirety, thus encompassing the entire landscape of the Badger-Two Medicine.[4] They recognized the Pikunni understanding of a whole, intact, interconnected place of sacred lands and waters.

Efforts to protect the Badger-Two Medicine, by the Blackfeet and many allied individuals and organizations, like the Glacier-Two Medicine Alliance, have had impressive results. The last of the original seventeen leases was retracted in 2023. This holy area was to be protected, after all. Perseverance on the part of the Pikunni has paid off. They understand that the land, in all its sacred magnificence, has a certain power to protect itself, a power that insinuates itself into the core being of those who visit there. It might not find the visitor receptive the first, second, or even third time, but eventually it will find its way into the hearts of those who come, and their way of knowing the world will change. That was certainly true for me. ✢

NOTES

Chapter 1: Moncacht-apé's Incredible Journey

[1] See Paul Logan Allen's discussion of fledgling French geographical knowledge of the American Northwest in the seventeenth century in his book *Lewis and Clark and the Image of the American Northwest*, Dover, 1975:13-14.

[2] The English translation is woefully inadequate. See Gordon Sayre, "A Native American Scoops Lewis and Clark: The Voyage of Moncacht-apé." Commonplace, June 2005 http://commonplace.online/article/a-newly-discovered-map https://blogs.uoregon.edu/lpdpanddumont/histoire-de-la-louisiane-vol-iii-chap-7/

[3] Taken from Choctaw Creation Myth, Indian Legend website Archived 26 January 2013 at archive.today where it is listed as being in the public domain

[4] English edition.

[5] Chiwere, the language of the Missouria, is a Siouan language closely related to Ho-Chunk. The language of the Kaw, their neighbors up the Missouri River, is a member of the Dhegiha branch of the Siouan-Catawban language family. Although the two are related in the very distant past, they are not mutually intelligible.

[6] This concept of a woman needing to be back home for "lying in"—interpreted as time to give birth—is very European. Native women of the Northwest were at home wherever their seasonal rounds took them.

[7] Sayre, Gordon, "Dumont de Montigny and Le Page du Pratz," https://blogs.uoregon.edu/lpdpanddumont/2016/10/27/hello-world/2010. Sayre, Gordon, "Newly Discovered Manuscript Map by Antoine-Simon Le Page du Pratz," 2010. https://www.academia.edu/95129287/A_Newly_Discovered_Manuscript_Map_by_ Antoine_Simon_Le_Page_du_Pratz.

Chapter 2: The Moccasin Telegraph, 1805

[1] *The Journals of the Lewis and Clark Expedition*, Vol. 5, Gary E. Moulton, ed. Lincoln: University of Nebraska Press, 1983, 102.

[2] *Journals*, 5:126-127.

[3] https://wiki.bugwood.org/Lewis_and_Clark_sighted_by_the_Assiniboine_Indians

[4] *Journals*, 5:136.

[5] *Journals*, 5:161-162.

[6] "Assiniboine Chief Rosebud Remembers Lewis and Clark." DVD sent to all Montana schools through OPI.

[7] "Assiniboine Chief Rosebud Remembers Lewis and Clark." DVD sent to all Montana schools through OPI.

[8] Snake Butte is an important landmark, now on the Fort Belknap Reservation.

[9] *Journals*, 5:211.

[10] Montanans refer to the Pikunni as Blackfeet, due to the naming of their reservation. Members of the Confederacy in Canada are called Blackfoot.

[11] Darrell Martin, Sally Thompson interview, 2002.

[12] *Journals*, 5:241.

[13] *Journals*, 5:263.

[14] Ewers, John C., *The Blackfeet: Raiders on the Northwest Plains*. (The Civilization of the American Indians Series 49.) Norman: University of Oklahoma Press, Rep.1958:200.

[15] *Journals*, Vol. 5, Lewis entry, June 13, 1805.

[16] A "wythe" is a masonry term indicating a facing that is one-brick thick. Perhaps this width is what Lewis was referencing in his description.

[17] Gary Moulton, editor of the Lewis and Clark journals, notes the similarity to a Blackfeet medicine lodge, except for the lack of mention of the characteristic center pole. In addition, a Pikunni medicine lodge has no central fire and the structure is secured by a length of rope cut from the entirety of a single buffalo robe rather than willow brush.

[18] Vaughn, Robert, *Then and Now; or, Thirty-Six Years in the Rockies*. Minneapolis: Tribune Printing Co., 1900, 395.

[19] Sikey-kio witnessed the Malcolm Clarke murder in 1869, and helped to prevent the killing of his wife. Mr. Lewis came to Fort Benton in 1857, shortly after the Lame Bull (Judith River) Treaty had been ratified. He did various jobs and found himself herding horses in the Sun River country in 1868 and spending the winter at the abandoned Catholic Mission at Ulm. The next spring he made a preemption claim on 160 acres nearby, which became a successful "stock ranch." – [OBIT – July 1, 1914, *Great Falls Tribune*]

[20] Also spelled Pikuni or Pikunni, these people are the southernmost of the Blackfoot Confederacy tribes.

[21] *Journals*, 5:410.

Chapter 3: Never Give Up

[1] J. Nielson Barry, "Madame Dorion of the Astorians," *Oregon Historical Quarterly*, Vol 30, No. 3 (1929):272-278; Peter Stark, *Astoria: John Jacob Astor and Thomas Jefferson's Lost Pacific Empire*. HarperCollins.

[2] Denham, Danielle, "Marie Dorion: The Most Badass Woman in Oregon History." *The Oregon Life*, September 11, 2021. https://thatoregonlife.com/2021/09/marie-dorion-oregon-history/

[3] Irving, Washington, *Astoria, Or, Enterprise Beyond the Rocky Mountains*. New York: G. P. Putnam's Sons,1836. https://www.gutenberg.org/files/1371/1371-h/1371-h.htm *The Adventures of Captain Bonneville, U.S.A., in the Rocky Mountains and the Far West*. rev. ed. New York: G. P. Putnam's Sons, 1868; J. Nielsen Barry, "Madame Dorion of the Astorians," *Oregon Historical Quarterly*, Vol. 30, No. 3. Sept. 1929:273.

[4] The first post was in the vicinity of current-day Vale, Oregon, and the second post was a little west of Parma, Idaho.

[5] Their trappers' camp was in the vicinity of present-day Caldwell, Idaho.

6 Ross, Alexander. Adventures of the First Settlers on the Oregon or Columbia River. 1904: 265-270.

7 Gayle C. Shirley, *More Than Petticoats: Remarkable Oregon Women.* Helena, MT: Falcon Publishing, 1998.

8 Although there are no remaining fluent speakers of Chiwere, the language of Marie's mother, the Ho-chunk language is closely related. Wilbert Cleveland, a Ho-chunk language speaker, spoke with me about the concept of "giving up." June 29, 2022.

9 Cox, Ross. Adventures on the Columbia Rive. J. & J. Harper. 1832:129-138.

10 Gabriel Franchère,. *Narrative of a Voyage to the Northwest Coast of America in the Years 1811, 1812, 1813, and 1814.* Thwaites, Reuben Gold. ed. *Early Western Travels.* Vol. 6. Cleveland, OH: The Arthur H. Clark Company, 1904.

Chapter 4: William Hamilton's Questionable Adventure

1 *Billings Gazette,* May 9, 1907, p7.

2 *Billings Gazette,* June 30, 1927, p47.

3 W. T. Hamilton. "A trading expedition among the Indians in 1858 from Fort Walla Walla to the Blackfoot country and return." Helena, MT: Historical Society of Montana, Vol. 3. 1900.

4 The only route across the mountains from St. Mary's Lake that could conceivably fit the details of Hamilton's story is up to Swiftcurrent Pass and down along Logging Lake into the basin of the North Fork of the Flathead River. This was a well-used Kootenai trail.

5 Capt. Thomas Blakiston of the Palliser Expedition learned from the Kootenai that "white people always come in the fall, remaining the winter trading with them, and returning to Colvile, eight or ten days' journey, in the spring." Spry, Irene M. (1963) *The Palliser Expedition: The Dramatic Story of Western Canadian Exploration, 1857-1860.* Toronto: MacMillan. Republished Toronto: Fifth House Publishers, 1995.

6 Blakiston was in the Tobacco Plains a few months before Hamilton arrived, and his work proved that the trading post was a fraction of a degree to the south of the boundary line at 48 degrees 55' 5". Until that time, the HBC folks had all believed they were north of the line.

7 Chance, David H. "The Kootenai Fur Trade and its Establishments, 1795–1871." Unpublished report for the U.S. Army Corps of Engineers. Seattle. 1981:64.

8 *The Diary of Dr. Augustus Thibido of the Northwest Exploring Expedition, 1859.* Fairfied WA: Ye Galleon Press, 1990.

9 The "Mission," according to a report by Blakiston (who had preceded Hamilton in the the Tobacco Plains by a few months), was at the site of an earlier HBC post at the mouth of Tobacco River, consisting of two tiny cabins and "a somewhat larger building, lacking a chimney, which he was informed was 'the Kootanie chapel' which had been erected the previous spring when a priest was there." Linklater told Thibido that the two priests were Fr. Bellcour and Fr. Belomena. These priests were not part of the Missouri Jesuits Rocky Mountain Mission. Father Bellcour was a Frenchman, about forty years old, who spoke broken English. He had been visiting there, from the Canadian side of the border, for six years.

[10] This HBC Kootenai post was established in 1846 by Edouard Berland on the Tobacco Plains about five miles south of the 49th parallel. John Linklater took over when Berland died in 1853 and until its closing in the early 1860s. The first post was on east side of the Kootenai River, but after Blackfeet attacks in 1853, they moved it to the west side. (Chance, "The Kootenai Fur Trade")

[11] Claude Schaeffer Papers, Glenbow Library Archives M1100-160, now transferred to University of Calgary.

Chapter 5: Kootenai Oral History and Glacial Lake Geology

[1] This was the largest volcanic eruption in the Cascades during the last million years, and the blast created the deepest lake in America, Crater Lake.

[2] http://acip.sd79.bc.ca/transcripts/ktunaxa_creation_story.pdf

[3] One version of this origin story, told by Joe Pierre, says that Naⱡmuqǂin's head goes down toward the south to a place known as Tuhuⱡnana, now called Missoula, Montana. http://acip.sd79.bc.ca/transcripts/ktunaxa_creation_story.pdf

[4] I would like to thank Violet Birdstone (St. Mary's Band of Ktunaxa) for her suggestions for improvement of this material.

[5] Dr. James Sears, personal communication, July 2019.

[6] J. E. O'Connor, et al. "The Missoula and Bonneville floods—A review of ice-age megafloods in the Columbia River basin." *Earth-Science Reviews*, 208 , Article No.103181, 2020. Hanson, Michelle A., Olav B. Lian, John J. Clague. "The sequence and timing of large late Pleistocene floods from Glacial Lake Missoula," *Quaternary Science Reviews*, 31, 2012:67–81.

[7] In the 32 miles between the spring-water source of the Columbia River and the outlet of Lake Windermere, the elevation difference is only 140 feet. Once Columbia Lake settled into its post-glacial elevation, it was stranded only about 13 feet below the level of the Kootenai River, enough to stop its southward flow.

[8] William Gingras in Ella Clark, Indian Legends from the Northern Rockies, University of Oklahoma Press, 1966, 141.

Chapter 6: A Big Surprise on the Trail of Father De Smet

[1] De Smet, Pierre-Jean, S.J., *Oregon Missions, and Travels Over the Rocky Mountains, 1845–1846.* Edward Dunegan, 1847.

[2] Wm. Davis Papers, Jesuits of Oregon Province Archives, formerly at Gonzaga University and now at the Jesuit Archives in St. Louis.

[3] Point, Nicolas, *Wilderness Kingdom*. Loyola University Press, 1968:174.

[4] Chittenden and Richardson, Vol. 2:490. Olga Johnson (1969, note 24, p. 274) provides an update on this location. "This spot is said to be on what is now an abrupt little 'island' rising above the broad cultivated flats which have been drained for farming, west of the town of Bonners Ferry." The lake shown on the south side of the river no longer exists.

5   Claude Everett Schaeffer Papers, Simon Francis interview. M1100-160. Glenbow Archives. Calgary, Alberta.

6   De Smet, Pierre-Jean. *Letters and Sketches*, p. 357.

7   *Life, Letters and Travels*, Vol. 2:498. The flat between the two rivers is actually only a mile wide. De Smet noted that it "receives a portion of its waters during the great spring freshet."

8   Chittenden & Richardson,Vol. 2:496.

9   De Smet, Oregon Missions, pp. 209-210. Olga Johnson reported that Berland and Morigeau arrived in 1818 with NWC. Three years later, at time of merger, Morigeau "turned free trapper, and moved into the Upper Columbia country, via Canoe River, with *Chief Ken-pe-skut* and his followers, traveling by canoe." (p. 275) Called by the Whites Peter Kinbaskit, this well-known North Thompson chief was highly spoken of by early explorers. He and his fifty or sixty people of mixed tribal blood allied themselves with the Stonies, Assiniboine people who often came to the Lakes country to fish. Descendants of the Morigeaus live throughout the region.

10   Chittenden, Hiram Martin and Alfred Talbot Richardson, *Life Letters and Travels of Father Pierre-Jean De Smet, S.J., 1801–1873*. New York, 1905, II:498.

11   Chittenden & Richardson, Vol. 2:499.On De Smet's map of the Columbia Lakes region, the cross is shown to the northeast of the Lower Lake, now known as Lake Windermere, in the modern vicinity of Invermere, British Columbia. Across from the far end of Lake Windermere, De Smet showed Thompson River (now Toby Creek), to indicate the location where David Thompson had established a trading post known as "Kootenae House" in 1807.

12   Researchers have suggested that Point's sketch was from atop Lewis and Clark Pass, despite the title of the sketch (See Sara A. Scott, "Indian Forts and Religious Icons: The Buffalo Road (Qoq'aalx 'Iskit) Trail Before and After the Lewis and Clark Expedition," *International Journal of Historical Archaeology*, 19:384-415, 2015. Point would not have mistaken the Missouri headwaters with those of the Saskatchewan. Furthermore, no evidence supports the conclusion that Father Point ever stood atop Lewis and Clark Pass. I believe that Fr. Point made his sketch from one drafted on-site by Fr. De Smet, who made simple sketches in his field journals. Although De Smet's original sketch has not been found, my assumption is based on comparable evidence from the one known field journal from 1858-1859. (See "The Strange Tale of Dueling Agents.") Point was not the only one to render De Smet's sketches. Matt Hastings prepared illustrations for his publications and also the Linton Album held by the Jesuit Archives.

Chapter 7: A Summer Like No Other

1   These materials had been acquired by Princeton University in 2013, then processed and uploaded for public viewing.

2   In 1853, Congress authorized four exploratory surveys to find a feasible route for a transcontinental railroad from the Mississippi River to the Pacific Ocean. Of these, the Northern Pacific Survey traversed present-day Montana between the 47th and 49th parallels; at the Rocky Mountain Front, spanning from just south of Rogers Pass to today's border with Canada.

Notes

3   *Journals and Letters of Major John Owen*, Vol I:90.

4   Adams, Thomas. Journal I, Princeton University Archives. C1452.
    https://findingaids.princeton.edu/catalog/C1452_c0000003

5   Adams, Journal "Volume II" April 14, 1854.

6   Adams letter to Stevens on January 16, 1855. Adams Letter Book. Princeton University
    Archives. C1452. https://findingaids.princeton.edu/catalog/C1452_c0000003

7   April 25, 1855 letter, Adams to Stevens. Adams Letter Book.

8   Oct. 16, 1855 letter from Tappan to Stevens from a camp near Fort Benton, NARA.

9   Tappan, Oct. 16, 1855 letter report.

19 Tappan, Oct. 16, 1855 letter report.

11 Adams Journal III, Princeton University Archives. C1452.

12 Lt. James H. Bradley, "Affairs at Fort Benton from 1831 to 1869 from Lieut. Bradley's
    Journal," Helena: MHS Contributions, 1900:372.

13 Bradley 1900:372

14 Fort Campbell, operated by the Missouri Fur Company, is a competitor to Fort Benton.
    The two forts were located less than a mile apart.

15 Oct. 16, 1855 letter from Tappan to Stevens from a camp near Fort Benton, NARA.

16 Adams, Letter report to Stevens, NARA.

17 Adams learns that the name "Musselshell" is what White people call the river.
    The Blackfeet call it" Bear Creek," and the "Western Indians," call it the "Catfish or
    "Bearded Fish" River."

18 Meldrum's Post was officially known as Fort Sarpy, an American Fur Company post on
    the north bank of the Yellowstone about five miles below the mouth of Rosebud Creek.
    It was abandoned and burned in May of 1855. Roobert Meldrum, known as Round Iron
    (Papásh Uuwatash) by the Crow, had managed the fort. https://www.legendsofamerica.com/
    fort-sarpy-montana/

19 Crows had killed two Gros Ventre men and stolen fourteen of their horses. On the other
    side, the Gros Ventre had killed four Crows, three men and a woman.

20 Adams, Journal III

21 The mouth of the Musselshell has been flooded by Fort Peck Lake Reservoir since 1940.
    Fort Peck Dam is one of the largest earthen dams in the world.

22 Farr, "When We Were First Paid."

23 See William E. Farr, "'When We Were First Paid': The Blackfoot Treaty, The Western
    Tribes, and the Creation of the Common Hunting Ground." *Great Plains Quarterly*,
    Vol. 21, No. 2, Spring 2001, 131–154, for full discussion of this aspect of the treaty.

24 See George F. Weisel, *Men and Trade on the Northwest Frontier*, (Missoula, MT, Montana
    State University Press), 1955:88–93; Granville Stuart, *Forty Years on the Frontier*, Arthur H.
    Clark Co.,Vol. 1, 1925.

25 Stuart, Vol. 1, 1925:227. Presumably this is a child from his marriage in 1855 since he
    is referred to as a boy, not a baby, and he doesn't speak English (which a baby would not
    be expected to do).

26 Weisel, *Men and Trade*, 89.

Chapter 8: The Strange Story of How a Crow Chief Found His Way Home

1 Joe Medicine Crow interview by author, Cody, Wyoming, 2007, when Joe was 95 years old.
2 "A great chief comes home." *Billings Gazette*, Sept. 10, 1978, p. 9.
3 Bauerle, Phenocia, ed., *The Way of the Warrior: Stories of the Crow People*. Bison Books, 2004.
4 Mauricio, Victoria, *The Return of Chief Black Foot*, Virginia Beach: Donning Publishers. 1981.
5 http://lib.lbhc.edu/about-the-crow-people/chiefs-and-leaders/#:~:text=Aw%C3%A9%2K%C3%BA alawaachish%2FSits%20In%20The,the%20borders%20of%20Crow%20Country.
6 The wooden bridge became known as Corbett's Crossing northeast of Cody along U.S. Highway 14A at the location of a shallow ford. In 1880, John Corbett and Vic Arland established a trading post along an established Indian travel route on Trail Creek just a few miles northwest of Cody. *Cody Enterprise*, Brian Beauvais, Nov. 15, 2021, https://www.codyenterprise.com/news/opinion/article_7d2ff814-4653-11ec-95df-ff84b277bc28.html
7 Yellowstone became the nation's first national park in 1872.
8 Buffalo Bill Dam, completed in 1910 and located in a narrow canyon on the Shoshone River about six miles above Cody, was one of the first concrete dams to be built in the country.

Chapter 9: Abraham Maslow's Surprising Summer at Siksika

1 Abraham Maslow, with John Honigman, "Northern Blackfoot Culture and Personality." Unpublished manuscript. p19. Undated, but post-1943. Fortunately, psychologist Sidney Stone Brown (Blackfeet) retrieved a copy of this manuscript and included it in her book *Transformation Beyond Greed: Native Self-Actualization* (2016), bringing into print the only compilation of Maslow's observations from Siksika.
2 Brown, Sidney Stone, *Transformation Beyond Greed: Native Self-Actualization*. 2016. p. 46. Similar understandings of human nature can be found throughout indigenous societies worldwide. In the U.S., for example, the Navajo Beauty Way ceremony restores balance similarly to what is described for the Siksika and their relatives.
3 Maslow, A. H. "Dominance-Feeling, Behavior, and Status." *Psychological Review*, 44(5), 1937: 404–429. Maslow, A. H. (1954b). *Motivation and personality*. New York: Harper & Row. Throughout his later life he regretted that he had never credited his Hierarchy of Needs theory to what he learned among the Siksika.
4 Brown, *Transformation Beyond Greed*, 49.
5 Michel, Karen Lincoln. (2014) Maslow's Hierarchy Connected to Blackfoot Beliefs. Online blog, accessed March 10, 2019.
6 Kaufman, S. "Who Created Maslow's Iconic Pyramid?" *Scientific American*. April 23, 2019.

Chapter 10: Disturbing the Sleeping Buffalo

1 Tauhindali, Laktcharas, "A Rock, A Stone," The poem is quoted by Theodoratus, D. J. and F. LaPena, "Wintu Sacred Geography of Northern California," in *Sacred Sites, Sacred Places*, Carmichael D, Hubert J and Reeves B., editors. London: Routeledge. 1994.

Notes

[2] Grinnell, George Bird, *Blackfoot Lodge Tales*. Bison Book, 1968:262-3.

[3] Ewers, John C., "The Medicine Rock of the Marias." In *The Red Man's West: True Stories of the Frontier Indians*, Michael S. Kennedy, editor. Hastings House, 1965:165-169. The referenced story was passed to Short Face by Spotted Calf.

[4] John Strachan, quoted in McDermott, Paul D., Ronald E. Grim, and Phillip Mobley, *The Mullan Road, Carving a Passage through the Frontier Northwest, 1859–62,*140 – Note 32.

[5] Snake Butte on the Fort Belknap Reservation blog. https://bigskywalker.com/2017/11/04/snake-butte-in-north-central-montana/

[6] So durable a material, this basalt was mined for construction of Fort Peck Dam.

[7] Hyndman, Donald and Robert Thomas, *Roadside Geology of Montana*, 2nd Edition, Missoula: Mountain Press, 2020.

[8] Prior to the ice sheet's arrival, the Missouri River flowed northeasterly to Hudson's Bay. The ice sheet forced the Missouri's course to follow the southern edge of the ice, flowing eastward and eventually into the Mississippi River. The Milk River emerged as the Laurentide continental glacier receded and worked its way into the abandoned channel of the Missouri.

[9] Long, James (First Boy), *Land of the Nakoda*, Helena: Riverbend Publishing, 2004:81.

[10] Stuart, Granville, *Forty Years on the Frontier*, Lincoln: Bison Books, 2004:15, 41.

[11] Jiusto, Chere, "Sleeping Buffalo and Medicine Rocks," Phillips County, Montana. Montana State Historical Preservation Office, National Register of Historic Places nomination, 1996.

[12] Archambault, Donovan (Gros Ventre), Inteview with Don Wetzel, Montana State Historical Society, 1995. National Register of Historic Places nomination.

[13] *Great Falls Tribune*, December 10, 1937.

[14] Yellow Kidney interview with Don Wetzel, Chere Jiusto, and Paul Putz, Montana State Historical Society, 1995. National Register of Historic Places nomination.

[15] Chere Jiusto, National Register of Historic Places nomination "Narrative Description."

[16] Horowitz, Joshua, "Tatanga Ishtima hinkna Iyá Waká: Sleeping Buffalo and Medicine Rock and Assiniboine Dislocation and Persistence." *Native American and Indigenous Studies*, Vol. 5, No. 2 (Fall 2018), pp. 123-145.

[17] Interview by the author, 2001. Thanks to Smith's daughter, Terry Lodmell, for providing additional information.

Chapter 11: Old Mindsets Die Hard

[1] An earlier version of this chapter was published in the January 30, 2007, *Great Falls Tribune* as "Indian Education for All signals inclusion for all Americans."

[2] Article X of the Montana Constitution—Education and Public Lands—has, as one of its educational goals, the statement: "The state recognizes the distinct and unique cultural heritage of the American Indians and is committed in its educational goals to the preservation of their cultural integrity." Legislation known as Indian Education for All (20-1-501, MCA) recognizes the distinct and unique cultural heritage of American Indians and commits Montana in its educational goals to the preservation of their cultural heritage.

Chapter 12: History Day in Jordan

[1] https://www.youtube.com/watch?v=yJxyMHft5tM

Chapter 13: Clark Fork Journey, Winter 1859

[1] John Owen, *The Journal and Letters of John Owen*, 2 vols., ed. Seymour Dunbar, notes by Paul Philips. New York: Edward Eberstadt, 1927.

[2] De Smet Letter to Captain Pleasonton from Coeur d'Alene Mission, February 12, 1859. NARA RG 393 – Pt 1 – E 3573 – Letters Recd, 1858-1860.

[3] Splawn, A. J. *Ka-Mi-Akin, the Last Hero of the Yakimas*, Published by Splawn, Mrs. A. J., 1917:119. Reprinted in 2009.

[4] Linton Album, letter to the monsignor at St. Louis University in November 1859, Midwest Jesuit Archives, St. Louis.

[5] De Smet to S.J. to the Monsignor, Saint Louis University, November 1, 1859. Midwest Jesuit Archives.

[6] De Smet to S.J. to the Monsignor, Saint Louis University, November 1, 1859. Midwest Jesuit Archives.

[7] P. De Smet to A. Pleasonton, May 25, 1859, RCA, NA.

[8] P. De Smet to A. Pleasonton, May 25, 1859, RCA, NA.

[9] These groups include some Yakamas, "people of the Naches," referring to a river within the Yakama territory.

[10] Owen, *Journal and Letters*, 208.

[11] Thompson, Sally, "John Owen's Worst Trip: A Journey Across the Columbia Plateau, 1858." *Montana, Magazine of Western History*. Vol 8 (61): Montana Historical Society Press, Helena, 2018.

[12] These entries are in French. The translations have not been proofed by a scholar.

[13] Letter from Father De Smet, S.J. to monsignor SLU, November 1, 1859; Chittenden, Hiram Martin and Alfred Talbot Richardson, *Life Letters and Travels* Vol. p. 767.

[14] *Dalles Journal*, March 28, 1859; J. Owen to E. Geary, May 31, 1859, WIA, NA.

[15] Owen's journal, as reported by the editor, stops abruptly in the middle of a sentence (page 39) and is not resumed until April 9, 1860.

[16] This man was called Andrew "Seltice" by De Smet, and noted as one of the chiefs.

[17] The Indian name for Garry provided by Harney is possibly an error, given that the name appears only in this reference. His childhood name of Slough-Keetcha (the meaning of which is unknown), was found in the Hudson's Bay Company archives on a letter he wrote to his parents from the Red River school. The meaning remains unknown. See "Local historians find proof of Chief Garry's original tribal name," *Spokesman-Review*, September 1, 2013. https://www.spokesman.com/stories/2013/sep/01/in-the-name-of-history/

[18] NARA RG393 – Pt 1 – E 3573 – Letters Received, 1858–1860.

[19] Letter from Father De Smet, S.J. to the Monsignor, Saint Louis University, November 1, 1859.

[20] I want to thank George Capps for alerting me about this 1899 letter and subsequent 1939 newspaper article. The original letter and photograph are held in the Howard McBride papers, Whitman College archives.

Notes

[21] P. De Smet to A. Pleasanton, May 25, 1859, RCA, NARA.

[22] Letter, Bvt Maj P. Lugenbeel, Capt 9th Infantry to Lt. J. Mullan at the Colville Depot, dated July 13, 1859, *Frontier Duty: The Army in Northern Idaho, 1853–1876*. Donna M. Hanson, compiler, transcriber, and editor. Northwest Historical Manuscript Series. University of Idaho Library, Moscow, 2005.

[23] *Dalles Journal*, March 28, 1859; J. Owen to E. Geary, May 31, 1859, WIA, NARA.

[24] Splawn, A.J. 1917:119-120; Ruby & Brown 1970:150; Richard D Scheuerman and Michael O. Finley, *Chief Kamiakin: The Life and Legacy of a Northwest Patriot*, Washington State University Press, 2008.

[25] At the time of the treaty signing, a provisional reservation was established for the Salish in the Bitterroot Valley.

Chapter 14: Deer Lodge is in Warm Springs

[1] Ferris, Warren A. *Life in the Rocky Mountains*, edited by Paul C. Phillips. Far West Publishing Co., 1940:107.

[2] Mullan, John. *Report on the Construction of a Military Road from Fort Walla Walla to Fort Benton*. Government Printing Office, Washington, D.C. 1863:344.

[3] Elijah Nicholas Wilson, The White Indian Boy or Uncle Nick Among the Shoshones. Fenske Printing, Rapid City.1988:14.

[4] Carling Malouf. Economy and Land Use by the Indians of Western Montana, Garland Publishers. 1974.

[5] Granville Stuart. *New Northwest*, August 20, 1869.

Chapter 15: West Side Bison

[1] Clark, Ella E., *Indian Legends from the Northern Rockies*, Norman: University of Oklahoma Press, 1966:121-125. The story had been told to Angus McDonald by an "old Flathead chief" and was discovered among McDonald's papers.

[2] Site 24SB125 contained Late Prehistoric, Avonlea, and Old Women's period projectile points.

[3] Griswold, Gillette and David Larom, The Hellgate Survey. *Anthropology and Sociology Papers*, No. 16. Montana State University, Missoula. 1954: 33-35, 11. Site 24MO11.

[4] Jim Gilles, interview by the author, 1999.

[5] Pat McDonald, interviews by author, 1999.

[6] John Conn, interview by author, 1999. Oldest evidence in the form of Oxbow dart points and youngest in the form of tri-notched points and a fleshing tool made from an elk radius.

[7] Flint, Patricia Robins, *The Northern Rocky Mountain Region: Environment and Culture History*. Ph.D. dissertation, University of Oregon. University Microfilms International, Ann Arbor. 1982.

[8] Siria, Carl H. *Rock Creek, Past and Present*. n.d. Manuscript in possession of the author. Also published as "Not for Fish Alone" in the *Sunday Missoulian*, May 31, 1964.

[9] Oakley, Robert D. *The Philipsburg Story, The History of the Philipsburg Ranger District, 1905-1980*. USDA Northern Region, Deerlodge National Forest, Butte, Montana. 1980.

[10] *Weekly Missoulian*, July 22, 1875.

Chapter 16: Somebody's Daughter

1 *Missoulian,* "Skeleton of Indian Child is Unearthed in Excavation on West Broadway," December 12, 1950.

2 *Missoulian,* December 12, 1950.

3 Scott, G. Richard and Christy G. Turner II, *The Anthropology of Modern Human Teeth: Dental Morphology and its Variations in Recent Human Populations.* Cambridge University Press. 1997.

4 *Missoulian,* "Skeleton Found Here Possibly Child of Indian Fishermen," December 19, 1950, p. 12.

5 The date of 1855 was probably a reference to the treaty signing, to mark the time when everything began to change. In actuality, Native people continued their old practices in the Missoula Valley as long as they were able, essentially until someone built a home or business on previous campsites.

6 Weisel, George F., ed. *Men and Trade on the Northwest Frontier as Shown by the Fort Owen Ledger.* Montana State University Press. 1955.

7 *Missoulian,* December 12, 1950.

8 Phillips, Ruth B. *Trading Identities: A Souvenir in Native North American Art in the Northwest, 1700–1900.* University of Washington Press. 1998.

9 George Weisel, *Men and Trade,* 1955:115.

10 Adeline Pelkey gave birth to Jefferson Pelkey in Hell Gate's Ronde on Feb. 13, 1862, making him the first white child born in Missoula County. Kim Briggeman article, *Missoulian* 2/6/2009.

11 Cave, Will. "Shadows of Past Afford Striking Contrast with Present Garden City." *Missoulian,* September 26, 1940.

12 Palladino, Lawrence Benedict. *Indian and White in the Northwest.* J. Murphy & Co., 1894.

13 The building that served as the original hospital is believed to have been the home of the McCormick family.

14 Sisters of Providence, Chronicles of the Providence of Sacred Heart, Missoula, Montana, 1873-1901.

15 Sisters of Providence, *Chronicles:*3.

16 Sisters of Providence, Chronicles:18–19.

17 Woody, Frank. "A Sketch of the Early History of Western Montana." *Missoulian,* August 18, 1940. This land eventually was joined to existing land on the north side of the river by filling the channel.

18 Malouf, Carling. The Cultural Connections between the Prehistoric Inhabitants of the Upper Missouri and Columbia River Systems. Doctoral dissertation, Columbia University. 1956:216.

19 *Missoulian,* February 13, 1880.

20 Koelbel, Lenora. *Missoula The Way It Was, A Portrait of an Early Western Town.* Pictorial Histories Publishing Co., Missoula, Montana. 1972.

21 Baumler, Ellen. *The Life of the Afterlife in the Big Sky State, A History of Montana's Cemeteries.* University of Nebraska Press, Bison Books, 2021.

[22] *Parfleche* refers to a container made of this stiff rawhide that was created by overlapping folds that were laced closed.

[23] White, George M. *Craft Manual of North American Indian Footwear.* Self-published, St. Ignatius, Montana. [UM, Mansfield Library, Special Collections.]1969.

[24] The original piece measures 2.6 inches long and 1.25 inches at the squared end, estimated to have been a Woman's Size 1, based on the scale provided in Mr. White's pattern, a common shoe size for a seven- to eight-year-old girl, even taking into account that some shrinkage probably occurred. The sole piece is roughly 2.25 times the length of the tongue, resulting in a moccasin length of 7.85 inches.

[25] Stuart, Granville. *Forty Years on the Frontier.* Edited by Paul C. Phillips. 2 vols. Arthur H. Clark Co. Granville Stuart, *The Montana Frontier, 1852–1864,* Paul C. Phillips, editor. University of Nebraska Press (also 1977 reprint, Arthur Clark Publication). 1925.

[26] Patterson, Ida S. *Montana Memories: The Life of Emma Magee in the Rocky Mountain West, 1866-1950.* Salish-Kootenai College, Pablo. 1981:35.

[27] Malouf. 1956:215.

Chapter 17: Andrew Garcia and the Place Where it Happened

[1] http://granitecountyhistory.blogspot.com/2018/10/tough-tripandrew-garcia-and-in-who-lise.html

[2] They were camped near Beaver Creek.

[3] McKay Gulch is now shown as Maukey Gulch on the USGS topo map.

[4] Down the creek about a mile and a half they would find the Salish buffalo trail, which crossed Rock Creek near the mouth of Ross's Fork. After it left Rock Creek, it followed the West Fork to the divide, then crossed over to the Skalkaho and followed down this creek into the main Bitterroot Valley.

[5] Loraine Bentz Domine, personal communication, May 2022.

[6] *Missoulian* obituary, December 10, 1922.

[7] http://granitecountyhistory.blogspot.com/2019/09/the-tr-hess-family.html

[8] *Great Falls Tribune,* Dec. 19, 1933, 7.

[9] The Salish buffalo trail crossed Rock Creek near the mouth of Ross's Fork. After it left Rock Creek, it followed the West Fork to the divide, then crossed over to the Skalkaho and followed down this creek into the main Bitterroot Valley.

[10] *Lethbridge Herald* obituary, January 8, 1943.

Chapter 18: The Gift of a Park

[1] *Sunday Missoulian,* May 30, 1909, 27.

[2] *The Anaconda Standard,* September 5, 1902, 14.

[3] *Missoulian,* September 22, 1925.

[4] *Sunday Missoulian,* August 1, 1930.

[5] *Missoulian,* July 23, 1911, 11. Obituary

[6] *Weekly Missoulian,* June 1, 1883.

[7] *Weekly Missoulian,* October 3, 1884, 3.

8 *Sunday Missoulian*, August 1, 1930, 1; Deed books "Greenough," 32–44.
9 Devlin, Sherry, "Greenough Turns 100," *Missoulian*, May 30, 2002.
10 Missoula County Book 29, p. 208.
11 *The Anaconda Standard*, September 5, 1902, 14.
12 *The Anaconda Standard*, Sept. 5, 1902, p14.
13 *Missoulian*, May 30, 1909, p. 27.
14 *Anaconda Standard*, March 12, 1903, p. 14.
15 *Missoulian*, May 12, 1903, p. 1.
16 *Missoulian*, December 27, 1902, p. 3.
17 *The Anaconda Standard*, September 5, 1902, p. 14.
18 *Missoulian*, Sept 22, 1925.
19 Devlin, Sherry, "Greenough Turns 100," *Missoulian*, May 30, 2002.
20 *Missoulian*, April 4, 1906, p. 4.
21 *Missoulian*, February 23, 1906.
22 *Missoulian*, June 8, 1906, p. 5.
23 *Missoulian*, Mar 30, 1908, p. 8.
24 *Missoulian*, May 31, 1908, p. 8.
25 *Missoulian*, June 7, 1908, p. 12.
26 *Missoulian*, August 28, 1908, p. 5.
27 *Missoulian*, March 13, 1910, p. 1.
28 *Missoulian*, editorial, March 22, 1910.
29 Missoulian editorial, March 22, 1910
30 Devlin, Sherry, "Greenough Turns 100," *Missoulian*, May 30, 2002. *Missoulian*, April 10, 1910, p. 27.
31 *Missoulian*, June 7, 1910, p. 3.
32 Filmed interview with Ruth's husband, Arthur Mosby.
33 *Missoulian*, July 24, 1911, p. 1. (picture of mansion and portraits of T. L. and Tennie)
34 *Missoulian*, July 24, 1911, p. 1.
35 Quoted in Devlin, Sherry, "Greenough Turns 100." *Missoulian*, May 30, 2002.
36 *Missoulian*, July 23, 1911, p. 17.
37 *Missoulian*, July 25, 1911, p. 4.
38 *Missoulian*, Aug 7, 1911, p. 4.
39 *Missoulian*, July 2, 1912.
40 *Missoulian*, July 3, 1912, p. 6.
41 *Missoulian*, July 6, 1913, p. 11.
42 *Missoulian*, July 6, 1913, p. 11.
43 *Missoulian*, July 6, 1913, p. 11.
44 *Missoulian*, August 6, 1913, p. 10.
45 *Missoulian*, June 10, 1917, p. 6.
46 *Missoulian*, June 17, 1917, p. 11.
47 *Missoulian*, August 19, 1918.
48 *Missoulian*, July 15, 1922, p. 2.

[49] *Missoulian*, September 22, 1925.

[50] *Sunday Missoulian*, August 1, 1937.

[51] *Missoulian*, June 11, 1948, p. 11.

[52] Cave, Will, "Will Cave Gives More Facts about Western Montana Names," *Missoulian*, May 21, 1922, p. 9.

[53] *Missoulian*, June 11, 1948, p. 11.

[54] *Missoulian*, August 1, 1948, p. 18 (with photos)

[55] Betty Miller, personal communication.

[56] *Missoulian*, June 11, 1948, p. 11.

[57] *Missoulian*, May 22, 1951, p. 3.

[58] *Missoulian*, November 3, 1951.

[59] *Missoulian*, May 5, 1954, p. 4.

[60] *Missoulian*, June 18, 1954, p. 13.

[61] *Missoulian*, September 7, 1955, p. 5.

[62] Paul Hendricks, personal communication, January 2023.

[63] In March 2023, the beaver was set upon by a dog while on shore and has not been seen since. Loose dogs have become a problem that the Greenoughs, not surprisingly, failed to anticipate. The per capita number of dogs in Missoula would have been beyond their imaginings.

Chapter 20: Ancient Climate Refugees on the Sun River

[1] Greiser, Sally Thompson, "Predictive Models of Hunter Gatherer Adaptations on the Central High Plains." Plains Anthropologist Memoir No. 20. 1985.

[2] Greiser, Sally T., T. Weber Greiser, Susan M. Vetter, and Alan L. Stanfill. "Sun River (24CA74): A Stratified Pelican Lake and Oxbow Occupation Site near Great Falls, Montana." Report prepared for Department of the Army, Omaha District, Corps of Engineers, Omaha, Nebraska. Contract No. DACW45-82-C-0152. Historical Research Associates, Missoula, Montana. 1983. Much of this article is extracted from Greiser, Sally T, T. W. Greiser and Susan Vetter, "Middle Prehistoric Period Adaptations and Paleoenvironment in the Northwestern Plains." *American Antiquity* 50(4): 849 877.

[3] Livers, Michael, "Stone Circles in Yellowstone Archeology of the Airport Rings Site," *Yellowstone Science* 20(2), 2012:5-11. https://files.cfc.umt.edu/cesu/NPS/ UMT/2007/07_08MacDonald_YELL_archeo%20field%20school_YELLSci_art.pdf

[4] Stones used for seed-grinding appear in the archaeological record of the area around this time. An Oxbow site near the Crimson Bluff on the Missouri, some 130 miles south of the Sun River site (see Chapter 21, "Prayer Rocks and Sacred Paint along the Old North Trail"), contains evidence of seed preparation. Sally T. Greiser, "Artifact Collections from Ten Sites at Canyon Ferry Reservoir." *Archaeology In Montana*. 27 (1-2).1986.i

[5] Binford, Lewis R. *Nunamiut Ethnoarchaeology*. Academic Press, New York. 1978:50

[6] Wheat, Joe Ben, "The Olsen-Chubbuck Site: A Paleo-Indian Bison Kill." *Society for American Archaeology* Memoir No. 26. 1972:114

[7] Antevs, Ernst. "Climatic Changes and Pre-white Man. In The Great Basin, with Emphasis on Glacial and Post-Glacial times." *University of Utah Bulletin* 38(20):168-191. 1948. "Geologic-Climatic Dating in the West." *American Antiquity* 20:317-335. 1955.

[9] Frison, George C., Michael Wilson and Diane Wilson. "Fossil Bison and Artifacts from an Early Altithermal Period Arroyo Trap in Wyoming." *American Antiquity* 41(1):28-57. 1976.

Chapter 21: Prayer Rocks and Sacred Paint along the Old North Trail

[1] Walter McClintock, *The Old North Trail: Life, Legends & Religion of the Blackfeet Indians.* MacMillan Co, London, 1910. (1992 edition, University of Nebraska Press, Lincoln, 434-43. Peter Stark, "The Old North Trail," *Smithsonian Magazine,* June 30, 1997.

[2] *The Journals of the Lewis & Clark Expedition,* Gary Moulton, ed., University of Nebraska Press, 1987, Vol. 5:401. https://lewisandclarkjournals.unl.edu/item/lc.jrn.1805-07-18#lc.jrn.1805-07-18.02

[3] Reeves, B. (1990). "How Old is the Old North Trail." *Archaeology in Montana* 31: 1–18.

[4] *The Journals of the Lewis & Clark Expedition,* Gary Moulton, ed., University of Nebraska Press, 1987, Vol. 5:423-424.

[5] *The Journals of Patrick Gass: Member of the Lewis and Clark Expedition,* Carol Lynn MacGregor, editor. Mountain Press, Missoula, MT. 1997:112.

[6] Owen, John. *The Journals and Letters of Major John Owen.* Seymour Dunbar, ed. and trans., with notes by Paul C. Phillips, New York, Edward Eberstadt, 1927:30.

[7] Thomas Adams Journal III, Princeton University Archives. C1452.

[8] Duncan McDonald, 1890s, cited in Stone, Arthur L. Stone, Arthur L. Following Old Trails. Gateway Printing, Missoula. 1996:255.

[9] Claude Everett Schaeffer Papers, Ambrose Gravelle interview. M1100-160. Glenbow Archives. Calgary, Alberta.

Chapter 22: Lewis & Clark Pass and the Search for *Shishequaw*

[1] Scott, Sara A., "Indian Forts and Religious Icons: The Buffalo Road (Qoq'aalx 'Iskit) Trail Before and After the Lewis and Clark Expedition." *International Journal of Historical Archaeology,* Volume 19 Number 2, 2015 p. 396. Salish-Pend d'Oreille Culture Committee and Elders Cultural Advisory Council 2005, p. 54

[2] A new trailhead with interpretive signs provides access to Lewis and Clark Pass from Alice Creek. The moderate trail is only 1.7 miles to the pass. With a little extra effort, a great view can be found on the ridge to the south.

[3] He may have mistaken Crown Butte for Square Butte, since the former is more visible from atop the pass.

[4] Lichenometry dates from the feature average to 1847. Hall, D. (2005). Lichenometric Analysis of Stone Features: Lewis and Clark Trail/Cokahlarishkit Trail, Upper Blackfoot Valley, Lewis and Clark County, Montana. On file, Montana State Historic Preservation Office, Helena. Researchers have proposed that Jesuit missionary Nicolas Point is likely the one who "planted" the stone feature identified as a cross in 1842, but Father Point never traveled through this gap. (See "Nicolas Point's View of Life in the Rockies, 1841-1842.")

[5] Scott, Sara A. 2015.

[6] Since they are heading northward, "wright" means flowing to the east.

[7] The Dearborn River High Bridge was nominated to the National Register of Historic Places for its significance as a rare example of a half-deck Pratt truss bridge.

[8] See Lewis' journal entries for July 25-27, 1806.

[9] Wheeler, Olin D. *The Trail of Lewis and Clark, 1804-1904*. New ed. 2 vols. New York: G. P. Putnam's Sons, 1924, 311-313.

[10] Culbertson in Lt. James H. Bradley, "Affairs at Fort Benton, 1900," Bradley Papers, Montana Historical Society, Helena. VIII:135.

[11] Thompson, David. *David Thompson's Narrative of his Explorations in Western America, 1784-1812*. J. B. Tyrell, editor. Toronto, Champlain Society, 1916.

[12] Larpenteur, Charles. *Forty Years a Fur Trader on the Upper Missouri*, edited by Elliott Coues. 2 Vols. Francis P. Harper, New York. 1898:264.

[13] Add note about dismantling and moving Ft. Lewis across the river as the beginning of Fort Benton

[14] The Blackfeet word for "people" is *o'kia'pitapi. Matápii* means "person."

[15] The 1904 GLO map shows "Pend d'Oreille Trail" crossing the Dearborn about two miles below the canyon.

[16] De Lacy map of 1869 of Montana Territory.

[17] Gaff, A., and Gaff, M. (eds.) *Adventures on the Western Frontier: Major General John Gibbon*, Indiana University Press, Bloomington. 1994. Rockwell, Ronald V. *The U.S. Army in Frontier Montana*. Helena, Mont.: Sweetgrass Books, 2009.

[18] Larpenteur, Chas. 264-265.

[19] Upper Blackfoot Valley Historical Society. Gold Pans and Singletrees. 1994:247.

[20] It turns out that another researcher had already figured out the French derivation of the name. Hartley, Alan H. *Lewis and Clark: Lexicon of Discovery*. Corvallis: Oregon State University Press, 2004.

Chapter 23: Prayer Rocks and Sacred Paint along the Old North Trail

[1] Interestingly, these lands were also part of the Kootenai seasonal round. They would hunt buffalo along the mountain fringes during the winter when the Blackfeet were in camps along the Marias and Teton Rivers, farther east, and closer to the large herds of bison.

[2] The name Two Medicine Lodge River appears on the 1801 map made by Akomokki for Peter Fidler of the Northwest Company.

[3] Leon Rattler. Quoted in the *Glacier Reporter*, Jun 28, 2017, p 1.

[4] The TCD, as approved, was expanded from our original work to include the Hall Creek area. ✣

INDEX

Index

Campbell, Bethany, 173
Canal Flats, British Columbia, 58, 62, 75–76, **75–76**
canoes, 10, 16, 29, 143
Cantonment Jordan, 37
Cantonment Stevens, 83
Caras, Jim, 212–213
Casey, Michael, 257
catalo. *See* beefalo
Catholics, 71, 156, 177, 181
Catlin, George, 166, **167 map**
cattle, 102, 220–222
Cave, Will, 176, 180, 215
Ceded Strip negotiations (1895), 264
Chance, David, 47
Charlo, Chief (Salish man), 180
Chata (Choctaw man), 5
Chickasah (Choctaw man), 5
Chickasaw (tribe), 4–5
Chinese residents, 181–182
Chinook, and Chinookan speakers, 12
Choctaw, 5
churches, **33**, 79, **80**
Clark, William, 2, 4, 15–19, 20, 23–26, 133–134, 236, 239–241, 245
Clark Fork journey, **144 map**; at eastern destination, 147–148; evidence of, 156; travel eastward, 142–143, 145–147; travel westward, 148–153; at western destination, 153–154
Clark Fork River area, **144, 160–161 map**; beefalo in, 219–220; bison in, 166; as burial site, 172, 175; environmental issues in, 218; fishing in, 198–199; flood season in, 205, 208; geology of, 62, 143; gold prospecting in, 102; red soil in, 240–241
Clarke, Malcolm, 163
Clatsop (tribe), 12
climate change, 224, 233–234
clothing, 174, 185–186
Coeur d'Alene (tribe), 142–143, 154
coffins, wooden, 181
Cold Spring (geographic area), 165–166, 165
Colonel Wright (steamboat), 153
Colter, John, 28

Columbia Discovery Centre, 75
Columbia Lake, 56, 58, 63
Columbia River area, **59, 68–69, 72–73 map, 76;** atmosphere of, 75–77, 78; and expeditions, 27–29, 71, 142, 240, 247; geology of, 58, 62–63; in lore, 53–56, 63; storms in, 169
competition, cultural differences in, 114
Confederated Salish and Kootenai Tribes, 172–173, 186, 218
Conn, John, and family, 168
Continental Divide, 9, 29, 38, 86–87, 166, 255
Cordilleran ice sheet, 60–61, 63
Corps of Discovery, **18;** consequences of, 133–134; Natives watching, 19–20; inspiration for, 2, 4, 14; Missouri Breaks, approaching, 15–19; Missouri Breaks, leaving, 20–26; records of, 224
Corps of Engineers, 225–227
Coues, Elliott, 257
Craft Manual of North American Indian Footwear (White), 184
Craig, William, 84, 90, 91, 95
Crazy Dog (Blackfeet man), 258, **259**
Crazy Dog Society, 258, 262, 268
Creator, 32, 50, 52–53, 57, 58, 265
Cree Crossing, 122, **123,** 128
Cree, 100, 125–126
Crimson Bluffs, **241,** 242
Cross of Peace, **69**
Cross of the Assumption, 69, 71
Cross of the Nativity, 68, **68,** 74, 77–80, **79–80**
crosses, 66, **66–67,** 68–69, 80, 146
Crow (tribe), **105,** 126; in ceremonies, 258; and Kamiakin, 157; killings by, 97; peace council, invitation to, 90, 93, 95, 96; peace council, missing from, 100; and sacred rocks, 125. *See also* Black Foot, Chief (Crow man)
Crowfoot, Chief (Siksika man), 115
CSKT Bison Range, 166
Culbertson, Alexander, 89, 254
Cumming, Alfred, 88–90, **88**

D

Davis, William, 68, 80
De Smet, Pierre-Jean, **65, 66–67 MAP, 70 map, 72–73 map, 141, 145, 147, 150, 160–161 map;** about, 65–66; beliefs of, 77; at council, 154, 156–157; crosses associated with, 68–69, 79–80; expeditions of, 69, 71, 74–77, 142–143, 145–150, 152–153, 255; illness and death of, 158; journals of, 140–142, 150–152; Owen in conflict with, 142, 156–157
Dearborn River, 249, 251
Dearborn River High Bridge, **251**
deep history, 50–51, 58–64
Deer Lodge, and Deer Lodge County, Montana, 163
Deer Lodge Valley, 162, 163–164
Deer's Lodge (geological feature), 159, **160–161 map,** 162–164,**164**
Delaware Jim (Delaware man), 90, 91
dogs, 98, 229–230, 231
Dorion, Jean Baptiste, 29–32
Dorion, Little Lark, 30
Dorion, Marie: death of, 32; expedition of, 30–32; family life of, 27–28, 32–33; and Sacagawea, 28–29; significance of, 27
Dorion, O. David, 32–33
Dorion, Paul, 29–32
Dorion, Pierre, Jr., 27, 30
droughts, 82–83, 90–92, 229, 230–231, 232–233
Drouillard, George, 28, 253
dyes, for textiles, 12–13

E

earthquakes, 235
Edgar, Bob, 108
Elk Creek (Shishequaw Creek), 252
erratics, **120,** 121–122
Eugene, Pauline, 77–80, **78**
Euro-Americans, 116–117, 132, 153–154, 175–177, 185, 253–254

F

Feather Woman Mountain, 270, **270**

289

Index

Index

ACKNOWLEDGMENTS

Since beginning my career in anthropology in Montana more than forty years ago, I have found countless wonderful people who gave help when needed and kindly shared their stories with me. So numerous, in fact, they would overwhelm these pages if I listed them all. Many of them, though, deserve mention because they provided the fodder and the ballast to see me through the writing of this book.

First of all, the stories that fill this book would not exist without the generosity of many Native friends, young and old, who, over the last few decades, graciously shared their knowledge, challenged my view of their history, and, often, encouraged me to continue with the projects that have resulted in this book. Clover Anaquad and Robert Four Star (Assiniboine); George Horse Capture, Sr. and Darrell Martin (Gros Ventre); from the Blackfoot Confederacy tribes: Arlene and Wishy Augere, Leo Bird, Charlene and Bob Burns, Iris Heavy Runner, Tiny Man Heavy Runner, Linda Juneau, Darrell Kipp, Pauline Matt, Leon Rattler, Darnell and Smokey Rides at the Door, Lorrie Tatsey, and Curly Bear Wagner (Pikunni); Jeanette Many Guns (Siksika); Narcisse Blood, Alvine Mountain Horse, Amethyst First Rider, and Leroy Little Bear (Kainai); Francis Auld, Rosemary Caye, Gigi Caye, Margaret Friedlander, Cathy Hamel, Naida Lefthand, and Vernon Finley (Kootenai); Louis Adams, Myrna Dumontier, Arlene Adams, Johnny Arlee, Lucy Vanderburg and Germaine White (Salish-Qlispe); Allen Pinkham and Horace Axtell (Nez Perce) and Roberta Conner (Cayuse-Nez Perce).

I remember with gratitude many Montanans who freely shared their knowledge about local history and archaeology. They include (alphabetically, for lack of a better strategy), Hank Armstrong, Willie Bateman, Kim Briggeman, George Capps, Ted Catton, Jim Cusker, Les Davis, Annie Dellwo, John Douglas, Ken Egan, Roger Ereaux, Bill Farr, Leif Fredrickson, Keith Graybeal, Troy Helmick, Buss Hess, Dusty Hilmo, Norman Jacobson, Lon Johnson, Dale Karkenan, Bob Knight, Pat and Esther McDonald, Jack and Claire Nisbet, Bill Ohrmann, Lloyd Paul, June Siple, Diane F. Smith, Scott

Sproull, Peter Stark, Ron West, Gale Winn, Al Wiseman, and my dear friend Swain Wolfe. Many of them have passed on from this life but are surely not forgotten. For those of you who aided my efforts along the way but do not find your name on this page, I hope you will be able to take pleasure in whatever contribution you made and will forgive my forgetfulness.

I want to thank the HRA field crew that did such a meticulous job excavating the Sun River site and also those individuals involved in the Clark Fork River off-reservation treaty rights research, especially Phil Tourangeau. Thanks to the many who joined me along old trails through the years. Kim Lugthart and Ken Furrow, in particular, joined on many adventures as part of our work at the Regional Learning Project at UM (2001–2010). I smile at the memory of the many amazing people we met along the way. I also shared some wonderful travels to archives with archaeologist Becky Timmons in widespread places across North America, thanks to a grant she was awarded.

Thanks to archivists and historians who helped with locating research materials, including Donna McCrae and Mark Fritch (University of Montana), Keith Belcher (Missoula County records), Dana Kopp (Providence Archives, St. Patrick Hospital), David Kingma (Gonzaga University), David Miros (Jesuit Archives, St. Louis), Gregory Pass (St. Louis University), Jim Flatness and Ron Grimm (Library of Congress).

To the various individuals who helped with finding and providing images or granting permission to use their artwork, I also express my thanks. Among that list are Harriet Bakas, Rod Benson, Kelly Garcia, Rick and Suzy Graetz, Don Greytak, Adolph Hungry Wolf, Carla Hunsley, Dale Karkenan, Mary Ellen Little Mustache, Terry Lodmell, Becky Hess Metesh, Taylar Robbins, Patrice Schwenk, Sara Scott, and Tracey Vivar.

Although I didn't realize the good fortune at the time, the deep dive I made into early Missoula history, which resulted in the "Somebody's Daughter" story, came from a challenge to my research findings. The extra work led me to a fine-tuned understanding of the difficult transitional years for Native people after the 1855 treaty was ratified. The mundane particulars brought the story to life. In retrospect, I am grateful for the shove.

Some of my travels were made possible by the Humanities Montana Speakers Bureau. This wonderful nonprofit affiliate of the National Endowment

Acknowledgments

for the Humanities is a major supporter of historical research and outreach, and I am grateful for their support through the years. A couple of these stories came about through Ellen Knight with a small grant from Five Valleys Land Trust, and others through support from the Charles Engelhard Foundation.

To those who took the time to review and comment on particular chapters, I extend my great appreciation: Johnny Arlee, Francis Auld, Tim Bernardis, Viola Birdstone, Kim Briggeman, Rosemary Caye, Loraine Domine, Shannon Gilbert, Weber Greiser, Beth Judy, Donna Erickson, Becky Hess Metesh, Betty Miller, Sally Mueller, Charlene Burns, Leon Rattler, Darnell and Smokey Rides at the Door, and Peter Stark. Thanks, also, to my pals who took the time to brainstorm titles with me and to others who reminded me of the flower sequence on Lewis and Clark Pass. So many blessings.

I count myself lucky that my editor at Farcountry, Will Harmon, responded so positively and with real appreciation for this compilation of stories. His understanding made for a pleasant, respectful, and productive book-shaping process. I am so grateful to Will and Steph Lehmann for creating a book design that is so in keeping with what I imagined. Six other stalwart supporters took the time to read the entire manuscript: Joyce Hocker, Ken Egan, Beth Judy, Annick Smith, Peter Stark, and John Weaver. The sum of their thoughtful responses and suggestions has resulted in a much better book than I could have written alone. It takes a village. . . .

Most of all, I want to thank Joyce Hocker for encouraging me to write this book and John Weaver for supporting me in so many ways through the process, even to the last grueling details. ✣

ABOUT THE AUTHOR

PHOTOGRAPH BY NEVA OLIVER.

Anthropologist Sally Thompson's long career in the Rocky Mountains and American Southwest has spanned more than four decades. She received her Ph.D. at the University of Colorado in 1980, the same year she moved to Missoula. She has worked as an archaeologist, ethnohistorian, and tribal consultant and collaborator, and also filmmaker. She has published a monograph and numerous articles in professional journals as well as in *Montana, the Magazine of Western History*. Her 2015 book, *People Before the Park*, published by the Montana Historical Society, was a collaboration with the Kootenai Culture Committee and the Pikunni Traditionalist Association of the Blackfeet Tribe. ✢